A DREAMSPEAKER CRUISING GUIDE, VOLUME 3

New, Revised Second Edition

Vancouver, Howe Sound & the Sunshine Coast

INCLUDING
PRINCESS LOUISA INLET & JEDEDIAH ISLAND

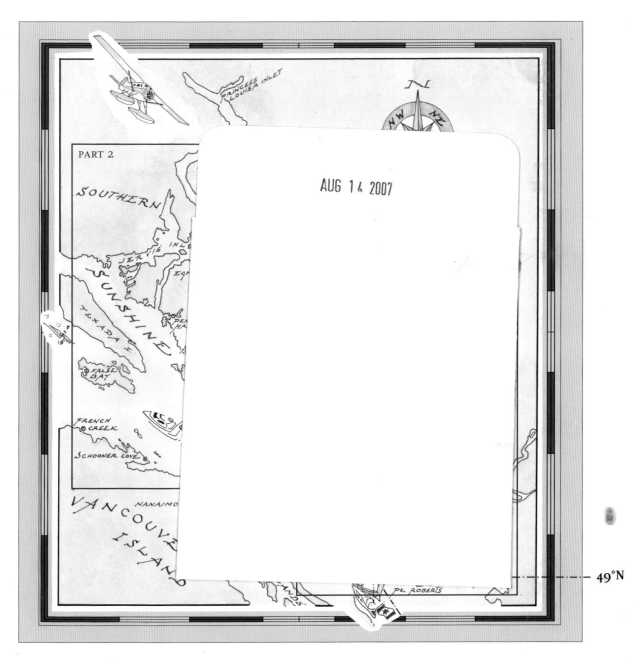

ANNE & LAURENCE YEADON-JONES

HARBOUR PUBLISHING

FEATURED DESTINATIONS
PART I: VANCOUVER & HOWE SOUND

TRAVEL

BY AIR: Vancouver International Airport — all scheduled and chartered international and regional airlines operate from this beautiful, modern airport.

Seaplane and helicopter services — both chartered and scheduled services operate from the S Terminal, Fraser River and Downtown Vancouver.

BY FERRY: B.C. Ferries offers several sailings daily from Horseshoe Bay, West Vancouver to Langdale on the Sunshine Coast; Bowen Island; and Nanaimo, Vancouver Island. Ferries to Victoria and the Gulf Islands run from Tsawwassen, Delta. For information call 1-888-223-3779 or visit www.bcferries.bc.ca.

BY BUS: Public transport is efficient and regular in Greater Vancouver and includes the bus, SkyTrain, Seabus and West Coast Express. For information call Translink at 604-642-0660 or pick up a map at the Infocentre 604-683-2000.

The West Vancouver Blue Bus operates between downtown Vancouver and Horseshoe Bay with an express bus for nifty ferry connections; call 604-985-7777 or visit www.natransit.com.

For Sunshine Coast Transit information call 604-885-3234.

Malaspina Coach Lines provides excellent road/ferry connections between Vancouver International Airport, downtown Vancouver and the Sunshine Coast; call 1-877-227-8287 or visit www.malaspinacoach.com.

BY TRAIN: The Euro-style Amtrak Cascades train from Vancouver to Seattle, Washington and points south is well worth the scenic adventure; call 1-800-872-7245.

TABLE OF CONTENTS
PART I: VANCOUVER & HOWE SOUND

Foreword by Simon Hill

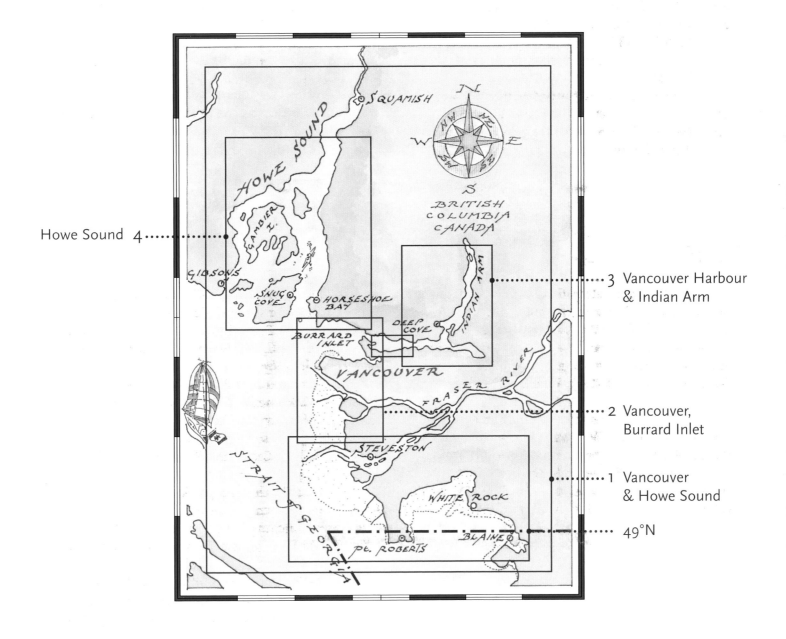

Howe Sound 4

3 Vancouver Harbour & Indian Arm

2 Vancouver, Burrard Inlet

1 Vancouver & Howe Sound

49°N

FEATURED DESTINATIONS
PART 2: THE SUNSHINE COAST

TABLE OF CONTENTS
PART 2: THE SUNSHINE COAST

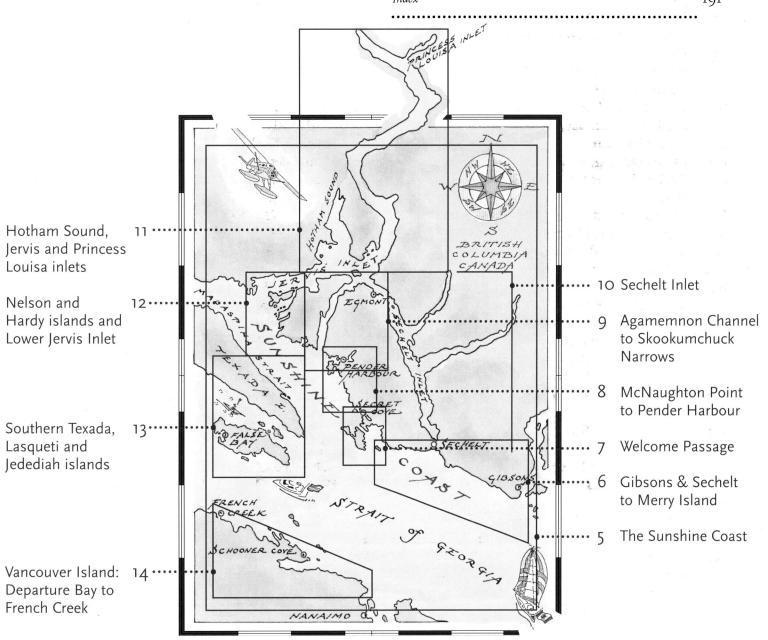

Hotham Sound, Jervis and Princess Louisa inlets   11

Nelson and Hardy islands and Lower Jervis Inlet   12

Southern Texada, Lasqueti and Jedediah islands   13

Vancouver Island: Departure Bay to French Creek   14

10 Sechelt Inlet

9 Agamemnon Channel to Skookumchuck Narrows

8 McNaughton Point to Pender Harbour

7 Welcome Passage

6 Gibsons & Sechelt to Merry Island

5 The Sunshine Coast

Text copyright © 2003 Anne and Laurence Yeadon-Jones, revised 2007. Photographs and illustrations copyright © 2003 Laurence Yeadon-Jones except page 150 top © Sunshine Coast Museum and Archive.

Harbour Publishing Co. Ltd.
P.O. Box 219
Madeira Park, BC
V0N 2H0
www.harbourpublishing.com

Edited by Scott Steedman
Layout by Teresa Bubela
Printed in China.

THE CANADA COUNCIL | LE CONSEIL DES ARTS
FOR THE ARTS | DU CANADA
SINCE 1957 | DEPUIS 1957

BRITISH COLUMBIA ARTS COUNCIL
Supported by the Province of British Columbia

Harbour Publishing acknowledges financial support from the Government of Canada through the Book Publishing Industry Development Program and the Canada Council for the Arts, and from the Province of British Columbia through the British Columbia Arts Council and the Book Publisher's Tax Credit through the Ministry of Provincial Revenue.

Library and Archives Canada Cataloguing in Publication

Yeadon-Jones, Anne
     A Dreamspeaker cruising guide / Anne Yeadon-Jones and Laurence Yeadon-Jones. – 1st Harbour Publishing ed.

Includes bibliographical references and index.
Contents: v. 1. The Gulf Islands and Vancouver Island, from
     Sooke to Nanaimo – v. 2. Desolation Sound & the Discovery
     Islands – v. 3. Vancouver, Howe Sound & the Sunshine Coast :
     including Princess Louisa Inlet & Jedediah Island – v. 5. The
     Broughton Islands.
ISBN 1-55017-402-9 (v. 1). – ISBN 1-55017-404-5 (v. 2). –
ISBN 1-55017-397-9 (v. 3). – ISBN 1-55017-406-1 (v. 5)

     1. British Columbia–Guidebooks. 2. San Juan Islands (Wash.) –
Guidebooks. 3. Boats and boating–British Columbia–Guidebooks.
4. Boats and boating–Washington (State)--San Juan Islands–Guidebooks.
I. Yeadon-Jones, Laurence II. Title.
FC3845.P2A3 2006   797.1'09711   C2005-907723-9

FOREWORD

When Duart Snow, then editor of *Pacific Yachting* magazine, first saw a manuscript from Anne and Laurence Yeadon-Jones, he made a decision that has paid dividends for the magazine and the boating community ever since. It was an easy decision — sign these writers up, and don't let them go. Since that first cruising article appeared in *Pacific Yachting* in June 1996, Anne and Laurence Yeadon-Jones have grown to become favourite cruising authorities within the B.C. boating community, and have established a reputation for providing informative, entertaining and in-depth information about our favourite cruising grounds. With the 1998 publication of *Gulf Islands & Vancouver Island,* the first *Dreamspeaker Cruising Guide*, Anne and Laurence really came into their own as cruising writers, and their reputation began to spread.

Over the years of working with Anne and Laurence, I've had the delightful privilege of meeting with them on many occasions and had the opportunity to venture forth into unfamiliar destinations armed with their hot-off-the-press articles. From these meetings and explorations, I've come to realize that one of the things that make Anne and Laurence such first-rate cruising writers is their obvious delight in unearthing and sharing the hidden treasures to be found in the areas they visit — that, and Laurence's habit of incorporating little visual treats into the beautiful, detailed, hand-drawn illustrations he creates to accompany the text.

In this third volume of their immensely popular *Dreamspeaker* series, Anne and Laurence tackle what is perhaps the most under-rated cruising area on our coast. The region encompassing Vancouver, Howe Sound and the Sunshine Coast doesn't command the sort of attention afforded the Gulf Islands or Desolation Sound, but it's one of the largest, most varied and historically fascinating sections of B.C.'s coast. From the bustle of downtown Vancouver to the charming villages and islands of Howe Sound and the delights of Welcome Passage, this area rewards close exploration. And there's no better guide to close exploration than the one you're holding in your hands.

Simon Hill
Former Editor
Pacific Yachting magazine

Corilair 'Beaver' Floatplane – Pilot, Anne
and Dreamspeaker at Pender Harbour

SPECIAL THANKS TO:

The Team at Corilair — Mike Farrell, Bill Dutch and Pat Hadikin —
who generously helped connect the *"Dreamspeaker* Team" with all the
coastal communities

GRATEFUL APPRECIATION TO OUR INDUSTRY SUPPORT:

Boss Systems, Snug Cove, Bowen Island; *computer services.*
C-Tow, Vancouver; *marine assistance network.*
Canadian Hydrographic Services; *charts and nautical publications.*
Canon Canada Ltd. Mississauga, Ontario; *camera and lenses.*
Corilair, Campbell River; *floatplane services.*
Custom Colour, Vancouver; *professional film processing.*
McElhanney; *aerial image & mapping resources,* www.mcelhanney.com.
Mustang Survival Ltd. Vancouver; *personal floatation devices.*
Nautical Data International, St Johns, Newfoundland; *electronic charts.*
Nobeltec, Beaverton, Oregon; *navigational software.*
Sea Com Marine Electronics, Campbell River; *electronic services.*
Sign Factory, Vancouver; Dreamspeaker's *stern lettering.*
HUB International TOS Ltd.; *specialist marine insurance services.*

ACKNOWLEDGEMENTS

Ken and Brenda, M.Y. Office, for their consistent support and quality service.
B.C. Provincial Parks, Garibaldi/Sunshine Coast District, GVRD Regional Parks
and the District of Sechelt for all their kind help.
City of Vancouver, Blueways Initiative.
Simon Hill, Editor, Pacific Yachting Magazine, for all his support.
All the coastal people who generously gave us their time and encouragement.
Scott Steedman, Ingrid Paulson, Teresa Bubela, Cindy Connor, Tessa Vanderkop and
Danielle Johnson.
Finally our family and friends for their patience and enthusiastic support.

To our friends old and new

and to all the coastal people who generously gave us their time.

PART I

Chapter 1

VANCOUVER & HOWE SOUND

"Vancouverites like to boast that you can go skiing in the morning, sailing in the afternoon and still be home in time for a night out on the town."
— *Chris Wyness, Vancouver (Lonely Planet, 1999)*

A floatplane landing in Vancouver harbour.

Chapter 1
VANCOUVER &
HOWE SOUND

CUSTOMS

Call 1-888-226-7277—7 days a week, 24 hours a day.
The ports of entry covered by this guide for recreational boaters entering Canadian waters are located in:
White Rock — at White Rock Pier (public wharf) and Crescent Beach Marina
Steveston — at the gas dock
Vancouver — at False Creek Public Wharf, Burrard Inlet, Coal Harbour and all marinas

NO-SEWAGE-DISCHARGE SITES

Current sites where the use of holding tanks is mandatory:
False Creek, Burrard Inlet, Coal Harbour, Deep Cove, Bedwell Harbour and Halkett Bay. All craft are required to use holding tanks; pump-out stations are available in Lower Mainland marinas and public wharves.
Note: Check Transport Canada (www.tc.gc.ca) for current Pleaure Craft Sewage Pollution Prevention Regulations.

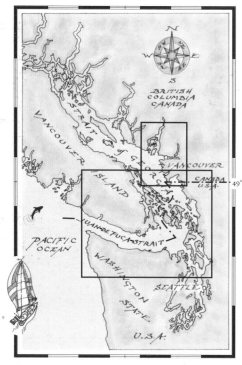

The cruising waters of Vancouver and Howe Sound.

On Canada's western Pacific seaboard lies the intangibly vast and intricate coastline of British Columbia. In the very south, tucked behind Vancouver Island's mountainous backbone and natural breakwater, a strip of silver sea known as the Strait of Georgia plays host to one of the world's finest recreational boating playgrounds.

Volume 3 of the Dreamspeaker series covers the Strait of Georgia's captivating eastern shoreline north of the 49th parallel, including the metropolitan mix of Vancouver and its popular local cruising area in Indian Arm and Howe Sound. Northwest from Gibsons lie the delights of the Sunshine Coast, an area blessed with more clear blue days than boaters would ever believe possible on this temperate raincoast.

Volume 3 has been divided into two parts: Vancouver and Howe Sound (Part 1) and the Sunshine Coast (Part 2). This is because Burrard Inlet, Indian Arm and Howe Sound form a distinctive region that differs significantly, both in character and climate, from the Sunshine Coast.

One of the most beautiful cities in the world, Vancouver has a spectacular natural setting, surrounded by mountains and interlaced with waterways. In spring, Vancouverites brag that they can ski the local slopes before lunch and spend the rest of the afternoon sailing in English Bay. Although Vancouver is known as a port city with a large commercial harbour, it is also renowned for its abundance of green spaces, with downtown Stanley Park the jewel in the crown. Thanks to the city's colourful, multicultural mix there is an overwhelming selection of excellent restaurants and cafés for all pocketbooks, and in the summertime English Bay celebrates the warm outdoor weather with the Celebration of Light, a magnificent four-night display of fireworks that the boater can enjoy up close from the comfort of the cockpit.

Howe Sound is a deep-water inlet fringed by spectacular snow-capped mountains. In the entrance to the sound lie three diverse islands — Bowen, Gambier and Keats islands — which attract unique personalities from summer cottage-owners to full-time residents. The indented shorelines provide a host of anchoring opportunities for visiting boats, and the gentle summer breezes that blow through the protected channels between the islands make these waters a sailor's paradise.

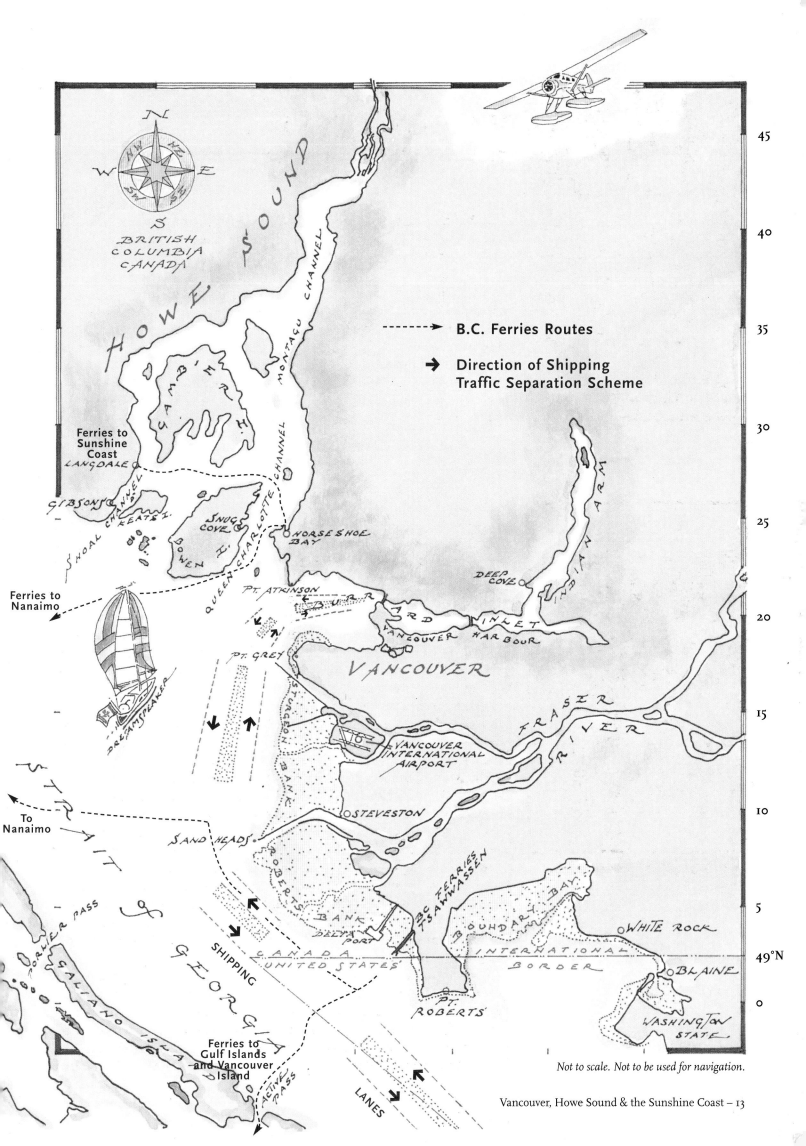

N
NW   NE
W   E
SW   SE
S

BRITISH
COLUMBIA
CANADA

HOWE SOUND

MONTAGU CHANNEL

- - - - → **B.C. Ferries Routes**

→ **Direction of Shipping
Traffic Separation Scheme**

GAMBIER I.

Ferries to
Sunshine
Coast
LANGDALE

GIBSONS

SHOAL CHANNEL

KEATS I.

SNUG
COVE

BOWEN I.

QUEEN CHARLOTTE CHANNEL

HORSESHOE
BAY

INDIAN ARM

DEEP
COVE

PT. ATKINSON

BURRARD INLET

VANCOUVER HARBOUR

Ferries to
Nanaimo

DREAMSPEAKER

PT. GREY

STURGEON BANK

VANCOUVER

VANCOUVER
INTERNATIONAL
AIRPORT

FRASER RIVER

STEVESTON

STRAIT

To
Nanaimo

PORLIER PASS

GALIANO ISLAND

SAND HEADS

ROBERTS BANK

DELTA
PORT

OF

GEORGIA

SHIPPING

CANADA
UNITED STATES

BC FERRIES
TSAWWASSEN

BOUNDARY BAY

INTERNATIONAL BORDER

WHITE ROCK

49°N

BLAINE

Ferries to
Gulf Islands
and Vancouver
Island

ACTIVE PASS

LANES

PT.
ROBERTS

WASHINGTON
STATE

45

40

35

30

25

20

15

10

5

0

Not to scale. Not to be used for navigation.

WEATHER & WIND

Fun for some! Strong wind and surf pound First Beach in Vancouver.

MARINE WEATHER FORECASTS

Listening to the marine weather forecast should be every boater's number one priority before heading out on the water. Setting up a regular routine to tune into the marine forecast is an invaluable asset.

MARINE FORECASTS

Marine forecasts and warnings are broadcast as continuous marine weather recordings and are available VHF: WX1:162.55, WX2:162.40, WX3:162.475, 21B:161.65
PHONE: VICTORIA 250-363-6492

VANCOUVER 604-666-3655

For further information on weather, visit Environment Canada at www.weatheroffice.ec.gc.ca.

ENVIRONMENT CANADA WEST COAST WEATHER PUBLICATIONS

Mariner's Guide: West Coast Marine Weather Services
Marine Weather Hazards Manual — West Coast: A Guide to Local Forecasts and Conditions
The Wind Came All Ways, by Owen Lange (GDS, 1999)

●   **Marine Weather Reporting Station**
▲   **Marine Weather Buoy**
◉   **Bowen Island Weather 3**
✳   **Weather Office**

NOTE: FORECAST TIMES

04.00, 10.30, 16.00 and 21.30. These times remain the same throughout the year.

To the untrained ear, marine forecasts take a little getting used to; however, they are quite straightforward. The forecast content is valid for 24 hours, with an outlook for the following 24 hours. The big weather picture for the entire British Columbia coast is provided by the synopsis.

SYNOPSIS: The synopsis is broadcast at the beginning of the marine forecast. It is a description of the location and intensity of the weather system that will affect BC coastal waters and how this system is expected to evolve over the next 24 hours. A general description of the present and forecast winds is also included.

FORECAST AREA: After the synopsis, specific reports for the forecast areas will be given. First is the Strait of Georgia, followed by Howe Sound (the areas covered in this volume). Local reports from the marine weather stations and buoys come later — listen to them carefully.

WIND SPEEDS: These are given in knots and are the average winds expected over the open water.

Light Winds	0–10 knots
Moderate Winds	11–21 knots
Strong Winds	22–33 knots
Gale Force Winds	34–47 knots
Storm Force Winds	48–65 knots
Hurricane Winds	64 knots plus

WIND DIRECTIONS: These refer to the direction from which the wind is blowing; they are based on True North, not on magnetic bearings.

WEATHER AND VISIBILITY: A brief description of the sky condition and weather, for example, sunny, cloudy, rain, drizzle or fog. This is followed by a statement about the visibility if it is expected to be reduced beyond 1 nautical mile.

MARINE WARNINGS: These are issued whenever the winds are expected to rise to above 20 knots. In a Small Craft Warning, 20–33 knots, recreational craft should seek safe and secure shelter from the forecast wind direction. Small Craft Warnings are issued for southern inner coastal waters, beginning in April and ending in November. Never wait for gale and storm warnings prior to seeking shelter.

WAVES, TIDES & CURRENTS

TIDE AND CURRENT TABLES provide essential navigational information and must be acquired prior to venturing into these waters. A working knowledge of tides and currents, and their interplay with winds, is especially important in this region.

Each chapter begins with Volume 5 of the *Canadian Tide and Current Tables* referenced. Tides (reference port and secondary ports) and currents (reference station and secondary stations) are followed

by a note describing any local tidal peculiarities or currents that may occur within the boundaries covered by the chapter.

OFFICIAL PUBLICATIONS
Refer to *Canadian Tide and Current Tables, Volume 5: Juan de Fuca Strait and Strait of Georgia.*

Beware First Narrows, where currents can reach 6.5 knots on both the flood and the ebb.

In the summer, the coastline and islands of the Strait of Georgia experience remarkably mild weather and relatively calm waters. The Georgia Basin, as this area is often referred to, lies in the rainshadow of Vancouver Island, an almighty breakwater that takes the full frontal attack of Pacific weather systems. The island's shoreline deflects Pacific storms and seas, and its mountainous backbone takes the brunt of the precipitation. As a result, the southern coastal mainland enjoys one of the most balanced climates in Canada, with a mean daily maximum of over 20°C (70°F) in the summer months.

WIND: Due to the NW/SE orientation of the Strait of Georgia, the predominant winds funnel along this axis. Northwesterly winds blow southward as the high pressure builds, bringing clear, sunny skies. The wind then switches around to a southeasterly as a low-pressure front approaches the coast, bringing overcast skies and wet weather.

WAVES: Hazardous wave action develops as a result of the wind interacting with the tidal current. In general, sea conditions are potentially dangerous when the wind opposes the current. A strong northwesterly meeting the outflow current from the Fraser River will create wave-sailing conditions at Spanish Banks and massive, steep surf will break over the shallows around sandheads.

TIDES: Although the rise and fall (range) of the tide is large — 4.8 m (15 ft) — this in itself is usually not a problem, although care should be exercised while anchoring and closing the shoreline. Tidal dangers can arise where land mass restricts tidal flow and currents can build to a significant force.

CURRENTS: In the area covered, strong currents of 6 knots or more on both the ebb and the flood exist at First and Second Narrows; fortunately these are well tabulated in the *Tide and Current Tables*. Lesser currents of 2–3 knots, on a large tide, flow NW and SE in the Strait of Georgia and in and out of Burrard Inlet, adding significant time to boaters' passage time. *Note: Always be aware of the state of the tide and current, as it is prudent to travel with the tidal flow and transit narrows and passes at slack water.*

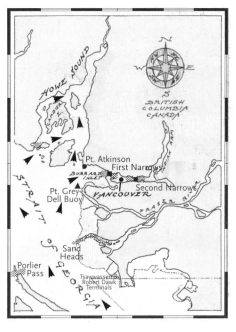

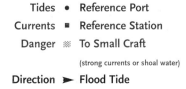

Tides • Reference Port
Currents ■ Reference Station
Danger ※ To Small Craft
(strong currents or shoal water)
Direction ➤ Flood Tide

CHARTS & NAUTICAL PUBLICATIONS

We have carefully designed this cruising guide to work in conjunction with the Canadian Hydrographic Service (CHS) charts and publications, and above each destination we have referenced the appropriate charts.

For their safety, all operators of ships and boats are required to have official, up-to-date charts and publications on board that cover the area they are navigating. These charts can be referenced from the *Pacific Coast Catalogue, Nautical Charts and Related Publications,* edited by the CHS and available free of charge at any chart dealer.

Individual charts are the primary tools used by professional mariners and recreational boaters, and those listed below cover the entire area included in this volume (Volume 3): Charts: 3458, 3459, 3493, 3495, 3512, 3514, 3526, 3534, 3535 and 3536.

Strip Charts 3311: Strait of Georgia — Sunshine Coast — Vancouver Harbour to Desolation Sound covers the majority of Volume 3. These charts are less cumbersome than the full-sized charts and are specifically designed for recreational boaters and small craft.

The Cruising Atlas (Chart 3312) is especially useful for Volume 3 as it covers Jervis Inlet and Lasqueti and southern Texada islands, and has been designed with the recreational boater in mind. This comprehensive navigational resource gives extensive supplementary information, extracts from *Sailing Directions* (see Nautical Publications section, below) and approach photographs to certain anchorages and passages. All charts referenced are metric editions.

ELECTRONIC CHARTS

Electronic charts are raster scans of CHS individual charts, produced under licence by Nautical Data International (NDI). They may be viewed independently on your computer or with the appropriate navigational software as an on-board aid to navigation. We recommend the following navigational software (compatible with NDI charts): Nobeltec Inc. Visual Navigation Suite, call 1-800-495-6279 Maptech: Marine Software, call 1-888-839-5551 Fugawi: Moving Map Software, call 416-920-0447 Note: In 2002, paper charts were still a legal, on-board requirement for all craft.

APPROACH WAYPOINTS

Approach waypoints are latitude and longitude positions based on NAD 83 and shown in degrees, minutes and decimals of a minute. They are located in deep water, at positions from which the illustrated features will be readily discernible in daylight.

PUBLICATIONS

We recommend the following publications to accompany your copy of Volume 3 of *A Dreamspeaker Cruising Guide.* For further reading, consult the Selected Reading list on page 188.

NAUTICAL PUBLICATIONS, CHS

Canadian Tide and Current Tables, Volume 5: Juan de Fuca Strait and Strait of Georgia
Pacific Coast Catalogue, Nautical Charts and Related Publications
(also includes a full list of available nautical publications and chart dealers)
Symbols and Abbreviations Used on Canadian Charts: Chart 1
Sailing Directions: British Columbia Coast (South Portion)

WEATHER PUBLICATIONS, ENVIRONMENT CANADA

Marine Weather Hazards Manual — West Coast: A Guide to Local Forecasts and Conditions
Mariner's Guide: West Coast Marine Weather Services
The Wind Came All Ways by Owen Lange (GDS, 1999)

BOATING SAFETY PUBLICATIONS, CANADIAN COAST GUARD

The Canadian Aids to Navigation System: Marine Navigation Services Directorate
List of Lights, Buoys and Fog Signals: Pacific Coast
Protecting British Columbia's Aquatic Environment: A Boaters Guide

EMERGENCY PROCEDURES & HOW TO USE THIS BOOK

THE CANADIAN COAST GUARD is a multitask organization whose primary role of search and rescue is supported by the following roles: maintaining the Aids to Navigation, operating the Office of Safe Boating and, in association with Environment Canada, the Marine Weather Forecast. For a copy of the *Safe Boating Guide*, call 1-800-267-6687. For search and rescue, call:

TELEPHONE	1-800-567-5111
CELLULAR	*311
VHF CHANNEL	16

EMERGENCY RADIO PROCEDURES
MAYDAY: For immediate danger to life or vessel.
PAN-PAN: For urgency but no immediate danger to life or vessel. For MAYDAY or PAN-PAN, transmit the following on VHF channel 16 or 2182 kHz.
1. MAYDAY, MAYDAY, MAYDAY (or PAN-PAN, PAN-PAN, PAN-PAN), this is [vessel name and radio call sign].
2. State your position and the nature of the distress.
3. State the number of people on board and describe the vessel [length, make/type, colour, power, registration number].

NOTE: If the distress is not life-threatening, the Coast Guard will put out a general call to boaters in your area for assistance. A tow at sea by a commercial operator can be expensive; however, C-TOW, 1-800-747-8877, operates a marine-assistance network in B.C. waters. HUB International TOS Ltd., 1-877-986-5265, Platinum Bluewater Contact, provides marine towing insurance.

HOW TO USE THIS BOOK
This sample layout identifies the various features of this cruising guide that will help you to reach your destination safely, and give you plenty of information.

Chapter & featured destination reference —
Chapter legend —
Destination locator —
* Approach waypoint latitude & longitude —
Tips on best approach & anchorages —
Cautionary note —

Depth contour (approximate position). Depths reduced to lowest normal tide (zero tide) —
Solid black line indicates HW mark —
Green area indicates land above HW mark —
Sepia area indicates shoreline that covers & uncovers with the tide —
Blue area indicates shallower water —
White area indicates deeper water that is safe for navigation —
* Asterisk indicates approximate position of approach waypoint —
Boats at anchor —
Red broken line indicates a safe approach course —
Aerial approach or ambient photograph —
HW: high water
LW: low water

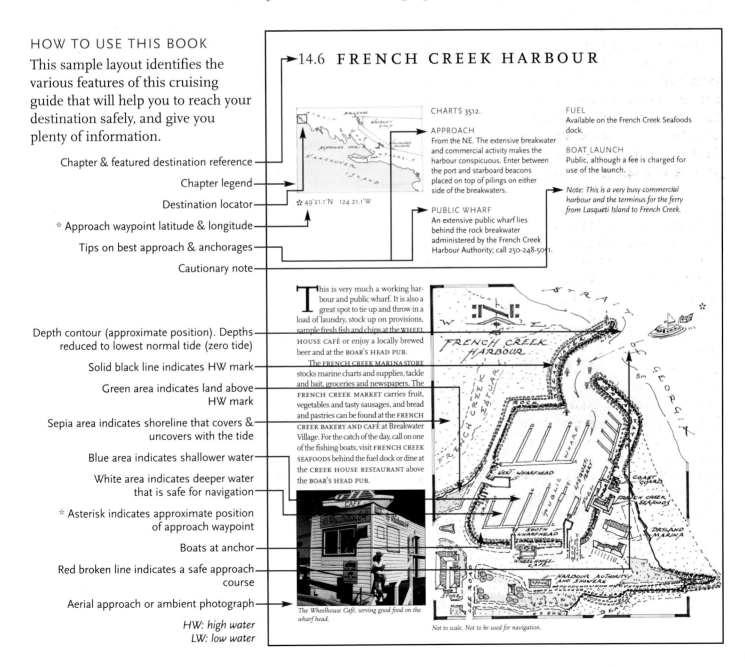

14.6 FRENCH CREEK HARBOUR

* 49°21.1'N 124 21.1'W

CHARTS 3512.

APPROACH
From the NE. The extensive breakwater and commercial activity makes the harbour conspicuous. Enter between the port and starboard beacons placed on top of pilings on either side of the breakwaters.

PUBLIC WHARF
An extensive public wharf lies behind the rock breakwater administered by the French Creek Harbour Authority; call 250-248-5051.

FUEL
Available on the French Creek Seafoods dock.

BOAT LAUNCH
Public, although a fee is charged for use of the launch.

Note: This is a very busy commercial harbour and the terminus for the ferry from Lasqueti Island to French Creek.

This is very much a working harbour and public wharf. It is also a great spot to tie up and throw in a load of laundry, stock up on provisions, sample fresh fish and chips at the WHEELHOUSE CAFÉ or enjoy a locally brewed beer and at the BOAR'S HEAD PUB. The FRENCH CREEK MARINA STORE stocks marine charts and supplies, tackle and bait, groceries and newspapers. The FRENCH CREEK MARKET carries fruit, vegetables and tasty sausages, and bread and pastries can be found at the FRENCH CREEK BAKERY AND CAFÉ at Breakwater Village. For the catch of the day, call on one of the fishing boats, visit FRENCH CREEK SEAFOODS behind the fuel dock or dine at the CREEK HOUSE RESTAURANT above the BOAR'S HEAD PUB.

The Wheelhouse Café, serving good food on the wharf head.

Not to scale. Not to be used for navigation.

49° NORTH

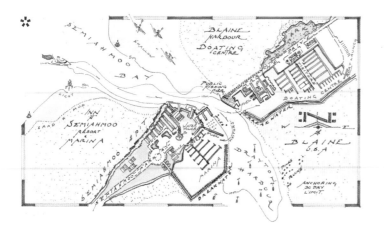

❉ 48°59.7'N 122°47.1'W

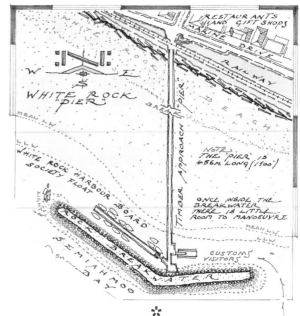

❉ 49°00.9'N 122°48.3'W

1.1 BLAINE, U.S.A.

APPROACH
The water tower is conspicuous within the Semiahmoo development. Enter the Drayton Harbour entrance channel by leaving the port (green) buoy to the E.

MARINAS
BLAINE HARBOR BOATING CENTER, 360-647-6176.
SEMIAHMOO MARINA, 360-371-0440.
Note: Blaine is a U.S. Customs Point of Entry, call 360-332-6318.

1.2 WHITE ROCK PIER, CANADA

APPROACH
From the SW. Masts of moored boats silhouetted over the breakwater are conspicuous.

PUBLIC WHARF
The NW finger is private. The SW float is strictly for customs clearance.
Note: White Rock is a Canada Customs Point of Entry, call 1-888-226-7277.

PASSAGES NORTH

The coastline from 49° North to Vancouver is low-lying, Fraser River delta country. This part of the Lower Mainland sees more than its fair share of mist and fog. When a wind is blowing, shallow waters make for a rough ride and heavy commercial shipping requires constant monitoring.

When cruising north, the recreational boater who chooses the Strait of Georgia's eastern shore will find four convenient destinations that straddle the international border — as this is border country, customs entry requirements need to be strictly adhered to. *Note: Fuel is available in Blaine, Point Roberts Marina and Steveston.*

1.1 Blaine: You have a choice of access: downtown Blaine Harbor with its newly refurbished facilities or Semiahmoo with its restaurants, golf course and other resort facilities. Boats are also able to swing at anchor in Drayton Harbor.

1.2 White Rock Pier: International visitors can clear customs on the southwest float.

1.3 Point Roberts Marina: This modern concrete affair has a no-nonsense marine chandlery and repair facility. The hike to Lighthouse Park, where you can watch the local orca pods from a viewing platform, is well worth the effort.

1.4 Steveston: What was once a fishing village is today more like a maritime heritage town as tourism is now the main revenue source. It is a fun place to visit, with fishermen at work while visitors vie for seats at the many renowned fish and chips stores.

Sandheads marks the seaward end of the Fraser River, South Arm.

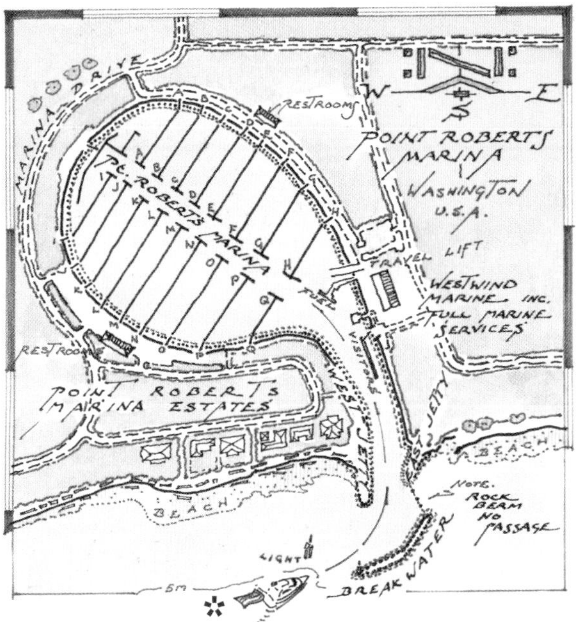

✲ 48° 58.3'N 123° 4.0'W

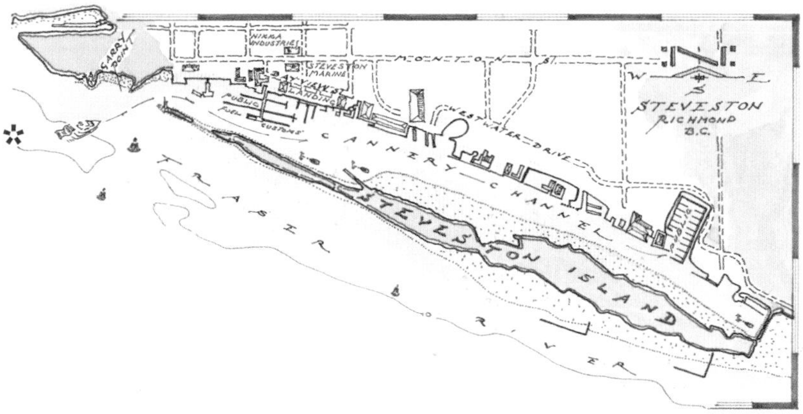

✲ 49°7.4'N 123°11.8'W

1.3 POINT ROBERTS, U.S.A.

APPROACH

From the SW. A dredged channel lies close to the breakwater. Enter the marina between the E and W jetties.

MARINA

A visitor float lies in the entrance channel to POINT ROBERTS MARINA; call 360-945-2255.

Note: Point Roberts is a US Customs Port of Entry, call 360-945-2314.

1.4 STEVESTON, CANADA

APPROACH

Via the Fraser River's southern arm leaving the Steveston Jetty to the N. Enter Cannery Channel close by the E tip of Steveston Island and Garry Point.

PUBLIC WHARF

Two extensive wharves lie either end of Cannery Channel.

Note: Steveston is a Canada Customs Point of Entry, call 1-888-226-7277.

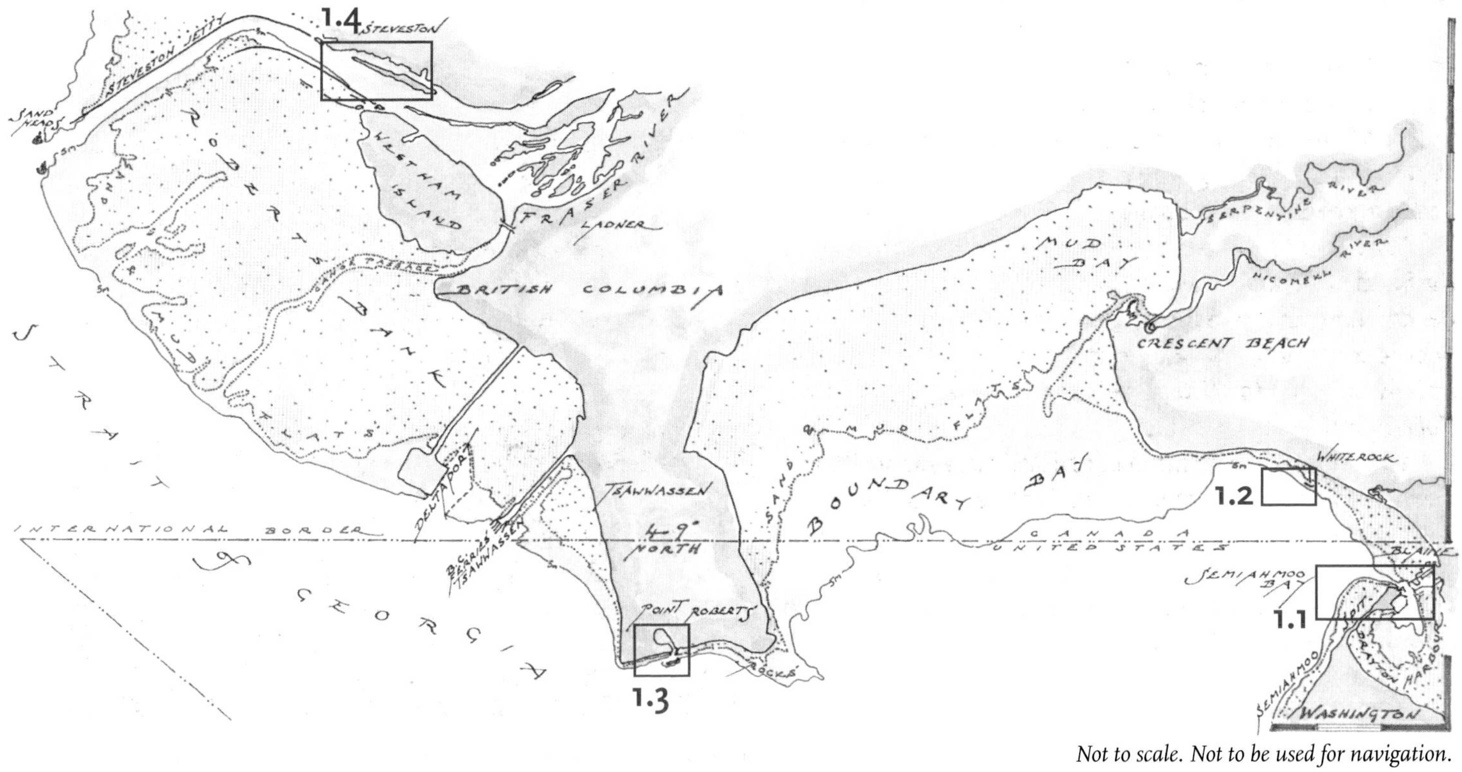

Not to scale. Not to be used for navigation.

CROSSING THE STRAIT

For boaters used to the sheltered Gulf Islands, the open waters of the Strait of Georgia are a little daunting. The Strait is no kids' playground, and crossing it needs careful planning. Listen to the weather forecast and go with wind and tidal current. Here are a few of the more popular routes.

TO VANCOUVER

1. Active Pass to Point Grey (25 N miles); because of ferries, shipping lanes and shoal water off Sturgeon Bank, this route is not recommended.
2. Porlier Pass to Point Grey (20 N miles) is a favoured route from mid-Gulf Island points of departure, sailable on both NW and SE winds.
3. Gabriola Passage. The Flat Top Islands to Point Grey (17 N miles) is our preferred route. After Gabriola Passage, take a breather in Silva Bay until conditions are favourable; a good sail to Vancouver or Howe Sound is then possible on both a NW and a SE wind.

TO HOWE SOUND

4. Nanaimo to Horseshoe Bay or Snug Cove on Bowen Island (28 N miles); keep an eye out for ferry traffic.
5. Nanaimo to Gibsons (20 N miles); Shoal Channel is navigated by small craft, best crossed on a rising tide, mid to high water.

TO THE SUNSHINE COAST

6. Nanaimo to Welcome Passage (20 N miles) is a straight run north if Whiskey Golf is not active; a good sail on a SE wind.
7. Schooner Cove to Pender Harbour (20 N miles) is only a slight detour if Whiskey Golf is active. A favoured route with power boaters; a good sail is possible on a southerly wind.

TO LASQUETI

8. French Creek to False Bay (8 N miles). This is a short, open water crossing and a good route if exploring the Lasqueti and Jedediah anchorages.

Wishing you a safe and enjoyable crossing.

Not to scale. Not to be used for navigation.

Chapter 2

VANCOUVER, BURRARD INLET

A rowing shell and crew in Coal Harbour set up for a sunset run to Canada Place.

Chapter 2
VANCOUVER, BURRARD INLET

Fireworks at the Festival of Light.

TIDES
Canadian Tide and Current Tables, Volume 5
Reference Ports: Point Atkinson (west of First Narrows), Vancouver (east of First Narrows)

CURRENTS
Reference Station: First Narrows
Note: Maximum current on a large tide, 6 kts on the flood and 5.4 kts on the ebb.

WEATHER
Area: Strait of Georgia
Reporting Stations: Sand Heads, Jericho and Point Atkinson

Note: In summer there tends to be a 50/50 mix of northwesterly and southeasterly winds. The buildup of a high-pressure ridge brings clear skies and westerly winds into Burrard Inlet. The wind switching around to the SE generally signals rain and unsettled weather.

CAUTIONARY NOTES: *It is unadvisable to travel N from Point Roberts and Tsawwassen to Point Grey in Vancouver when strong NW winds are blowing onto Sand Heads and an ebbing current is draining out from the Fraser River. Seas can build over the shallows of the Fraser delta and be dangerous to small craft. When proceeding north of Sand Heads, skippers should stay to the inside of the shipping channel, taking care not to stray onto Sturgeon Bank off Lulu Island or Spanish Banks off Point Grey.*

On rounding Point Grey, the first-time visitor is often surprised by the cluster of high towers that mark Vancouver's downtown skyline, contrasting with the low-rise neighbourhoods and abundance of green spaces. Voted one of the most beautiful cities in the world, Vancouver is a winner well worth the detour. Blessed with a spectacular natural setting, the city offers a wonderful combination of cosmopolitan urban living and outdoor activities in close proximity to mountains, forests and the ocean. Although Vancouver Harbour is primarily commercial, it is endeavouring to facilitate visits from recreational boaters by providing additional moorage and a designated anchorage in False Creek.

Burrard Inlet extends from Point Atkinson along the base of the spectacular North Shore mountains, through Vancouver Harbour east to Port Moody and Indian Arm. It continues around Stanley Park into English Bay and False Creek and along Kitsilano, Jericho Beach and Spanish Banks to Point Grey — a total shoreline of 152.6 km (95 miles), much of it fringed by a stone promenade, the Sea Wall.

Vancouver Harbour is a commercial port, Canada's largest and second only to Long Beach, California, on the West Coast. The busy cruise liner terminal at Canada Place recently counted its millionth passenger. International freighters waiting to load or unload their cargo can be seen anchored in designated stations near the entrance to Burrard Inlet, within the harbour limits.

Within Vancouver Harbour, Coal Harbour has undergone huge redevelopment in the past ten years, with the southern shore now prime waterfront property housing million-dollar high-rises, manicured parks and a large marina favoured by visiting mega-yachts. THE VANCOUVER ROWING CLUB, a heritage landmark, is in an ideal location backed by Stanley Park. It is a fun place to stay when moorage can be arranged.

Both moorage and designated anchorage are available in False Creek, the north shore of which has undergone major development since Expo 86. Conveniently close to the delights of Granville Island and the downtown sights, shops and restaurants, False Creek is a wonderful spot to spend time getting to know Vancouver while living in the heart of the city.

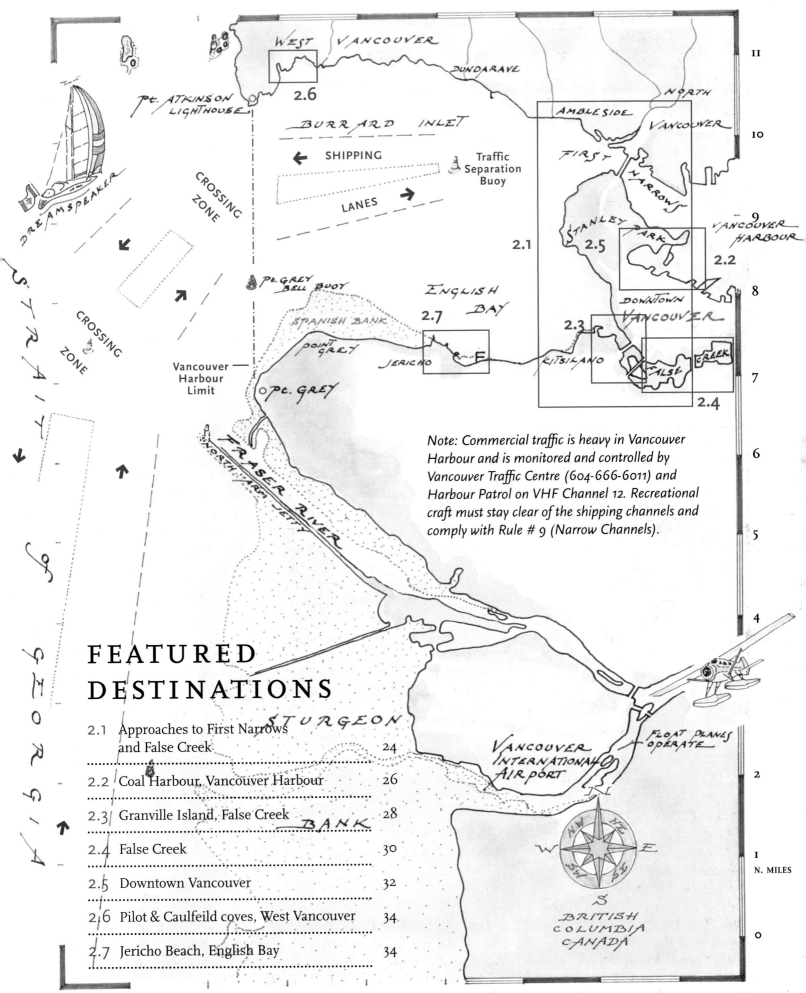

WEST VANCOUVER

DUNDARAVE

NORTH

AMBLESIDE

VANCOUVER

PT. ATKINSON
LIGHTHOUSE

2.6

FIRST NARROWS

BURRARD INLET

← SHIPPING

Traffic
Separation
Buoy

LANES →

STANLEY PARK

2.5

VANCOUVER
HARBOUR

2.2

DREAMSPEAKER

CROSSING
ZONE

2.1

DOWNTOWN
VANCOUVER

↓

PT. GREY
BELL BUOY

ENGLISH
BAY

2.7

2.3

↑

CROSSING
ZONE

SPANISH BANK

JERICHO

KITSILANO

FALSE CREEK

2.4

S T R A I T

POINT
GREY

Vancouver
Harbour
Limit

PT. GREY

Note: Commercial traffic is heavy in Vancouver
Harbour and is monitored and controlled by
Vancouver Traffic Centre (604-666-6011) and
Harbour Patrol on VHF Channel 12. Recreational
craft must stay clear of the shipping channels and
comply with Rule # 9 (Narrow Channels).

o f

NORTH ARM JETTY

FRASER RIVER

G E O R G I A

↑

FEATURED DESTINATIONS

STURGEON

BANK

VANCOUVER
INTERNATIONAL
AIRPORT

FLOAT PLANES
OPERATE

NW N NE
W   E
SW S SE

BRITISH
COLUMBIA
CANADA

11

10

9

8

7

6

5

4

2

1

N. MILES

0

Not to scale. Not to be used for navigation.

2.1 APPROACHES TO FIRST NARROWS AND FALSE CREEK

✳ (A) 49°18.8'N 123°10.0'W
  (B) 49°17.5'N 123°10.0'W

Approaching First Narrows, a cruise ship leaves the harbour under the Lion's Gate Bridge.

The water slide on English Bay Beach is a summer landmark.

A charter boat approaches Burrard Bridge.

Moorage facilities for recreational craft in the city of Vancouver can be found beyond Lions Gate Bridge in Coal Harbour, and moorage and protected anchorage can be found beyond Burrard Bridge in False Creek.

(A) The city's northern entrance along West Vancouver's affable shoreline takes the visiting boater under Lions Gate Bridge, built across First Narrows in 1939. The classic suspension design and splendid curved lines have made this structure a prominent city landmark. On entering the Inner Harbour, visiting boaters are often overwhelmed by the sight of sleek cruise liners, international freighters and tugs towing large barges slipping under Lions Gate, while commercial float planes and helicopters fly overhead.

The south shore of the harbour entrance is dominated by Vancouver's pride and joy — Stanley Park. Encircled by a busy Sea Wall crowded with walkers, bikers and in-line skaters, this wonderful expanse of green leads to Brockton Point Lighthouse. Once the Burnaby Shoal light has been rounded, the impressive tent-like sails of Canada Place come into view. Home to the VANCOUVER TRADE AND CONVENTION CENTRE, an expansive cruise ship terminal and the PAN PACIFIC HOTEL, this unique structure will confirm your arrival in Vancouver's modern and cosmopolitan downtown (see 2.2, pages 26–27, and 2.5, pages 32–33).

(B) To reach False Creek (also within the Port of Vancouver boundaries), boaters enter English Bay and pass the legendary Siwash Rock, Third and Second beaches in Stanley Park and the West End beaches of English Bay. Kitsilano Beach, the distinctive A-frame structure of the Maritime Museum — housing the famous *St. Roch* — and the green lawns of Vanier Park come into view on the starboard side, before passing under Burrard Bridge and past the Kitsilano Coast Guard Station into the hustle, bustle and delights of Granville Island (see 2.3; pages 28–29). On a blue-sky summer's day the sandy beaches are filled with colourful umbrellas, frolicking Vancouverites and happy visitors taking advantage of the good weather. Even in the most fickle of winds, exotic kites fly high above the open expanse of Vanier Park.

CHARTS 3493. 3311 Sheet 1

APPROACH

(A) FIRST NARROWS: Lions Gate Bridge crosses First Narrows and a shipping channel runs to Brockton Point. Inbound craft need to stay to starboard after rounding Prospect Point light. Deep water extends to the outside of the bridge supports.

Note: Strong tidal currents with associated overfalls and tide rips may be experienced in First Narrows.

APPROACH

(B) FALSE CREEK: The entrance lies in the SE portion of English Bay and is conspicuous by the span of Burrard Bridge. The approach is best made in the white sector of the light on the north pier of the bridge and in centre channel. Keep to the 5-knot speed limit (2–3 knots is even safer) once under the bridge.

MARINAS

See 2.2; Coal Harbour.

ANCHOR

Possible off Kitsilano and English Bay beaches for short stays. Protected from all quarters except the W and NW, holding good in sand.

MARINAS

See 2.3 Granville Island; and 2.4 False Creek.

BOAT LAUNCH

Public, W of the Kitsilano Coast Guard Station in Vanier Park.

Note: It is safe in the summer to overnight off the beaches, although they are not designated as anchorages.

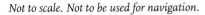

Not to scale. Not to be used for navigation.

2.2 COAL HARBOUR, VANCOUVER HARBOUR

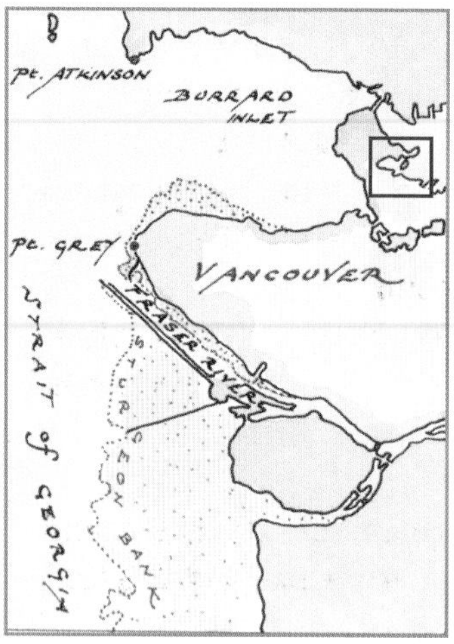

✲ 49°17.6'N 123°7.0'W

The Brockton Point light signals Burnaby shoals.

The cruise liner terminal, docks and downtown.

The rowing club at the head of Coal Harbour.

Coal Harbour's coal seam never proved as substantial as anticipated and it was the Union Steamship Company that finally put Coal Harbour on the map in 1891, by assembling three ships in a makeshift yard on the south shore. This encouraged an assortment of ship and engine builders to move in, establishing Coal Harbour as British Columbia's major marine centre.

Today Coal Harbour's northern shoreline is backed by Stanley Park, the heart and soul of downtown Vancouver. The park's 405-hectare reserve includes forests, meadows and picnicking lawns, encircled by a 10.5-km (6.5-mile) stone Sea Wall and interlaced with hiking, biking and jogging trails that lead to Beaver Lake and Lost Lagoon. Once an extension of Coal Harbour, this is now a freshwater lake and wild-bird sanctuary (see 2.5, page 32).

THE VANCOUVER AQUARIUM is Canada's largest and the Salmon Stream Project leading from the Aquarium into Coal Harbour is also worth a visit.

Deadman's Island, surrounded by muddy shallows at LW, is connected to the mainland by a causeway. Once a First Nations burial site, it is now a naval reserve. An interesting collection of hand-carved totem poles from a number of First Nations communities can be found behind Brockton Point. The Nine O'Clock Gun on Hallelujah Point is an electrically fired cannon whose boom is a familiar sound to Vancouver residents at 9 each evening.

Once industrial, Coal Harbour's southern shoreline is now prime waterfront property housing million-dollar high-rises, restaurants, parks, a community centre, the WESTIN BAYSHORE HOTEL, HARBOUR FERRIES, yacht brokerages, charter companies and a large new marina. WRIGHT MARINER, the only chandlery on the new Sea Wall, has been in the neighbourhood longer than most of the old salts care to remember; it is well stocked with boating hardware and marine necessities. The LIFT BAR GRILL and CARDERO'S RESTAURANT AND MARINE PUB are popular waterfront meeting places while homey BOJANGLES CAFÉ takes care of the coffee crowd.

Built in 1911, the VANCOUVER ROWING CLUB is now a heritage landmark sitting comfortably on its piles at the head of Coal Harbour. Club facilities include showers, a downstairs pub and an upstairs bar with a view of downtown from the patio. The lower deck and club dock are especially busy on weekends and after 5 p.m. on weekdays.

CHARTS 3493. 3311, Sheet 1

APPROACH
Inbound visitors should first round the lighted starboard (red) aid over Burnaby Shoal before heading S/SW to the entrance to Coal Harbour. Note that locals often use an inside channel west of the fuel barges. The speed restriction of 5 knots is enforced by the Harbour Patrol.

ANCHOR
Anchoring is prohibited south of a line from the tip of Deadman's Island.

PARKS FLOAT
A new 500-ft parks float off Harbour Green Park is available to visiting boaters, to clear customs and make arrangements for overnight moorage. Maximum stay is 3 hours.

MARINAS
COAL HARBOUR MARINA, 604-681-2628. VHF channel 66A. Extensive moorage with summer berths for visitors.
BAYSHORE WEST, 604-689-5331
HARBOUR CRUISES, 604-687-9558

ROYAL VANCOUVER YACHT CLUB, 604-224-1344. Reciprocity only.
VANCOUVER ROWING CLUB, 604-687-3400. Visitor and reciprocal moorage if space is available; call ahead to confirm.
BBX wireless internet is available at all marinas except Harbour Cruises.

FUEL
A fuel barge E of Deadman's Island provides water, ice, bait and snacks.

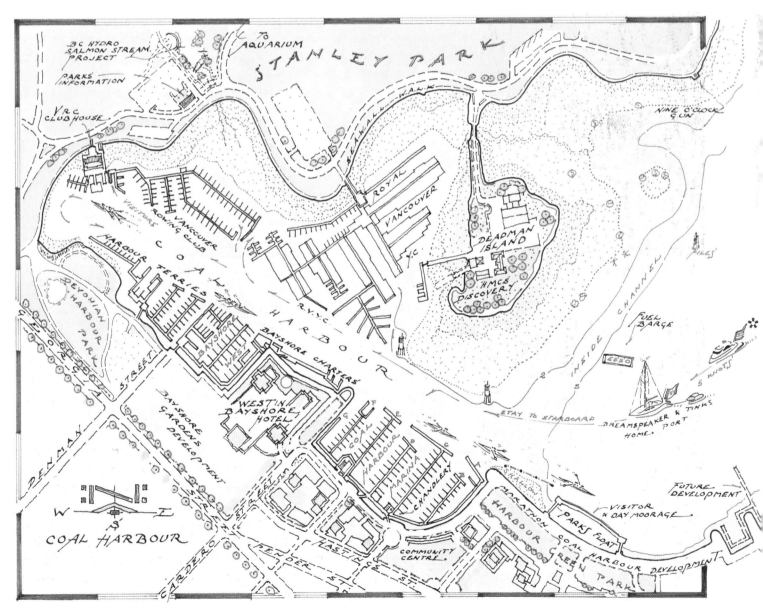

Not to scale. Not to be used for navigation.

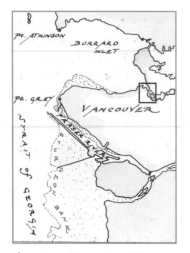

✿ 49°17.0'N 123°9.0'W

After passing under Burrard Bridge, the island and market are well signposted.

The island is full of colour and music.

Note: The waters between Burrard and Granville bridges are a hive of activity in the summer months with local and visiting boats, tugs pulling barges, fishing boats, charter yachts, rowers, kayakers, rental runabouts and a fleet of mini-ferries crossing to and from the island, all converging in one small space. Be sure to keep a constant and vigilant watch and maintain a cool and courteous demeanour at all times.

Situated under Granville Bridge on the southern shore of False Creek, the small peninsula that is Granville Island was originally two sandbars favoured by the Squamish First Nation as a winter fishing ground. Transformed into an industrial island servicing the maritime industry in 1916, it was redeveloped in 1979 into a friendly mix of industry, businesses, markets, restaurants, theatres, artists' studios and galleries (including the EMILY CARR INSTITUTE OF ART AND DESIGN), a hotel and a kids' water park and picnic area. OCEAN CONCRETE, one of the original industries, still operates on the island.

The major attraction is the Granville Island Market. Open 9 a.m.–7 p.m. seven days a week, this lively market is bursting at the seams with fresh produce, artisans, buskers, local shoppers and tourists. It offers an overwhelming choice of greengrocers, butchers, fishmongers, bakeries, European delicatessens, specialist food and wine merchants and coffee shops. The Thursday Farmers' Market sells delicious "just picked" and organic produce in the summer.

The MARITIME MARKET along Duranleau Street, on the west side of the island, offers a variety of marine supplies, boat maintenance services and a busy travel lift. It also houses a museum, a scuba diving school, an ocean kayak centre offering day rentals and tours, and a choice of yacht brokers and charter companies. Local and specialty tours and cruises are also available.

THE QUARTERDECK specializes in local and international charts in a dedicated section of the store alongside their excellent range of books and guides, while RED SKY AT NIGHT concentrates on casual clothing and footwear for boaters and JUSTIN STITCHES customizes clothing and accessories for just about anyone. While on your walking tour be sure to visit FEATHERCRAFT KAYAKS, near the end of Cartwright Street; THE GRANVILLE ISLAND BREWERY offers tastings and tours and is a great place to rehydrate if you enjoy specialty beers.

FALSE CREEK FERRIES and AQUABUS (with designated ferries for bicycles) transport visitors between Granville Island and other points on the inlet, as far east as Science World. At night the island is transformed into a fairyland of lights, bustling restaurants, live music and performing arts, all offering diverse and multicultural experiences.

APPROACH
In the white section of the light on the north pier of Burrard Bridge, keep to starboard of the centre channel between Sunset Beach and Kitsilano Coast Guard Station. Proceed slowly and refrain from overtaking. A 5-knot speed limit is in place, but 2–3 knots is advisable.

ANCHOR
There are no facilities for anchoring in this portion of False Creek (see 2.4, page 30).

MARINAS
BURRARD CIVIC — 604-733-5833; FISHERMANS WHARF 604-733-3625 BBX wireless internet available; PELICAN BAY — 604-263-5222.
Granville Island Public Market has day moorage for visitors up to a maximum of 3 hours; it is well policed by the island wardens, so don't overstay your welcome.

BOAT LAUNCH
Public, W of the Kitsilano Coast Guard Station in Vanier Park.

FUEL
False Creek Esso, NW of Burrard Bridge, at the entrance to False Creek.

Not to scale. Not to be used for navigation.

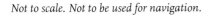

2.4 FALSE CREEK

✤ 49°17.0'N   123°9.0'W

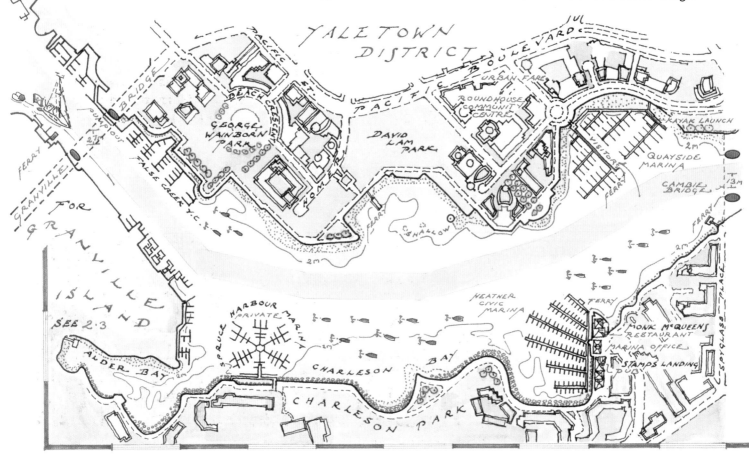

An eclectic array of craft anchored in Charleson Bay.

CHARTS 3493. 3311, Sheet 1

APPROACH
Inbound and outbound, stay to starboard within the navigational channel.
Note: Cambie Bridge has a minimum clearance of 13 m (42 ft).

ANCHOR
In the designated areas only. Depths 2–4 m (6–13 ft), holding good in soft mud. Anchor via free permit for up to 14 days, April 1–September 30. Permits available at the Boating Welcome Centre. Call 1- 866-677-2628.

MARINAS
QUAYSIDE MARINA offers some transient moorage; HEATHER CIVIC MARINA — 604- 874-2814
Note: False Creek is a definite NO-SEWAGE-DISCHARGE ZONE and a pump-out station is located under the Granville Street Bridge.

Beyond Granville Island and the south shore's houseboat community, False Creek opens up to a protected basin of flat water with reasonable depths for anchoring. It is a boaters' paradise in the heart of Vancouver.

On a typical busy summer's day, the creek will gaily embrace a mix of craft from mini-ferries, rowing shells, canoes, kayaks and dragon boats to the steady procession of commercial charters and tugs pulling barges. This is a glorious spot to spend time visiting the city, as shopping and sightseeing are close at hand and easily accessible by foot, bicycle or bus. MONK McQUEEN'S RESTAURANT and STAMPS LANDING PUB above HEATHER MARINA have waterfront views and the local supermarket and shops in LEG-N-BOOT SQUARE are close to both the anchorages and mooring buoys west of Cambie Street Bridge. Provisioning couldn't be easier with Granville Island Market just down the channel and an eclectic mix of specialty stores, cafés, restaurants and several parks on the north side, the original site of Expo 86. Beyond Pacific Boulevard are the renovated warehouses and lofts of Yaletown, once a neglected industrial zone, now a delightful mix of offices, shops and restaurants.

Modern architecture is in vogue at the Concord Pacific.

NOTE: *Yellow marks the navigational channel and designated no-anchoring zone. Anchoring is also forbidden in Alder Bay.*

Not to scale. Not to be used for navigation.

Dragon boat races in front of the Plaza of Nations.

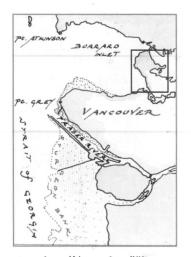

✛ 49°17.0'N 123°9.0'W

Second Beach, English Bay, summer playtime in the city.

Stanley Park Seawall.

West End architecture, old and new.

The visiting boater will find Vancouver's downtown easily accessible, whether you are moored in Coal Harbour or anchored in False Creek (see 2.2 and 2.4, pages 26 and 30). And as we have called it home for the past 14 years, we thought it only courteous to invite you on a walking/cycling tour of some of our favourite downtown spots.

One of our greatest pleasures is to jump on our trusty bikes (there are many rental stores at the N end of Denman) and take a quick trip around Stanley Park before the crowds take over the popular Sea Wall. We often end the tour with our reward — a long espresso accompanied by a sinful pastry or homemade ice cream at MUM'S GELATO AND COFFEE.

Friendly Denman Street is lined with coffee stops, cafés, bistros and restaurants and also houses a specialty magazine store and a mini-mall and hotel. One of the eclectic retail stores is a colourful condom emporium. If you need internet or office services, try M.Y. OFFICE at the S end of Denman street. For the tastiest and most affordable Szechuan cuisine, WON MORE has great food and service. For something a little more up-market, RAINCITY GRILL serves creative West Coast cuisine in a fusion of tastes. On the E side of Denman, a stroll through tree-lined streets will take you to Barclay Heritage Square, lined with eight restored houses dating from 1890 to 1909. That will take you back to a time before high-rises consumed the West End.

Davie Street, another well-populated residential centre with a lively style all its own, hums day and night. It too is filled with great places to eat, drink and be merry, as well as provision, rent a video or buy a book. ROMANO'S MACARONI GRILL, in a restored Queen Anne stone mansion near the foot of Davie, features a warm and relaxed Italian interior that welcomes families.

A leisurely stroll along the English Bay Park Sea Wall takes you past English Bay Beach, jammed on sunny days with locals and visitors claiming favourite logs. Standing tall on the peninsula breakwater is an elegant 6 m (20 ft) Inukshuk, modelled on a traditional Inuit navigational aid. The promenade continues to Sunset Beach and the Aquatic Centre, where a quick mini-ferry detour can be made to Granville Island (see 2.3, pages 28–29) or the Maritime Museum, Planetarium and Vanier Park. Avoid the detour and have coffee or a light lunch at FIDDLEHEAD JOE'S overlooking the hustle and bustle of False Creek.

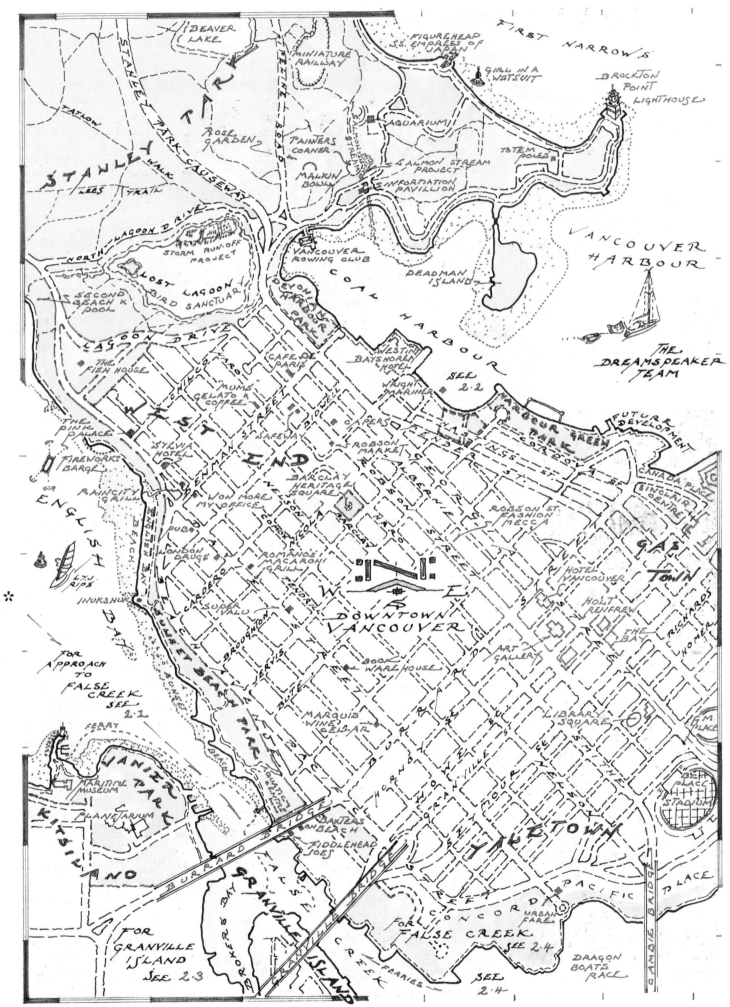

Not to scale. Not to be used for navigation.

2.6 PILOT & CAULFEILD COVES, WEST VANCOUVER

CHARTS 3481. 3311, Sheet 1

APPROACH
Pilot Cove — at LW when the sand and gravel beach is exposed. Caulfeild Cove — with caution: private mooring buoys dot the cove.

ANCHOR
On the shelf, off the sand and gravel beach. Exposed to southerlies and inlet wash. This is a day/picnic anchorage with fair holding.

PUBLIC WHARF
In Caulfeild Cove there is a small day wharf for pickup and drop-off or short stays.

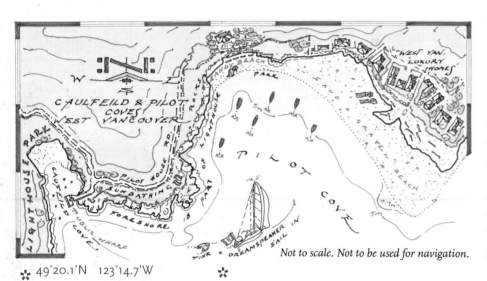

Not to scale. Not to be used for navigation.

❉ 49°20.1'N   123°14.7'W   ❉

On a sunny afternoon when the tide is out, the charming pocket beach in Pilot Cove is revealed. Just a hop and a skip from downtown Vancouver and popular with local families and their pooches, this lovely spot seems a world away from the crowds and hustle and bustle of the big city as you laze on the sun-warmed rocks or build sandcastles on the beach. At LLW the sand and rocky beach that fronts the waterfront homes is fully exposed and fun to explore.

2.7 JERICHO BEACH, ENGLISH BAY

CHARTS 3481. 3311, Sheet 1

APPROACH
Best made at LW. In the summer months, buoys mark the "no go" swimming area off the beach and a sailing zone to the west.

ANCHOR
Tuck in off the old float plane launch, where you will find fair protection from light westerlies and good protection from southerlies. This is primarily a day/picnic anchorage with good holding in sand.

MARINA
ROYAL VANCOUVER YACHT CLUB, JERICHO STATION; 604-224-1033. Reciprocity moorage only. BBX wireless internet is available.

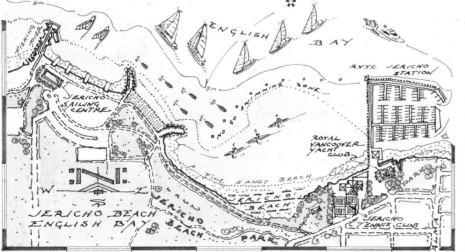

❉ 49°16.7'N   123°11.7'W

Not to scale. Not to be used for navigation.

Anchoring off Jericho Beach will give you a grandstand view of the tactical big-boat races put on by the ROYAL VANCOUVER YACHT CLUB. You might witness a dozen or so sailboats bearing down on you, only to tack at the last second to avoid the restricted beach area. On an altogether different scale, nifty small boats whip in and out of the JERICHO SAILING CENTRE and are thrilling to observe from the comfort of the cockpit with a pair of binoculars in one hand and a cool drink in the other.

Chapter 3

VANCOUVER HARBOUR & INDIAN ARM

At anchor in Indian Arm.

Lonsdale Quay in North Vancouver.

Chapter 3
VANCOUVER HARBOUR & INDIAN ARM

TIDES
Canadian Tide and Current Tables, Volume 5
Reference Port: Vancouver
Secondary Ports: Port Moody, Deep Cove and Buntzen Lake

CURRENTS
Reference Station: Second Narrows
Second Narrows is a constricted passage that runs under two bridges. The narrows is a restricted and controlled zone (see cautionary notes for details).

The flooding easterly current attains 6.5 knots in the passage while the ebbing westerly current seldom exceeds 5.5 knots and is best transited at or near slack water.

WEATHER
There is no specific reporting station for this area; however winds tend to be light in the summer (up-inlet during the day and outflow at night). Occasionally strong outflow winds do occur — be sure to listen for outflow wind warnings.

CAUTIONARY NOTES: *Keep in mind that while transiting Vancouver Harbour and Second Narrows, commercial vessels take priority over any other vessels. Sail only in the permitted zone and always listen in to Vancouver Harbour Control, Channel 12. The Second Narrows railway bridge has only 10.7 m (35 ft) clearance when fully down. If you require the lift span to be raised, establish communication with the bridge operator on VHF Channel 12. Remain 400 m (0.25 miles) from the bridge until the lift span has been raised and you are cleared for transit.*

The shoreline of Vancouver Harbour (western portion) from First to Second Narrows is home to the Port of Vancouver's many busy docks, quays and loading facilities and is a bustle of activity with freighters, cruise liners, hired runabouts, pleasure craft, float planes, tour boats, the North Shore/downtown ferry and tugs pulling barges.

Running north from upper Burrard Inlet to the Indian River estuary is a 17–km (11 mile) ocean fjord known as Indian Arm. Revealed when the last ice age receded 10,000 years ago, it is blessed with mainly protected and placid waters and some of the most gorgeous scenery on the West Coast. Indian Arm is popular with kayakers, canoeists and local runabouts, who can beach their craft easily. Boaters will find it hard to miss the monumental Buntzen Power Station (still operational), a surviving example of classic early-1900s industrial design visible from almost anywhere along the southern portion of the arm.

A wonderful weekend can be spent exploring the charm and splendour of Burrard Inlet and Indian Arm and its marine parks, using the protected summer anchorage in Bedwell Bay or the moorage facilities in Deep Cove as a base.

Established in 1996, Indian Arm Provincial Park covers over 9,500 hectares (23,750 acres) and protects the arm's entire shoreline. Co-managed by the Tsleil Waututh First Nation, it includes major old-growth forests, watersheds, alpine lakes, waterfalls and abundant marine and land life. Artefacts over 3,000 years old have been excavated in a number of the village sites and a variety of fascinating pictographs are scattered along the arm and up the Indian River. There are five marine parks: Racoon and Twin islands in Burrard Inlet, Bishop Creek, Clementine Creek and Granite Falls.

Also included in the park are a number of private waterfront cottages and yacht club outstations whose boundaries should be respected. BURRARD YACHT CLUB is located near Clementine Creek, DEEP COVE YACHT CLUB is north of Granite Falls and the notorious WIGWAM INN at the head of the inlet is now home to the ROYAL VANCOUVER YACHT CLUB. A commanding sight after a journey through wilderness, the inn was built in 1910 as a luxury summer resort for the rich and famous. After World War II it became a gambling casino and was raided and shut down in 1962. The building was unused until the RVYC purchased and renovated it, retaining its original colonial charm and grandeur.

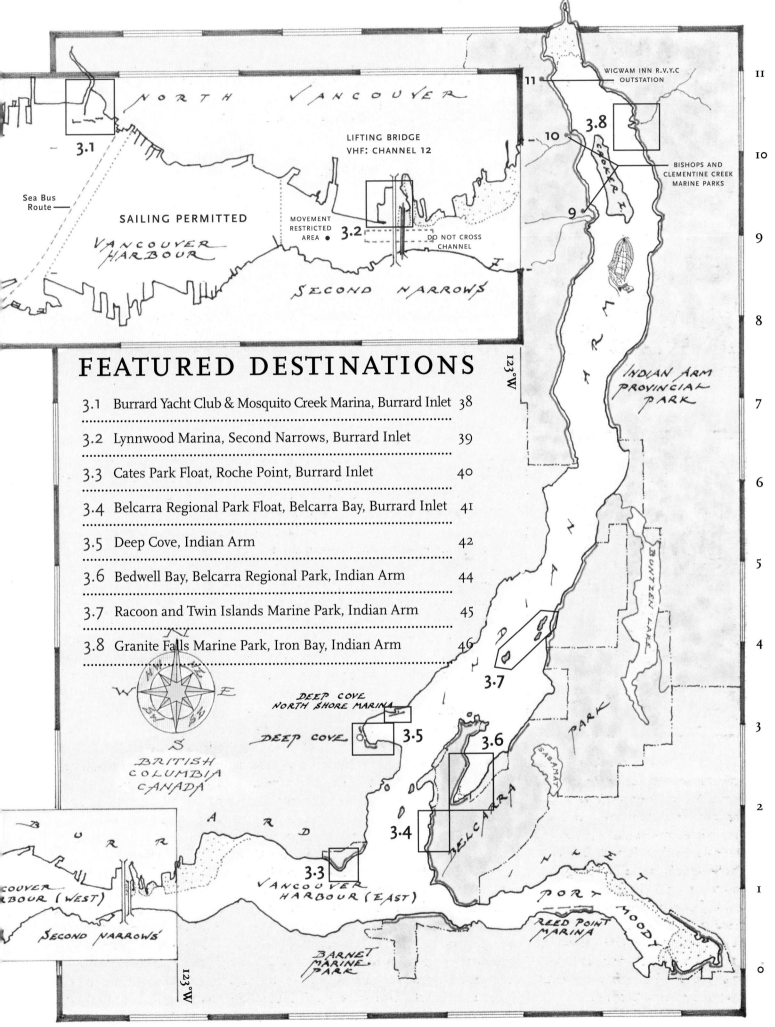

NORTH VANCOUVER

3.1

LIFTING BRIDGE
VHF: CHANNEL 12

Sea Bus Route

SAILING PERMITTED

VANCOUVER HARBOUR

MOVEMENT RESTRICTED AREA

3.2

DO NOT CROSS CHANNEL

SECOND NARROWS

WIGWAM INN R.V.Y.C OUTSTATION

11

3.8

10

9

BISHOPS AND CLEMENTINE CREEK MARINE PARKS

123°W

INDIAN ARM PROVINCIAL PARK

BUNTZEN LAKE

FEATURED DESTINATIONS

3.1   Burrard Yacht Club & Mosquito Creek Marina, Burrard Inlet   38

3.2   Lynnwood Marina, Second Narrows, Burrard Inlet   39

3.3   Cates Park Float, Roche Point, Burrard Inlet   40

3.4   Belcarra Regional Park Float, Belcarra Bay, Burrard Inlet   41

3.5   Deep Cove, Indian Arm   42

3.6   Bedwell Bay, Belcarra Regional Park, Indian Arm   44

3.7   Racoon and Twin Islands Marine Park, Indian Arm   45

3.8   Granite Falls Marine Park, Iron Bay, Indian Arm   46

BRITISH COLUMBIA CANADA

DEEP COVE NORTH SHORE MARINA

3.7

DEEP COVE

3.5

3.6

SASAMAT

3.4

BELCARRA

BURRARD

3.3

VANCOUVER HARBOUR (EAST)

PORT MOODY

INLET

REED POINT MARINA

VANCOUVER HARBOUR (WEST)

SECOND NARROWS

123°W

BARNET MARINE PARK

Not to scale. Not to be used for navigation.

3.1 BURRARD YACHT CLUB AND MOSQUITO CREEK MARINA, BURRARD INLET

✻ 49°18.6'N   123°05.5'W

CHARTS 3493. 3311, Sheet 1

APPROACH
From the south, the twin spires of St. Paul's Church are conspicuous. The floating breakwater is made up of old barges, coasters, etc., and the openings are not hard to spot.

ANCHOR
There is no designated anchorage within Vancouver Harbour.

PUBLIC WHARF
A parks float for transient moorage is available for "short visits" to North Vancouver and Lonsdale Quay.

MARINAS
BURRARD YACHT CLUB has reciprocal moorage only; call 604-988-0817. MOSQUITO CREEK MARINA has temporary visitor moorage, offers extensive marine repair facilities, a boat lift and a dry dock/hard space; call 604-987-4113. BBX wireless internet is available.

FUEL
At MOSQUITO CREEK MARINA.

The public pavillion with the city of North Vancouver float alongside.

North Vancouver's Lonsdale Quay is well worth a casual visit. The best access is via the Seabus, the ferry from downtown. However, if an annual refit or bottom paint job is due, the boat yard at Mosquito Creek is very handy for do-it-yourself or professional help.

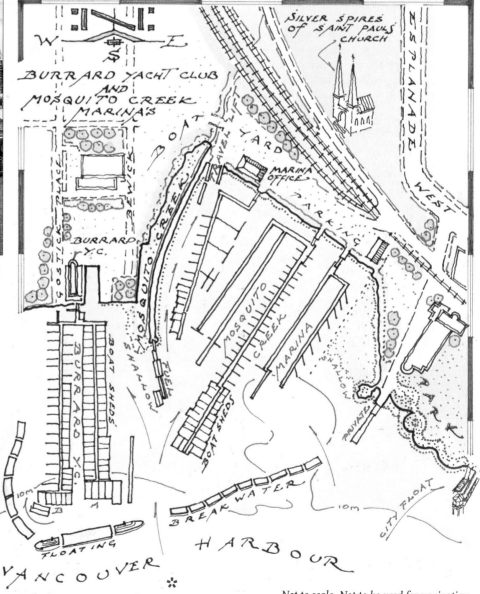

Not to scale. Not to be used for navigation.

LYNNWOOD MARINA, SECOND NARROWS, BURRARD INLET

CHARTS 3494. 3311, Sheet 1

APPROACH
The entrance lies west of the Second Narrows Bridge. Enter by rounding the end of Lynnterm Quay.

MARINA
LYNNWOOD MARINA (604-985-1533). No overnight moorage, but short-term (one month plus) is possible. A boat lift and extensive marine repair facilities are available on shore.

FUEL
At fuel barge E of Deadman Island.
Note: Currents around the entrance are similar in strength and direction to those tabulated for Second Narrows.

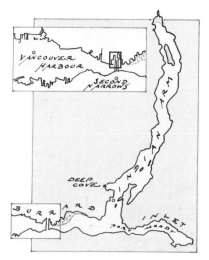

✳ 49°17.7'N 123°01.7'W

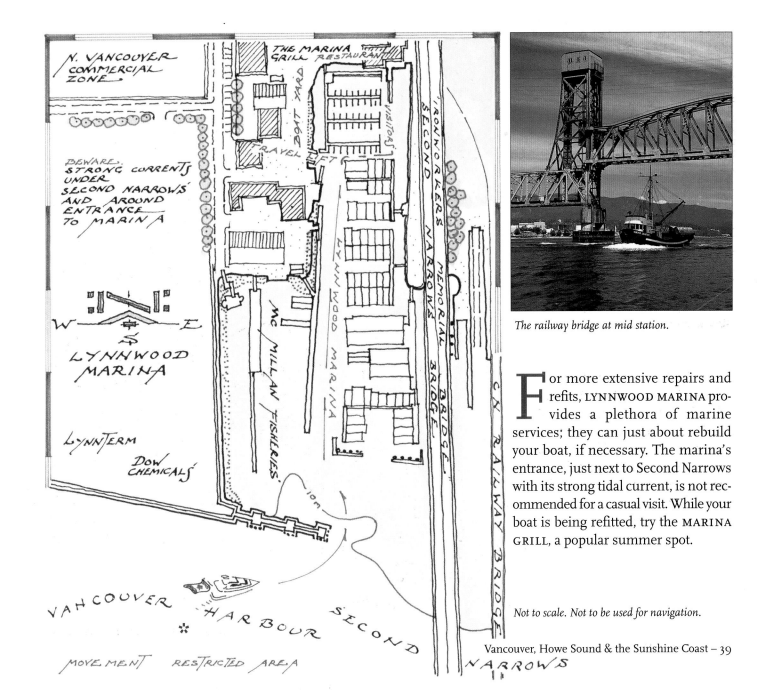

The railway bridge at mid station.

For more extensive repairs and refits, LYNNWOOD MARINA provides a plethora of marine services; they can just about rebuild your boat, if necessary. The marina's entrance, just next to Second Narrows with its strong tidal current, is not recommended for a casual visit. While your boat is being refitted, try the MARINA GRILL, a popular summer spot.

Not to scale. Not to be used for navigation.

3.3 CATES PARK FLOAT, ROCHE POINT, BURRARD INLET

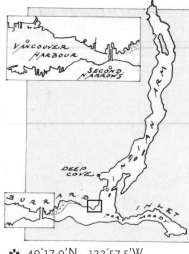

✿ 49°17.9'N 122°57.5'W

CHARTS 3495. 3311, Sheet 1

APPROACH
From the S. There are no obstructions on the approach.

ANCHOR
Possible NW of the float. Depth, holding and bottom condition unrecorded.

PARKS FLOAT
Used mostly by small recreational craft, though the outside offers day moorage to larger craft wishing to visit the park.

BOAT LAUNCH
The 5-lane public launch is open year-round. Fee charged; call 604-990-3800 for boat launch information. Very busy during summer weekends.

Dreamspeaker *visits Cates Park.*

Located at the tip of Indian Arm and named for the Cates family who founded a landmark tugboat company in North Vancouver, Cates Park provides boaters with a fun and convenient stopping-off point before Deep Cove. The park's 23 hectares (58 acres) include Roche Point Lighthouse and 6 km (4 miles) of waterfront trails that wind past sandy beaches and through a mixed forest of Douglas fir and big-leaf maple. A walk named for the notorious expatriate writer Malcolm Lowry takes you to a plaque noting the location of the squatter shack where he completed his most celebrated novel, *Under the Volcano* (1947). Park amenities include playgrounds, picnic lawns and tables, tennis courts, a concession stand and a swimming beach (lifeguards on duty Saturday and Sunday, July 1 to Labour Day). A cedar totem pole and a 15–m (50–ft) war canoe handcarved by Chief Henry Peter George are also displayed in the grounds.

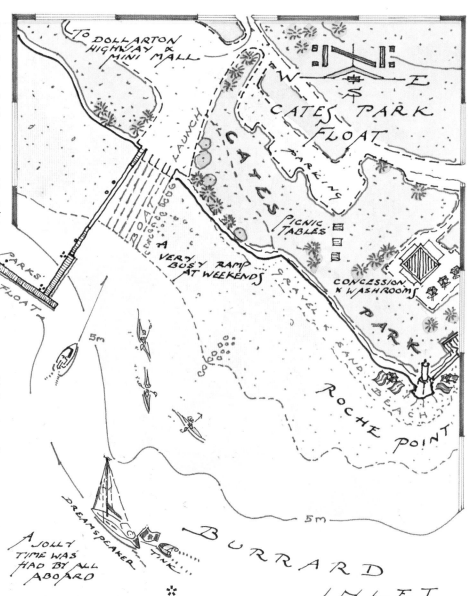

Not to scale. Not to be used for navigation.

BELCARRA REGIONAL PARK FLOAT, 3.4
BELCARRA BAY, BURRARD INLET

The park float is very popular with fishermen and picnic parties.

CHARTS 3495. 3311, Sheet 1

APPROACH
From the SW. There are no obstructions on the approach to the float.

ANCHOR
Anchorage is possible N or S of the float. Depth, holding and bottom condition unrecorded.

PARKS FLOAT
The extensive float is often very crowded. Charter vessels also dock here. No overnight moorage.

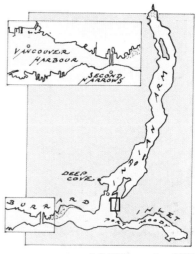

✿ 49°18.8'N   122°55.8'W

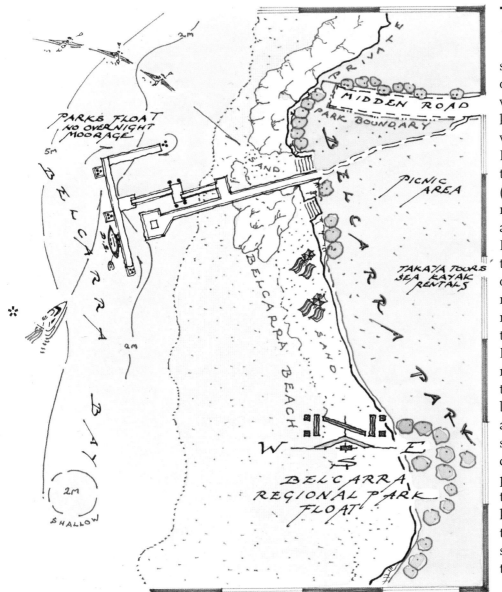

Not to scale. Not to be used for navigation.

When it's time for the kids to run off excess energy or the skipper and crew need to stretch boat-weary legs, Belcarra Park offers a convenient lunch or day stop with a sandy beach, picnic area and sea kayak tours and rentals. Once a major winter village of the Tsleil Waututh First Nation, who came here to harvest the abundant sea life, the park's 9 km (5.5 miles) of shoreline include a large midden that yielded several important archaeological finds when excavated. Hiking trails curve north along steep terrain to Jug Island Beach with views of Indian Arm and the North Shore mountains (2 hrs return). An easy 40-minute walk follows a gentle wooded trail to the muddy tidal flats of Bedwell Bay (see 3.6, page 48). The southern route hugs the shore's rocky coastline to Admiralty and Burns points, with beautiful vistas up Burrard Inlet (2 hrs and 2.5 hrs return). Certain trails are shared by hikers, horseback riders and cyclists, and are shown on the detailed park map, available from the information shelter; pets must be leashed and kept to designated areas. Just up from the public float is a LW pocket beach shaded by tall trees and strewn with twisted driftwood.

3.5 COMMUNITY OF DEEP COVE, INDIAN ARM

✼ 49°19.7'N 122°56.1'W

Approaching Deep Cove from Indian Arm.

The busy summer foreshore.

The cove's earliest residents were the Tsleil Waututh First Nation whose modern-day chief, Dan George, became a successful actor in his sixties and was nominated for an Academy Award for his part in *Little Big Man*. Deep Cove then became the site of a granite quarry and also provided access for lumber to be sent downstream to Dollar's Mill in Cates Park. In the 1930s it became a fashionable summer getaway for boat parties of daytrippers from Vancouver.

Today, fronted by lovely Panorama Park, the cove is as welcoming and friendly as ever. The park includes kids' playgrounds, an inviting sandy beach that's great for swimming, lush green lawns ideal for picnicking, and meandering paths and walkways that lead past the yacht club and public wharf to the ever-active DEEP COVE CANOE AND KAYAK CENTRE; call 604-929-2268.

A choice of restaurants, cafés, bistros, markets and ice-cream parlours line the main street, Gallant Avenue. DEEP COVE PIZZA, "a delicious landmark for 27 years" offers "the quintessential European pizza experience." HONEY DOUGHNUTS AND GOODIES, the local meeting place, is famed for its all-day breakfasts and yummy honey-glazed doughnuts. It also offers a kids' menu and mouth-watering freshly baked potato bread. CHEFI'S serves excellent "pasta to go" and casual fine dining indoors or on their relaxed street patio, where you can enjoy the hustle and bustle of "downtown" Deep Cove.

Indulging in gourmet ice cream is a popular pastime in "the Cove," with ORCA'S FAVOURITE serving up the most tempting flavours. DEEP COVE MARKET AND GRILL stock a selection of fresh produce and THE PANORAMA MARKET sells ice and basic groceries.

DOLLARTON SHOPPING CENTRE, a short bus ride from Deep Cove, houses a variety of shops including a large SUPERVALU and a B.C. Liquor Store. PARK GATE SHOPPING CENTRE is a little closer and includes a SAFEWAY store. The historic RAVEN PUBLIC HOUSE, a popular local pub, is a 15-minute walk from the public dock and also runs a cold beer and wine store.

Deep Cove Cultural Centre houses a 130-seat theatre and the Seymour Art Gallery, which offers excellent, ever-changing exhibits. The eastern end of the Baden-Powell Trail begins at Deep Cove (off Panorama Drive) and continues west along the north shore to Horseshoe Bay.

CHARTS 3495. 3311, Sheet 1

APPROACH
From the E, a speed restriction buoy lies at the centre of the entrance — there are no obstructions.

ANCHOR
Anchorage is possible close in. Depths of 5–15 m (16–50 ft) over mud and sand bottom. Holding unrecorded.

PUBLIC WHARF
The substantial wharf is the only available public moorage facility. Public facilities are available in Panorama Park.

Not to scale. Not to be used for navigation.

MARINAS
THE DEEP COVE YACHT CLUB has reciprocity moorage only; call 604-929-1009. DEEP COVE NORTH SHORE MARINA has very limited visitor moorage; call in advance to reserve, 604-929-1251.

FUEL
Available at DEEP COVE NORTH SHORE MARINA.

BOAT LAUNCH
Private, at DEEP COVE NORTH SHORE MARINA. (See below.)

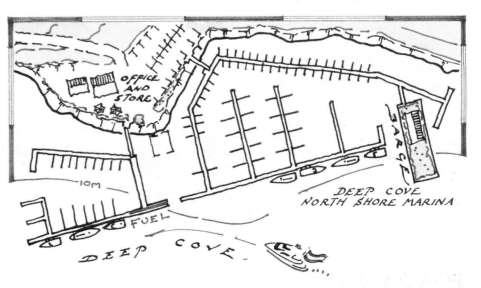

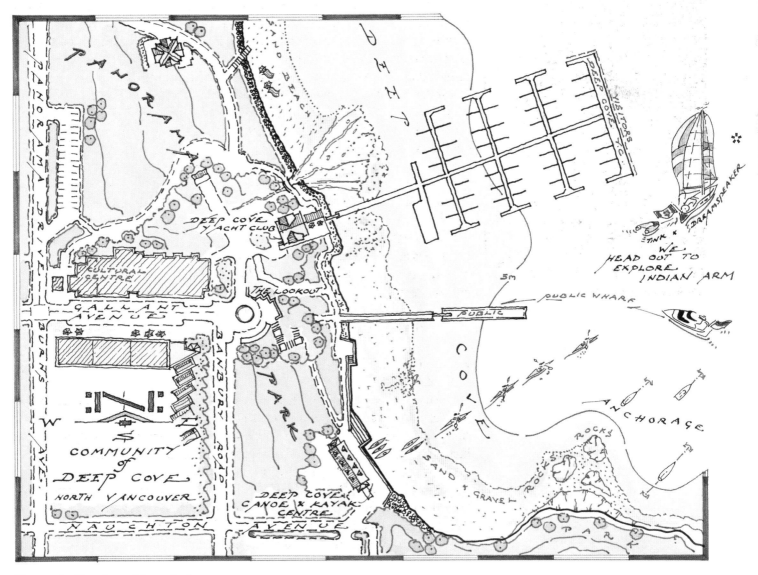

Not to scale. Not to be used for navigation.

3.6 BEDWELL BAY, BELCARRA REGIONAL PARK, INDIAN ARM

✳ 49°19.7'N   122°54.2'W

CHARTS 3495. 3311, Sheet 1

APPROACH
From the N giving Charles Reef a wide berth. The speed restriction buoy marks the northern extent of the anchorage.

ANCHOR
See plan — there is ample space although the bay does become crowded during summer weekends. Depth 5–15 m (16–50 ft), holding good in mud. Open to the N.

A nook below the lookout.

With terrific views to the north, Bedwell Bay is the best-protected summer anchorage in Indian Arm. Surrounded by the extensive Belcarra Regional Park with its multitude of hiking trails and a sandy beach in Belcarra Bay (see 3.4, page 41), this peaceful spot (on weekdays) is a local favourite and can be well used on summer weekends. All the trails, including the loop around Sasamat Lake and Woodhaven Swamp, can be accessed from the eastern shore at the head of the bay, where a small path connects to the park trail. The northern portion of Bedwell Bay is home to the VANCOUVER WATER SKIING CLUB and on summer weekends can become a popular rendezvous spot for jet-ski partners.

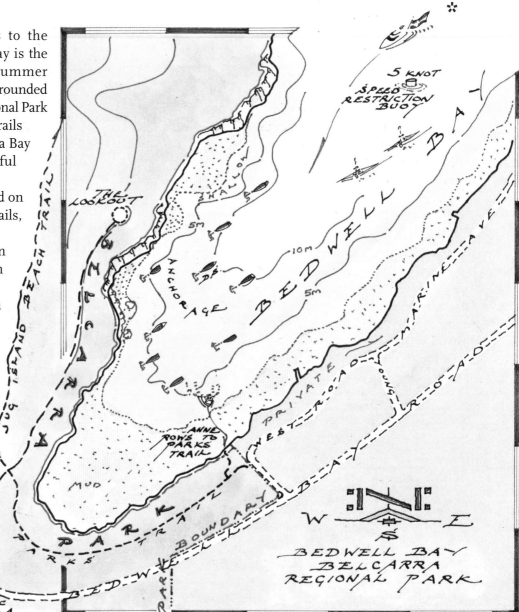

Not to scale. Not to be used for navigation.

RACOON AND TWIN ISLANDS MARINE PARK, INDIAN ARM

CHARTS 3495. 3311, Sheet 1

APPROACH
Both Racoon and Twin islands lie in deep water with shoals extending outward, and landing by larger recreational craft (9 m/30 ft plus) is exceedingly difficult.

ANCHOR
No protected anchorage available.

PUBLIC WHARF
A small parks dinghy float lies off the eastern shoreline of Big Twin Island. *Note: This destination is used primarily by kayakers and small boats, as are Bishop and Clementine Creek marine parks.*

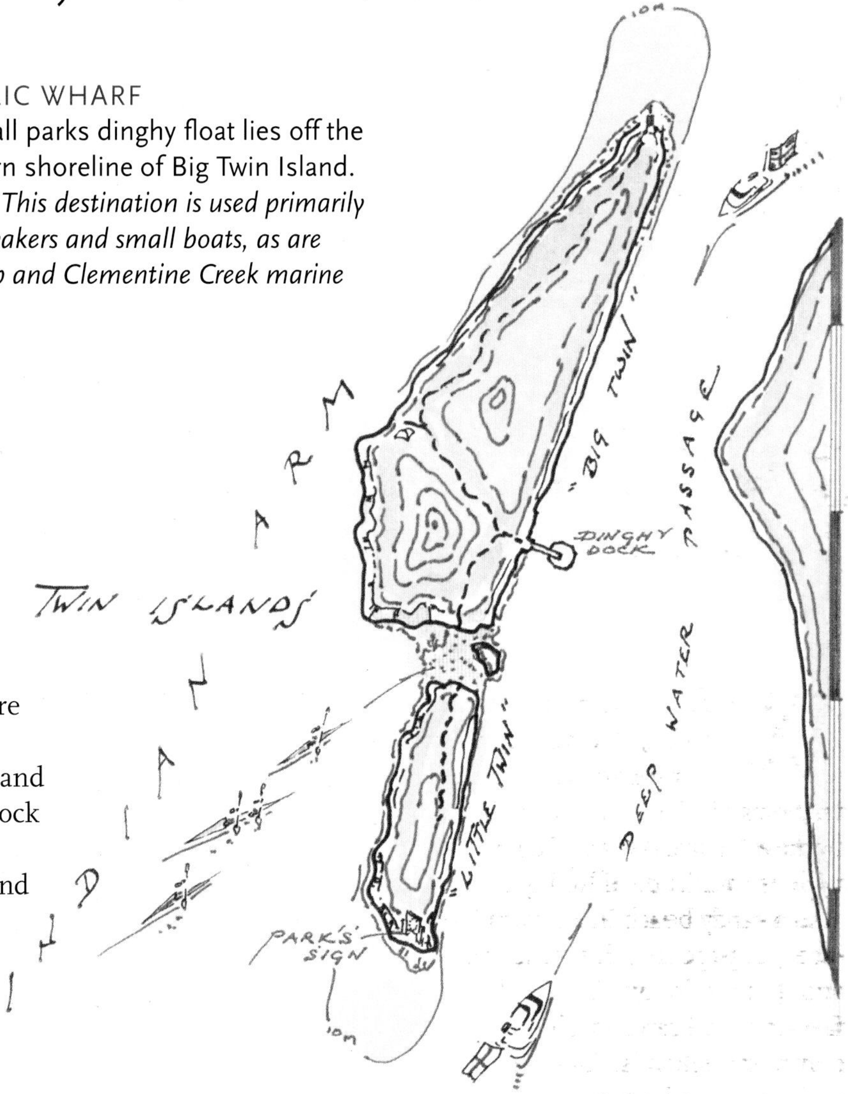

Within Indian Arm Provincial Park are five small marine parks, including Racoon and Twin islands, with Big and Little Twin being joined by a small shell-and-rock beach at LW. These undeveloped islets have steep, rocky shorelines and forested uplands and are popular picnic and camping spots for kayakers and small craft. The waters around Twin Islands are a favourite with divers and a hike to the light at the northern tip of Big Twin Island is well worth the effort for the splendid view up Indian Arm to snow-capped Mount Felix. Twin Islands has a dinghy dock, picnic tables, fire rings and a pit toilet. Although Racoon Island has no facilities, a site on its south side is great for swimming and scuba diving.

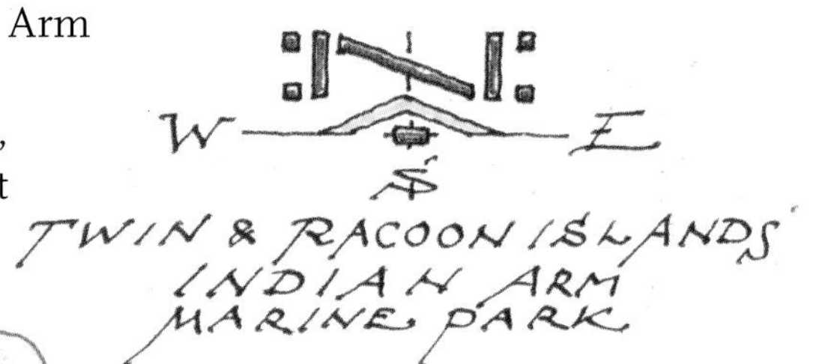

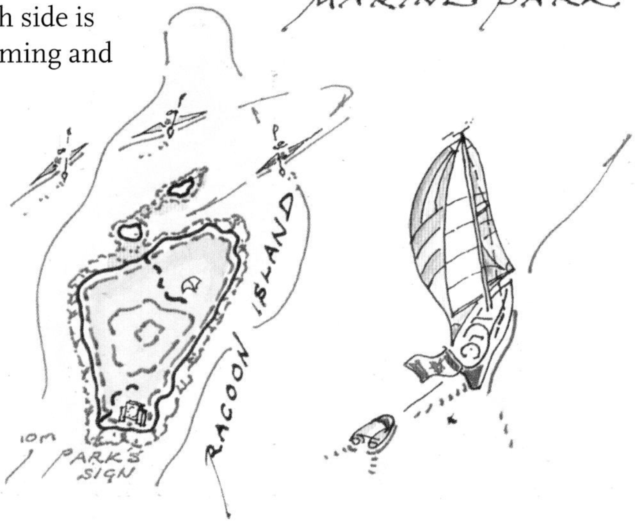

49°20.3'N 122°54.2'W

Not to scale. Not to be used for navigation.

Indian Arm, a summer sailing delight.

3.8 GRANITE FALLS MARINE PARK, IRON BAY, INDIAN ARM

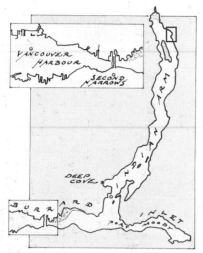

✳ 49°27.0'N 122°51.8'W

CHARTS 3495. 3311, Sheet 1

APPROACH
From the W. The falls are conspicuous and the parks float lies N of the delta.

ANCHOR
Temporary anchorage may be found off the delta. Overnight deep-water anchorage is possible N of the park float with a stern line ashore so long as strong outflow winds are not forecast. Alternative anchorage is also available S of the light, in a cove that affords reasonable protection from outflow winds. Depths 10–15 m (33–50 ft), fair in rock and gravel.

PARKS FLOAT
Small day boats and dinghies only.
Note: The drop-off from the shoreline is very deep.

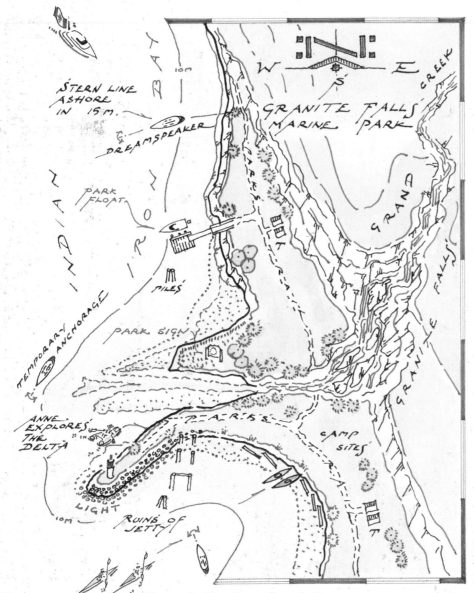

Not to scale. Not to be used for navigation.

Home to the biggest waterfall in Indian Arm, Granite Falls Marine Park has always been a popular destination and was once also the site of a quarry and homestead. The small-boat dock is used by daytrippers and there are pit toilets and a few cleared camping sites in the southern nook. When we visited in the summer, gallons of ice-cold water shot horizontally over the sheer rock face, the park was filled with birdsong and our deep-water, stern-to anchorage came with a view of the snow-capped mountains. Tranquility!

The falls tower over Anne and Tink.

Chapter 4

HOWE SOUND

A Vancouver Island ferry leaves Horseshoe Bay.

Chapter 4
HOWE SOUND

TIDES
Canadian Tide and Current Tables, Volume 5

Reference Port: Point Atkinson
Secondary Port: Gibsons

CURRENTS
There are no currents of note within this chapter.

WEATHER
Area: Howe Sound

Reporting Stations: Point Atkinson and Pam Rocks
Howe Sound has a climatic microsystem all its own. In the summer months, expect light to moderate inflow southerly winds during the day and outflow northerly winds at night.

Sailing into Centre Bay.

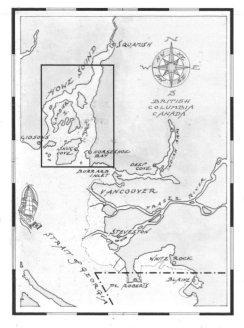

CAUTIONARY NOTES: *Listen out for inflow and outflow wind warnings. Hot, cloudless days can produce strong inflow winds and equally strong overnight outflow winds. Occasionally these winds reach gale force.*

Howe Sound cuts deep into the coastal range northwest of Burrard Inlet. Rising abruptly from the water's edge, these majestic mountains provide the recreational boater with stunningly beautiful vistas, especially in spring and early summer, when the sparkling snow-capped peaks contrast with the lush green of the lower, timbered slopes. The mini-cruising ground covered in this chapter has long been a favourite with local boaters and is an excellent introduction to West Coast cruising for the first-time visitor.

The delights of Snug Cove and Mannion Bay on Bowen Island are only 14 km (9 miles) from the hustle and bustle of Vancouver. This charming island is a popular destination in the busy summer months, as it is just a 20-minute ferry ride from Horseshoe Bay and offers a medley of village stores, bakeries, cafés, bistros and artists' studios.

The long finger-like inlets on Gambier Island's southern shoreline can provide many days of pleasant adventuring for the cruising boater. Undeveloped Halkett Bay Marine Park is a popular weekend retreat that reveals a tiny shell beach at low water and offers rustic campsites for kayakers. The laid-back anchorage in Port Graves has access to an enchanting, well-worn trail that rambles around the grounds of Camp Artaban. Centre Bay is home to many local yacht club outstations and also provides stern-to anchorage along both the western and eastern shorelines. Anchorage at the head of West Bay is now clear of obstructions and the undeveloped Sir Lipton Park makes a rewarding exploration detour. The New Brighton Public Wharf is home to the welcoming GAMBIER ISLAND GENERAL STORE AND DINER.

Popular as a year-round anchorage, Plumper Cove Marine Park on Keats Island is an easy cruise from Vancouver and conveniently close to all the amenities of Gibsons Landing. The parks float provides extensive boat and dinghy moorage, and park buoys are available in the cove for early arrivals. The grounds are kept in pristine condition with neatly laid-out campsites, picnic tables and a 90-year-old orchard. The pebble beach filled with squirting clams is fun to explore at low water and great for swimming.

FEATURED DESTINATIONS

Note: See C.H.S. chart 3534 for detailed plan of Squamish Harbour.

Note: To obtain a Gambier Island Information and Trail Map from Gambier Island Conservancy, or to become a member, call 1-604-886-8901.

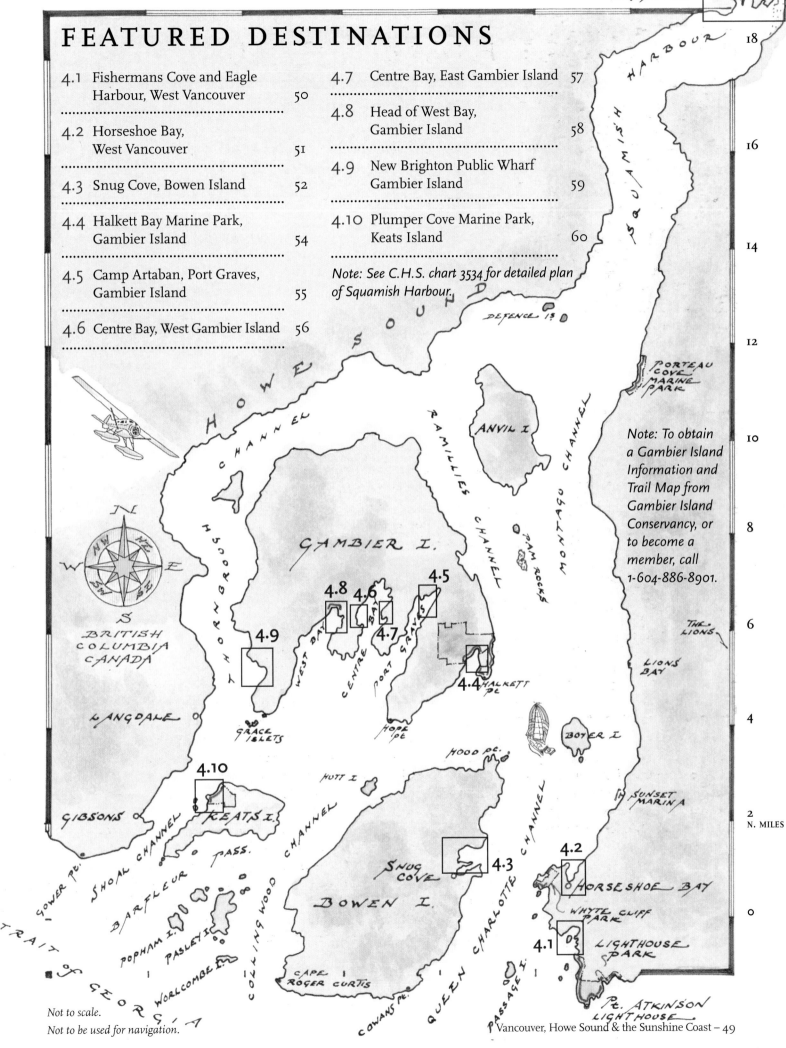

Not to scale.

Not to be used for navigation.

4.1 FISHERMANS COVE AND EAGLE HARBOUR, WEST VANCOUVER

❊ (A) 49°21.2'N 123°16.7'W
❊ (B) 49°21.1'N 123°16.3'W

CHARTS 3526. 3534. 3311, Sheet 1

APPROACH

(A) Fishermans Cove — from the W. Enter between the two rocky islets leaving the starboard (red) lighted aid to the S.

MARINAS

RACE ROCK YACHT SERVICES has no transient moorage but provides full marine repair facilities with a travel lift; call 604-921-7007.

WEST VANCOUVER YACHT CLUB only offers club reciprocity moorage; call 604-921-7575.
THUNDERBIRD MARINA has limited transient moorage; call ahead and they will accommodate visitors if space is available. A travel lift is available for boats up to 15 m (50 ft); call 604-921-7434. THUNDERBIRD MARINE SUPPLIES is open seven days a week most of the year (closed on Tuesdays from November to January) and carries an excellent selection of charts, books, guides and marine accessories; call 604-921-9011.

FUEL

Esso, operated by RACE ROCK YACHT SERVICES.
Note: Navigable water (2 m/6 ft plus) extends to the outer floats of Thunderbird Marina.

APPROACH

(B) Eagle Harbour — from the SW. Enter between the floating breakwater and the starboard (red) can buoys.

MARINA

EAGLE HARBOUR YACHT CLUB offers club reciprocity moorage only; call 604-921-7636.
Note: The channel between Eagle Island and the West Vancouver shoreline is navigable by small craft; however, at LW and on a large tide there are patches charted at 0.6 m (2 ft) or less.

Not to scale. Not to be used for navigation.

The approach to Fishermans Cove.

HORSESHOE BAY,
WEST VANCOUVER

CHARTS 3526. 3534. 3311, Sheet 2

APPROACH
From the NW by rounding Tyee Point and the minor (white) lighted aid. Enter the bay keeping W and clear of the B.C. Ferries operation zone.

PUBLIC WHARF
Used mainly by water taxis and local fishing boats.

MARINA
SEWELL'S MARINA will do their best to accommodate visiting boats; call ahead as it is usually full in the summer, 604-921-3474 or VHF channel 81A between April and end October.

FUEL
At SEWELL'S MARINA.

BOAT LAUNCH
Public launch next to THE LOOKOUT. THE BOAT CENTRE has a repair facility and travel lift; call 604-921-7438. *Note: Stay well clear of the busy ferry operation zone.*

❋ 49°22.9'N 123°16.3'W

Horseshoe Bay is well known as a major B.C. Ferries terminal serving the Sunshine Coast and Vancouver Island; however, local residents have successfully retained its waterfront village charm. Visitors will be treated to a superlative view looking up into mountain-fringed Howe Sound while strolling along the beach, sitting on a bench in the waterfront park or dining at the BOATHOUSE RESTAURANT. THE LOOKOUT, Sewell's original marina building, was established in 1931 and has been renovated into a cosy café/gallery that offers "art and conversation" and doubles as an INFORMATION CENTRE.

A spring vista, with snow on the mountain peaks.

Not to scale. Not to be used for navigation.

4.3 SNUG COVE, BOWEN ISLAND

❀ 49°23.0'N 123°19.0'W

On approach, watch for the Bowen ferry outbound from Snug Cove.

Union Steamship Marina office and store.

Scenic Mannion Bay.

The delights of Snug Cove and Mannion Bay on Bowen Island are only 14 km (8.5 miles) from False Creek and First Narrows, providing a convenient weekend escape for Vancouver's boaters. This charming island is also just a 20-minute ferry ride from Horseshoe Bay in West Vancouver.

A short walk from the busy public dock and marinas will take you to Government Road and a medley of stores, bakeries and cafes. "Downtown" Bowen Island has many great places to eat and drink, beginning with lively DOC MORGAN'S INN on the boardwalk. They serve everything from burgers to fresh seafood and are reputed for their summer barbeques. BLUE EYED MARYS BISTRO offers fine dining while TUSCANY has perfected its mouthwatering wood-oven pizza. THE SNUG CAFÉ serves tasty sandwiches.

SNUG GENERAL STORE at the top of the hill has a liquor store and a good selection of basics and produce. THE RUDDY POTATO is an organic alternative. Kids big and small will love to visit PHOENIX ON BOWEN and browse through their great selection of books, toys and games for all ages. After a kilometer or so (ask locals for the shortcut) you will reach "Artisan Square," home to eclectic studios, shops and art galleries. For alternative island transportation, jump on the "Community Shuttle."

To discover Bowen's history, pick up a copy of the "Heritage Walking Tour" from the information booth at The Cottage Museum. A right turn at the UNION STEAMSHIP COMPANY STORE (now the library and post office) leads to the anchorage in Mannion Bay. Linger a while in tranquil Memorial Gardens or continue on to the Bridal Lake Falls viewpoint and the Killarney Lake Loop Trail (moderate 4-km/2.5-mile/2-hr hike; trial map available).

The Lady Alexandra Promenade and boardwalk overlooks the UNION STEAMSHIP COMPANY MARINA (complete with shower and laundry facilities) and leads past the marina store, DOC MORGAN'S INN, DAVIES ORCHARD and the restored Union Steamship cottages to the lovely Snug Cove picnic lawn in Crippen Park. The Dorman Point Trail begins here (moderate 4-km/2.5-mile /1.-hr hike), climbing through arbutus groves dotted with mossy knolls to a viewpoint overlooking the Strait of Georgia.

CHARTS 3526. 3534. 3311, Sheet 2

APPROACH

From the E. The starboard (red) minor lighted aid sits on rocks at the tip off a peninsula. Mannion Bay lies to the N and Snug Cove to the S.

ANCHOR

In the NW corner of Mannion Bay is relatively protected from up-inlet and down-inlet winds but is open to the wash and wake of boats and ferries and boats in Queen Charlotte Channel. Depths and holding unrecorded.

MARINA

Both THE UNION STEAMSHIP COMPANY MARINA, 604-947-0707, VHF channel 66A and BOWEN ISLAND MARINA, 604-947-9710, offer transient moorage. BBX wireless internet access available at Union Steamship dock.

PUBIC WHARF

The wharf is used constantly by water taxis and transient visitors.

Not to scale. Not to be used for navigation.

4.4 HALKETT BAY MARINE PARK, GAMBIER ISLAND

✳ 49°26.5'N 123°19.3'W

CHARTS 3526. 3311, Sheet 2

APPROACH

From the S, off Halkett Point. Follow the eastern shoreline in as rocks and shallows extend out from the islets and prove to be keel-crunching material at LLW on a big tide.

ANCHOR

E and NE off the rocky islets. The bay affords good protection from outflow winds but is open to up-inlet winds, although these tend to die off in the early evening. Depths 4–10 m (13–32 ft). Holding good in mud and shingle.

Note: This is a popular weekend spot, especially during the summer months, and it is wise to limit the amount of scope used when anchoring.

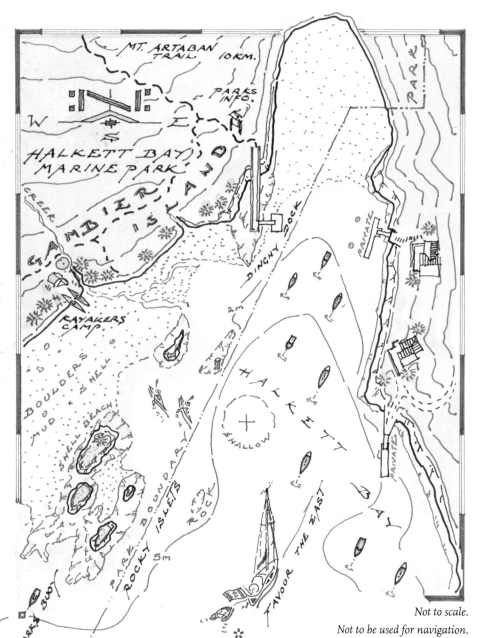

Not to scale.
Not to be used for navigation.

Undeveloped Halkett Bay includes 309 hectares (764 acres) that extend out from Halkett Point. Although it is the closest marine park for Lower Mainland boaters, it still manages to keep a peaceful, low-key charm, making it popular with local kayakers.

Rustic walk-in campsites and a pit toilet are provided, and the park trail winds along the water's edge overlooking the anchorage, where a lovely little shell beach appears between the rocky mini-islets at LW. These grass-covered islets support a variety of wildflowers and other plant life in the spring and summer months, and the shallows filled with squirting clams and mussel beds make this a pleasurable spot to poke about for a few hours.

Park facilities include a dinghy dock and ramp that leads to the information shelter and one coveted mooring buoy SW of the rocky islets. For the energetic, a 10–km (6–mile) trail leads from the shoreline through forested uplands to Mount Artaban (614 m/2,014 ft). The round trip takes about five hours, and the last third of the trail is said to be a little demanding.

CHARTS 3526. 3311, Sheet 2

APPROACH

The entrance to Port Graves lies beyond Potts Point and is an active log-booming area, although the head of the bay is clear and without obstructions.

ANCHOR

S of Camp Artaban and W of the rocks, as indicated in the shoreline plan.

Good protection from overnight outflow winds, moderately open to inflow winds. Depths 4–10 m (13–33 ft). Holding good in mud and gravel. Note: Logging debris is reported to be on the bottom.

PUBLIC WHARF

The small float is used by water taxis and dinghies.

✳ 49°28.0'N   123°21.6'W

Afternoon excercise: a row to the dinghy dock and a hike to Lost Lake.

Frequented by locals, Port Graves is a laid-back and friendly anchorage with room to spare. The modest public wharf has a half-hour time limit for small boats. From here an enchanting, well-worn trail rambles around the grounds of Camp Artaban. Another trail leads to Lost Lake, although private land blocks access to Halkett Bay.

Note: As the main trail passes through property owned and maintained by Camp Artaban, all visitors are asked to respect private property and camp boundaries.

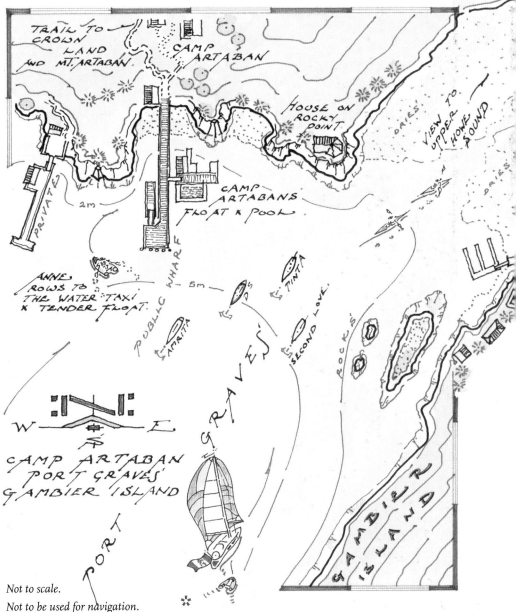

Not to scale.

Not to be used for navigation.

4.6 CENTRE BAY, WEST GAMBIER ISLAND

✱ 49°27.8'N 123°23.0W

CHARTS 3526. 3311, Sheet 2

APPROACH
From the S, free of obstructions.

ANCHOR
With a stern line below the HW mark and bow northwards. Good protection from up-inlet winds and moderate outflow winds. Depths 4–10 m (13–33 ft). Holding good in mud.

Rowing around helps keep the anchorage a "quiet zone."

Extensive Centre Bay has a pleasant, open feeling and is usually a peaceful spot to spend a few days, though on summer weekends it can be invaded by noisy runabouts for a few hours.

If "early to bed, early to rise" is your cruising motto, than "Sunrise Cove" (named by us) on Gambier's western shoreline is the ideal spot to drop your hook.

We were happy to discover that "Sunrise Cove" is frequented by locals who endeavour to keep the anchorage a "quiet zone" by either rowing or keeping their runabouts to an acceptable level of speed and noise.

Note: The western shoreline is changing yearly with the addition of private jetties, limiting anchoring possibilities.

Not to scale.
Not to be used for navigation.

CENTRE BAY, EAST GAMBIER ISLAND

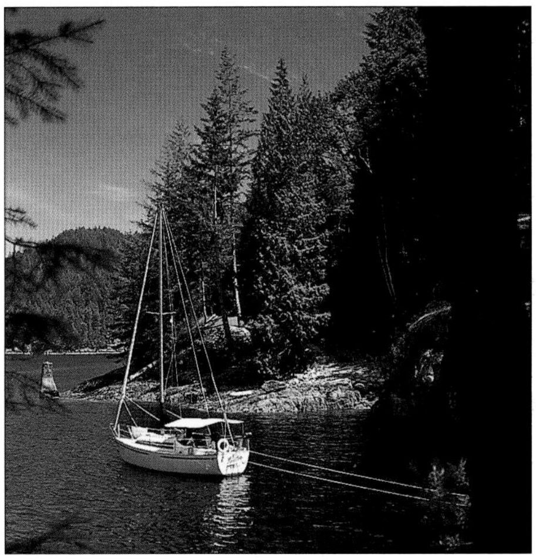

"Sunset Cove," known by friends as "Brent's Cove."

CHARTS 3526. 3311, Sheet 2

APPROACH
From the S. Centre Bay is deep and without obstructions.

ANCHOR
"Mackenzie Cove" (local name) S of "The Islet" provides good, all-round protection. Stern-to anchorage open to inflow winds is possible N of "The Islet" along the "Sunset Wall." Good protection can be found tucked into "Sunset Cove."

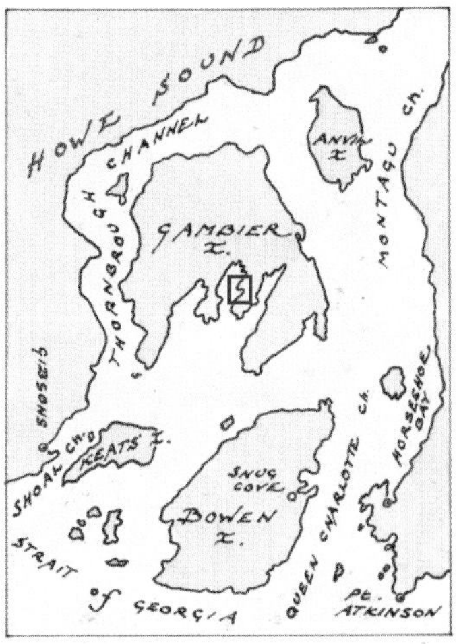

⁂ 49°27.8'N 123°23.0'W

The most coveted boat anchorage on Gambier's eastern shoreline is in "Sunset Cove" — it is well known by local boaters, but you just might get lucky. It is well worth the climb to read and meditate on the memorial plaque to Brent Henderson. If this spot is taken, consult the shoreline plan for alternatives. Backed by pine-clad hills and snow-capped mountains, the bay supports a large variety of wildlife. Nothing could be more heartwarming while at anchor than to watch a family of mergansers slipping effortlessly past your boat in the sun's soothing afterglow.

The small gravel beach south of "Sunset Cove" provides a convenient spot to pull up a dinghy or kayak and explore the shady, moss-covered rocky ledge. An energetic hike up the steep hill and along the old logging road leads to the lovely man-made Koi Lake.

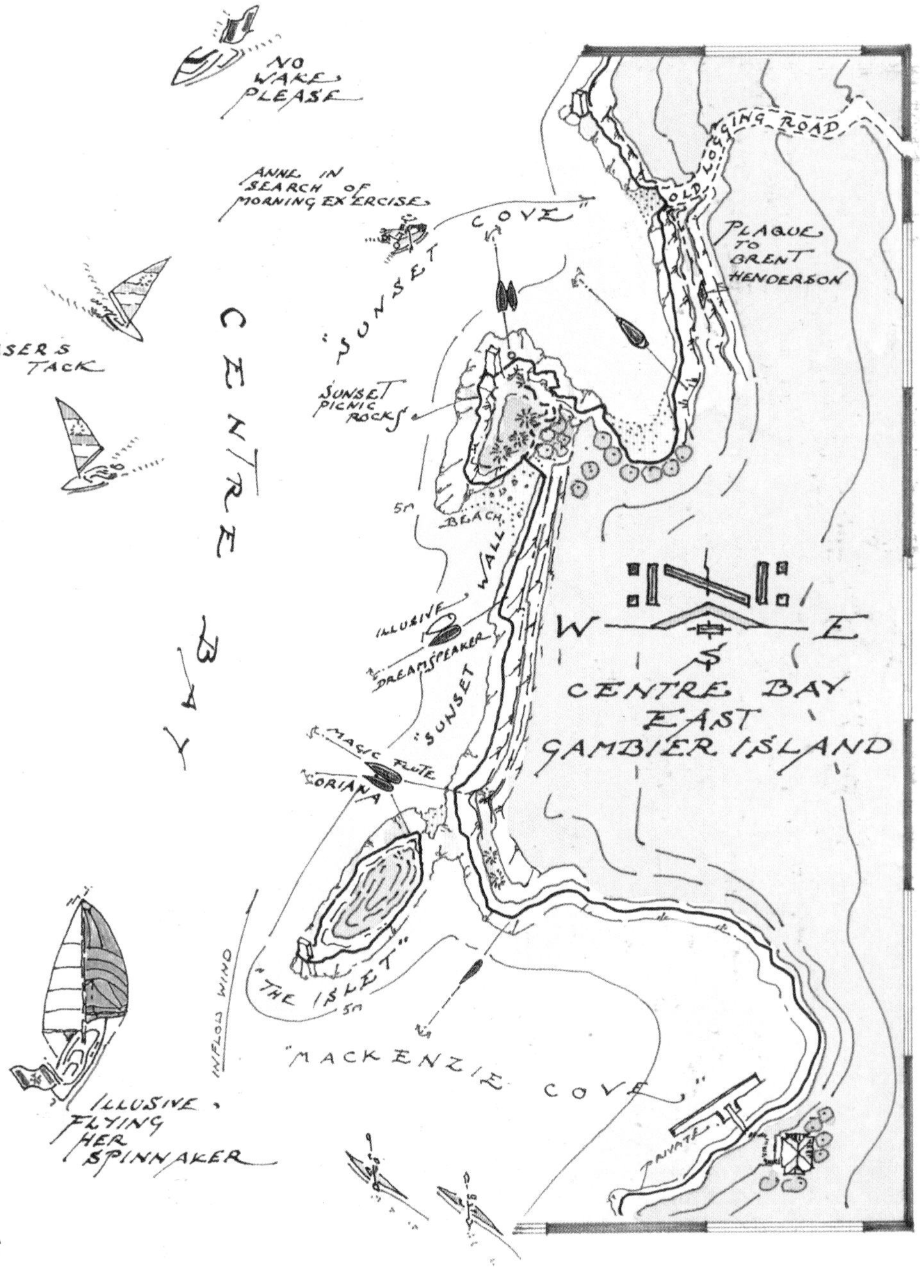

Not to scale.
Not to be used for navigation.

⁂

4.8 HEAD OF WEST BAY, GAMBIER ISLAND

✤ 49°28.0'N 123°24.2'W

CHARTS 3526. 3311, Sheet 2

APPROACH
Close-in deep water along either the E or W shorelines as charted, but unmarked rocks lie in the centre of the entrance to the bay and are covered at HW.

ANCHOR
Off Sir Thomas Lipton Park beach. Note that the drop-off to deep water is sharp. Alternative anchorage can be found in the eastern nooks, with a stern line ashore. Depths, bottom condition and holding vary.

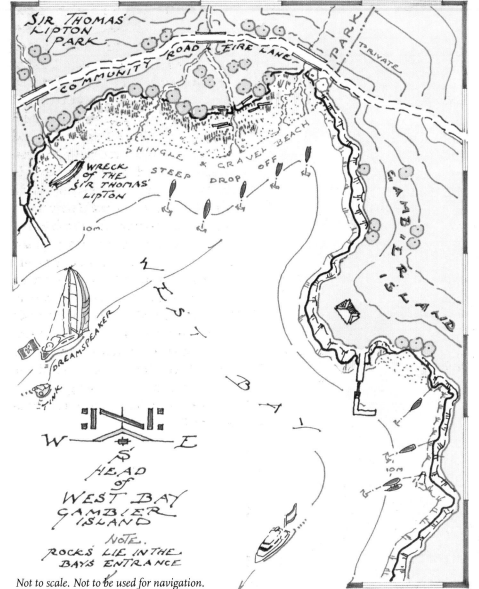

Not to scale. Not to be used for navigation.

Since the decline of active log-booming, anchorage at the head of West Bay is now clear of obstructions although boaters should note the position of the rocks in the bay's entrance that are only visible at LW.

The *Sir Thomas Lipton*, a lumber carrier built in 1919, was beached at the head of West Bay in 1941–42 to keep log booms from going aground on the shallows. The ship's remains now rest here with port side uppermost and her bow pointing north. Sir Lipton Park and beach are lovely to explore; try a hike across Butcher Brook, a swim on the rising tide or a fresh-water wash and brush-up in McDonald Creek.

Boat at anchor off the beach.

NEW BRIGHTON PUBLIC WHARF, GAMBIER ISLAND

CHARTS 3526. 3311, Sheet 2

APPROACH
From the W, out of Thornbrough Channel.

The general store and a local pioneer.

ANCHOR
Anchorage is possible to the NW of the public wharf although open to inflow winds. Depths 4–10 m (13–40 ft). Holding good in sand and shingle.

PUBLIC WHARF
The two floats are used extensively by local craft and water taxis, but there is generally room for visitors. The outside is exposed to chop from inflow winds in Thornbrough Channel.

BOAT LAUNCH
Public, adjacent to the wharf.

✳ 49°26.8'N 123°26.8'W

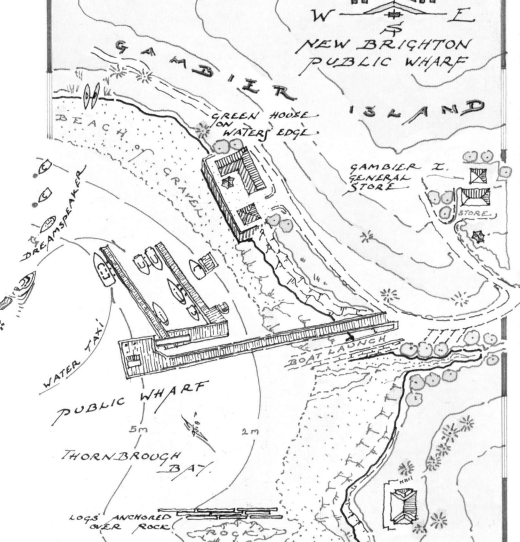

Not to scale. Not to be used for navigation.

Discovering New Brighton and the GAMBIER ISLAND GEN-ERAL STORE AND DINER brought our cruising day to life. The store is run on a cash-only basis and is open 9 a.m.–7 p.m. on weekends and 9 a.m.–6 p.m. weekdays, and until 8 p.m. in the summer. They stock a good selection of basic groceries and fresh produce, including homemade breads, berry and cheese scones and a variety of sinful delights. Hearty soups and delicious sandwiches (fresh turkey and roast beef being the most popular) are served daily and hamburgers and hot dogs are grilled on the outside barbecue. They are licensed to sell beer and wine with their meals and you can either eat in or retreat to the charming garden and make yourself comfortable on one of the shaded benches or swinging seats.

For more information call 604-886-3838.

4.10 PLUMPER COVE MARINE PARK, KEATS ISLAND

CHARTS 3526. 3311, Sheets 1 and 2

APPROACH
(A) In deep water — from the NW, between Observatory Point and Shelter Islets.
(B) In shallow water — from the SW, between Keats and Shelter Islets, 0.9 m (3 ft) on a zero tide.

ANCHOR
Pick up one of the parks eight mooring buoys or anchor to the S or W of the buoys. Depths 6–8 m (20–27 ft). Holding good in mud and shingle.

PUBLIC WHARF
The parks float provides extensive boat and dinghy moorage.

Note: A yellow buoy has been placed over the rocks off the end of the parks float. Anchorage and moorage at the floats can become somewhat rolly in strong outflow winds.

✳ (A) 49°24.3'N   123°28.5'W
✳ (B) 49°24.0'N   123°28.8'W

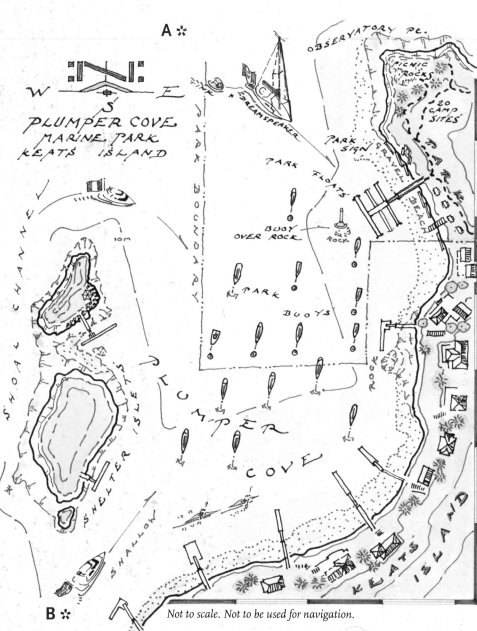

Not to scale. Not to be used for navigation.

Established in 1960, Plumper Cove is a popular year-round anchorage, an easy cruise from Vancouver and close to the amenities of Gibsons Landing (see 6.1, page 70). The park is kept in pristine condition with neatly laid-out campsites, picnic tables, fire rings, pit toilets and a water pump. The pleasant 1–km (half-mile) circular trail also cuts down to the moss-covered "Picnic Rocks" above Observatory Point, offering a panoramic view into Howe Sound. And a 2–km (1.2–mile) trail leads from the park to Keats Landing, serviced by a foot-passenger ferry service from Langdale.

A small cabin sits above the 90-year-old orchard and a picnic area overlooks the anchorage where as many as 75 boats can be counted on a busy summer weekend. The pebble and gravel beach is fun to explore and great for swimming.

Rowing the pooch ashore.

PART 2

Chapter 5

THE
SUNSHINE
COAST

Kayakers take a break in Sechelt Inlet.

A sunset anchor check in Pender Harbour.

Chapter 5
THE SUNSHINE COAST

CUSTOMS

There are no customs ports of entry within the cruising area described in the following nine chapters. Ports of entry covered by this guide are White Rock, Steveston and Vancouver (see page 18); contact Canada Customs at 1-888-226-7277. The main ports of entry to the south are Victoria, Sidney and Bedwell Harbour (see Volume 1); to the north, Powell River and Campbell River (see Volume 2).

NO-SEWAGE-DISCHARGE SITES

The only site where holding tanks were mandatory in 2002 was Smuggler Cove. The following areas are soon to become designated sites: Pender Harbour, Blind Bay, Ballet Bay, Harmony Islands, Princess Louisa Inlet, Nanoose Harbour and Jedediah Island Marine Park. Pump-out stations are available in Gibsons, Secret Cove, Pender Harbour and Schooner Cove. *Note: Check Transport Canada (www.tc.gc.ca) for current Pleasure Craft Sewage Pollution Prevention Regulations.*

The Sunshine Coast owes its alluring name to the visionary ideas of Harry Roberts and his grandmother, Charlotte Roberts. According to author Howard White, in the early 1900s Granny Roberts was "the first to refer to the little strip around Roberts Creek as the Sunshine Belt" while Harry advertised the area in "foot-high letters" across the steamer dock freight shed and "hatched the idea of combining all the coast's isolated settlements under one regional name."

The Sunshine Coast encompasses the coastal waters NW from Gibsons to the entrance to Jervis Inlet. To complete the *Dreamspeaker* trilogy, we have also connected Volume 3 to Volumes 1 and 2 by incorporating the "missing link" on Vancouver Island's eastern shoreline, from Departure Bay to French Creek.

Blessed with more hours of sunshine than most parts of Canada and stunningly beautiful scenery, the Sunshine Coast has become a popular cruising ground with both local and U.S. boaters. Marine facilities, fuel, and provisioning and launching stops are fairly well spaced along the coast and a cross-section of all-weather anchorages and well-maintained marinas offer comfortable shelter from summer storms. The area is also reputed for its stunning Class A marine parks, including the all-time favourite Princess Louisa Marine Park and the ruggedly beautiful Jedediah Island Marine Park. Snug hideaways, peaceful one-boat nooks and fun picnic stops indent many of the island's shorelines and you are never too far from an inviting beach or hiking trail. Warm-water swimming holes, lagoons and surprise waterfalls that ribbon down sheer granite cliffs are an added bonus.

Safe havens for a diverse selection of wildlife can be found in many of the quieter, less crowded anchorages, and on any given day you may be fortunate enough to encounter soaring bald eagles, graceful ospreys, bobbing flocks of surf scoters and belted kingfishers diving for their lunch. Boaters will often be treated to the playful antics of river otters and harbour seals, and there is nothing more rewarding than a visit from a pod of Dall's porpoises, which love to ride a boat's bow-wave.

Known for their quirky ways and straightforward, almost pioneering approach to life, the people of the "Sunshine Belt" are proud to share their coast's natural beauty with summer visitors. Their only request is that we help to protect and preserve the sensitive ecosystems of the shorelines and islands by keeping wake and noise to a minimum, packing out all garbage and being aware of the official "no-sewage-discharge sites."

The risk that our peaceful waterways will become noisy highways in the busy summer months is very real, and the delicate natural balance of these cruising grounds lies in the hands of every boater who comes to enjoy the rugged beauty of British Columbia's coastal waters. Please respect this sacred place, and leave it as you found it.

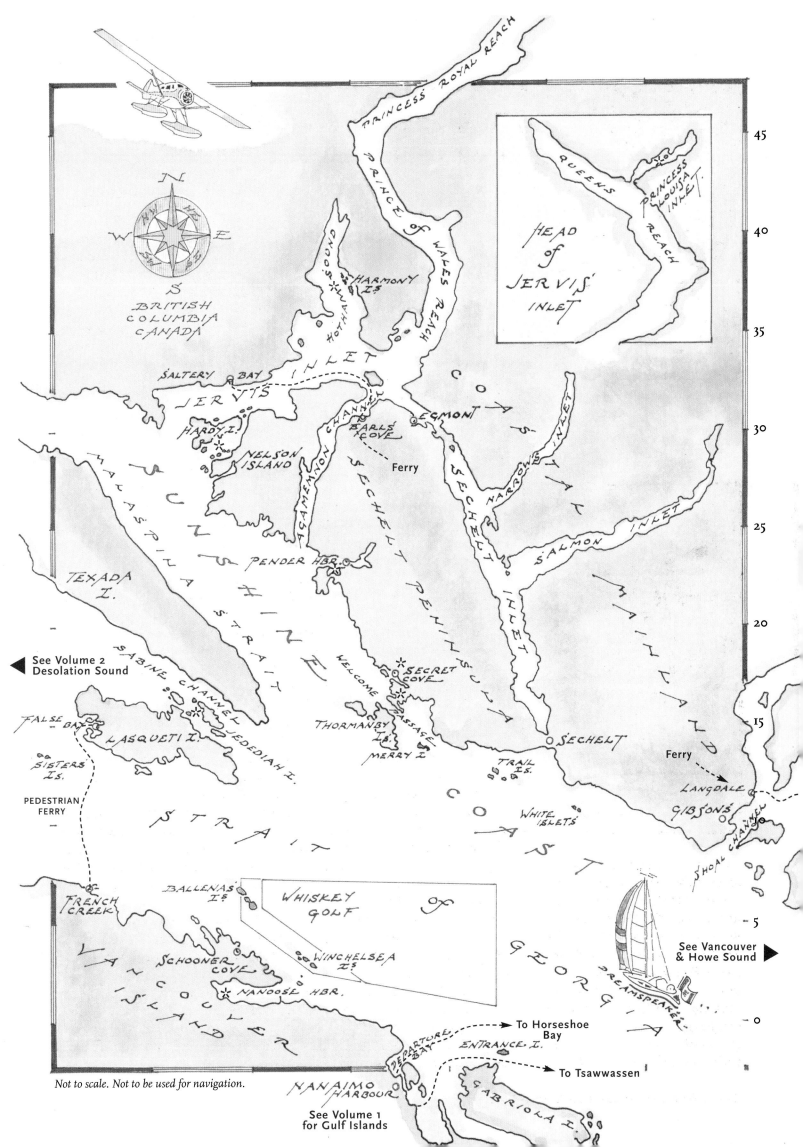

45

40

BRITISH
COLUMBIA
CANADA

HEAD
of
JERVIS'
INLET

35

PRINCESS ROYAL REACH

PRINCE OF WALES REACH

QUEENS REACH

PRINCESS LOUISA INLET

HOTHAM SOUND

HARMONY IS.

SALTERY BAY

JERVIS INLET

AGAMEMNON CHANNEL

EGMONT

30

HARDY I.

BARLS COVE

Ferry

NELSON ISLAND

NARROWS INLET

SECHELT PENINSULA

SECHELT INLET

SALMON INLET

COAST

MALASPINA STRAIT

25

TEXADA I.

PENDER HBR.

SUNSHINE

MAINLAND

20

See Volume 2
Desolation Sound

SABINE CHANNEL

WELCOME PASSAGE

SECRET COVE

SECHELT

Ferry

THORMANBY IS.

15

FALSE BAY

LASQUETI I.

JEDEDIAH I.

MERRY I.

TRAIL IS.

LANGDALE

GIBSONS

SISTERS IS.

STRAIT

WHITE ISLETS

COAST

SHOAL CHANNEL

10

PEDESTRIAN
FERRY

FRENCH
CREEK

BALLENAS IS.

WHISKEY GOLF

5

SCHOONER COVE

WINCHELSEA IS.

See Vancouver
& Howe Sound

GEORGIA

DREAMSPEAKER

NANOOSE HBR.

VANCOUVER ISLAND

0

To Horseshoe
Bay

Not to scale. Not to be used for navigation.

DEPARTURE BAY

ENTRANCE I.

To Tsawwassen

NANAIMO HARBOUR

GABRIOLA I.

See Volume 1
for Gulf Islands

WEATHER & WIND

A rainbow in Pender Harbour.

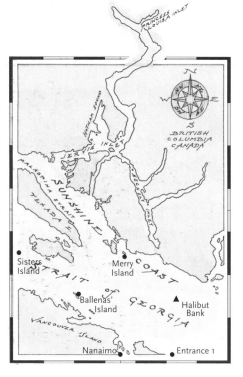

● **Marine Weather Reporting Station**

▲ **Marine Weather Buoy**

MARINE WEATHER FORECASTS

As a safety priority boaters need to be aware of local weather conditions, both current and expected. By developing a daily routine of listening to scheduled marine forecasts, you will be kept well informed with what is happening on the water.

Marine forecasts and warnings are available as continuous broadcasts on the following VHF channels and frequencies: WX1: 162.55; WX2: 162.40; WX3: 162.475; and 21B: 161.65. Alternatively phone the continuous marine weather recording: 604-666-3655.

For further information, visit Environment Canada at www.weatheroffice.ec.gc.ca.

ENVIRONMENT CANADA WEST COAST WEATHER PUBLICATIONS

Mariner's Guide: West Coast Marine Weather Services

Marine Weather Hazards Manual — West Coast: A Guide to Local Forecasts and Conditions

The Wind Came All Ways, by Owen Lange (GDS, 1999)

The Sunshine Coast is blessed with one of the highest average amounts of sunshine in Canada. From mid-June to mid-September, mean daily maximum temperatures hover over 20°C (70°F), with the Strait of Georgia having a moderating influence on coastal temperatures. High pressure is associated with clear skies and good weather, while low pressure brings overcast and rainy weather to the coast.

WINDS: When a ridge of high pressure tracks in from the Pacific, the wind switches around quite abruptly to the northwest. Initially the northwesterly is quite strong, 20 to 30 knots, with the Vancouver Island shoreline and Lasqueti Island taking the full force of the wind. Texada Island sometimes shelters the Sunshine Coast, but this is not always the case, as northwesterly winds have been known to rocket down Malaspina Strait and through Welcome Passage and then funnel up into Howe Sound with a vengeance, making the passage north a wet but sunny ride. If the high-pressure system anchors itself over the coast the wind moderates to a light northwest breeze and cools the coast under unbroken blue skies.

A small Pacific disturbance with a slight drop in pressure brings a day or so of southerlies and rain showers before the sunshine returns. The high pressure either weakens or tracks into the Interior with a low-pressure front following close behind, bringing rain and southeasterly winds. These southeasterlies gradually build in force and are known to produce gales of 30 to 40 knots or more in the Strait of Georgia, even during the summer months. Shelter in an all-weather anchorage or marina is advised as wind and sea conditions can range from moderately miserable to dangerous.

Outside of the summer season, especially during May and June and from late September to early October, the adventurous boater is often rewarded with excellent conditions. But in the winter months, the "raincoast" is best left to hardened commercial skippers while recreational boaters snuggle up next to the fire, engrossed in a good cruising guide.

WAVES, TIDES & CURRENTS

TIDE AND CURRENT TABLES provide essential navigational information and must be acquired prior to venturing into these waters. A working knowledge of tides and currents, and their interplay with the wind, is very important in this region.

Each chapter begins with Volume 5 of the *Canadian Tide and Current Tables* referenced. Tides (reference port and secondary ports) and currents (reference station and secondary stations) are followed by a note describing any local tidal peculiarities or currents that may occur within the boundaries covered by the chapter.

OFFICIAL PUBLICATIONS
Refer to *Canadian Tide and Current Tables, Volume 5: Juan de Fuca Strait and Strait of Georgia.*
Note: Vancouver Island shelters the Strait of Georgia from open ocean swells and extreme seas, creating relatively safe conditions for coastal cruising and making the Sunshine Coast and its island shores a popular destination for recreational boaters and kayakers.

A surf kayaker at Sechelt Rapids.

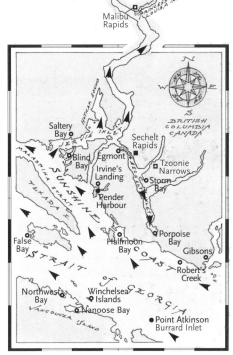

Hazardous wave action in this region develops as a result of the wind interacting with the tidal current. Sea conditions can be dangerous when the wind opposes the current, so it is best to travel when the winds are in the same direction as the current.

TIDES: The tides in the Strait of Georgia and mainland inlets require careful study and monitoring as the tidal range (rise and fall of the water) is large, with a maximum range of 5.5 m (18 ft) at Egmont and a mean range of 4.3 m (14 ft) throughout the coast. It is always advisable to explore new destinations for the first time at LW, when the extent of the shoreline and any dangers are visible.

CURRENTS: Along the coast, currents are generated by tidal streams (the direction of tidal movement). The flooding current streams northwest, while the ebbing current streams southeast. In the Strait of Georgia the current rarely exceeds 2 knots and only creates a potential danger in a wind-against-current situation, which may increase wave height dramatically. This wave action is more evident in constricted channels such as Shoal Channel, Welcome Passage and Sabine Channel. In severely restricted channels rapids will form. These occur at the entrance to Sechelt Inlet — Sechelt Rapids and the entrance to Princess Louisa Inlet — Malibu Rapids. Sechelt Rapids is world famous for a surfable standing wave, generated by current on a flood tide. To ensure a safe passage, it is best to negotiate tidal rapids at slack water.

CAUTIONARY NOTES:
Times of slack water (turns) at the rapids may differ significantly from the times of shore-side high and low water. For the safety of boat and crew, it is of paramount importance to be able to read and interpolate the tide and current tables accurately.

Tides	●	Reference Port
Currents	■	Reference Station
	▢	Secondary Station
Danger	▩	To Small Craft
		(strong currents or shoal water)
Direction	➤	Flood Tidal Stream
Tide	●	Reference Port
	○	Secondary Ports

Chapter 6

GIBSONS & SECHELT TO MERRY ISLAND

At anchor off the Shoal Channel shoreline at Soames Creek.

Chapter 6
GIBSONS & SECHELT TO MERRY ISLAND

TIDES
Canadian Tide and Current Tables, Volume 5
Reference Port: Point Atkinson
Secondary Ports: Gibsons and Roberts Creek

CURRENTS
No specific reference or secondary stations cover this chapter. Tidal currents flood north and ebb south at up to 1.5 knots.

WEATHER
Area: Howe Sound for Gibsons
Strait of Georgia (North of Nanaimo) for Gower Point to Merry Island
Reporting Stations: Halibut Bank and Merry Island

Note: Expect a 50/50 mix of north-westerly and southeasterly winds in the summer months for this open stretch of coast. It is advisable to plan your passage with the forecast conditions.

Merry Island lights: if you're this close, you're on the rocks!

FEATURED DESTINATIONS

CAUTIONARY NOTES:
A northwesterly over a flooding current and a southeasterly over an ebbing current produce short, choppy seas. Strong to gale-force winds over opposing tidal currents produce steep waves, creating potentially dangerous conditions for small craft.

White Islets, the halfway mark.

Tucked behind Steep Bluff at the Shoal Channel entrance to Howe Sound lies charming Gibsons Landing, the gateway to the Sunshine Coast and provision stop with a diverse selection of shops, art galleries, cafés and restaurants. Secret Cove, 48 km (30 miles) up the coast, is the next port of call for refueling.

When entering and exiting Gibsons via Shoal Channel, boaters should be aware that the south entrance is obstructed by a bar of sand and rock with a depth of 2.1 m (7 ft) over it. This is usually not a problem at mid-tide plus, but crossing the bar at LLW on a large tide, especially if you are in a wind-over-tide situation, may present a hazard for recreational craft, as long swells will reduce available depth and cause seas to break over the bar.

Originally inhabited by the Squamish Nation, the town gets its name from retired British naval lieutenant George Gibson, whose family were the first Europeans to settle in Gibsons, where they began farming and selling their produce to the growing city of Vancouver. Gibsons Landing is now known worldwide as the home of *The Beachcombers*, CBC's long-running TV show. The original MOLLY'S REACH is now a popular restaurant. Take a languid stroll along the picturesque Sea Walk from Charman Creek to the delightful roped-off swimming area at Amours Beach.

Beyond Gower Point lies 36 km (20 miles) of exposed water before the welcoming flash of the Merry Island lighthouse. This portion of the Sunshine Coast runs quite straight and parallel to the prevailing NW and SE winds. Take the opportunity to explore this often-forgotten coastline when settled weather and calm seas prevail.

The only all-weather protection to be found between Gibsons and Merry Island is at private Port Stalashen Marina, however visitor moorage is not currently available.

In Sechelt Village, take a self-guided studio "art walk" or a trip to the House of Hewhiwus to discover the history of the Sechelt band.

Sargeant Bay, just SE of Reception Point, is a truly idyllic anchorage when the weather is on your side. It has a lovely crescent-shaped beach backed by a preserved marsh and bird sanctuary, and the Triangle Lake trail will lead you to lily-pad ponds and magnificent views.

The bluffs mark the entrance to Shoal Channel.

Not to scale. Not to be used for navigation.

6.1 GIBSONS LANDING

✤ 49°24.0'N 123°30.0'W

The approach to Gibsons, with the public wharf to starboard and the marina to port.

Colourful downtown Gibsons.

View from the Winegarden Waterfront Park.

Gibsons truly is the gateway to the Sunshine Coast. It is also a charming town to visit at the start of a cruise north and a convenient location to pick up or drop off family and friends. Gibsons is known worldwide as the home of the *Beachcombers*, the long-running TV show. The original MOLLY'S REACH has been carefully renovated and is now a popular restaurant.

The friendly public wharf behind the northern breakwater is a colourful spot to tie up and take a walking tour of Lower Gibsons. Fresh fish and prawns can be purchased from work boats and it's fun to stroll along the docks and view the houseboats. Extensive upgrading has led to improved marine facilities, an enhanced Sea Walk and the beautiful Winegarden Waterfront Park. GIBSONS MARINA is tucked behind the southern breakwater. It has shower and laundry facilities and its store carries boating gear, books, charts, hardware and ice.

To discover the history and charm of Gibsons, pick up the "Take a Walk" pamphlet at the visitor information booth, call ARTWORKS WALKING TOUR (604-886-1200). Local buses provide regular service to Davis Bay and Sechelt.

A selection of "tried and true" spots in Gibsons include Gibsons Landing Gallery; Elphinstone Pioneer Museum & the Maritime Museum; COAST BOOKS; FONG'S MARKET AND GIFTS; MOLLY'S LANE MARKET (a Gibsons landmark); HAUS EUROPA RESTAURANT (European food, call 604-886-8326); GIBSONS FISH (good fish and chips); MIKE'S GELATO (also serves sandwiches and salads) and GRAMMA'S PUB, that has a cold beer and wine store. For the big shop, head to IGA in the Park Plaza in Upper Gibsons; a short taxi or bus ride or a hard walk straight up hill. Also in Upper Gibsons are the B.C. Liquor Store and London Drugs in the Sunnycrest Mall. For baked goods, try WILD BISTRO AND BAKERY in Seaview Place, Gibsons Way for picnic lunches and take out meals (604-886-1917) or WHEATBERRIES BAKERY for excellent bread (604-886-9107).

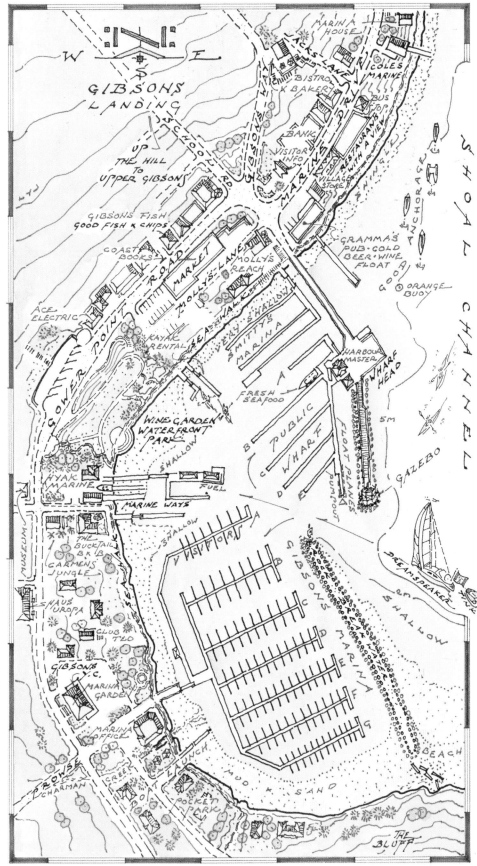

Not to scale. Not to be used for navigation.

APPROACH

From the E, leaving the port (green) lighted aid to the S. The village rising up behind the wharf head and breakwater is quite conspicuous.

ANCHOR

N of the wharf head where reasonable protection can be found in all winds excepting strong outflow winds. Holding good in mud and shingle.

PUBLIC WHARF

The well-run and orderly public wharf is situated behind the northern breakwater. Wharf assistance is on hand in the summer months (604-886-8017, VHF Channel 68). Even though there is extensive moorage, the wharf is often occupied by local craft and rafting is the norm. BBX wireless internet is available.

MARINAS

GIBSONS MARINA (604-886-8686). The extensive visitor moorage fills up fast and reservations are recommended.

✳

FUEL

At fuel dock operated by HYAK MARINE; call 604-886-9011.

BOAT LAUNCH

Private, at GIBSONS MARINA.

PUMP-OUT

At public wharf

Note: The public wharf and marina complex, with its mix of pleasure and commercial craft, makes for a busy place in the summer months.

6.2 WILSON CREEK COMMUNITY

✿ 49°25.8'N 123°42.6'W

CHARTS 3512. 3311, Sheet 3

APPROACH

Wilson Creek lies due N of White Islets. The pink and yellow low-rise condominiums to the N of the breakwater entrance are the most conspicuous landmark.

Note: A sign on the western breakwater cautions boaters that a sandbar lies between the two breakwaters, with a minimum depth of 0.9m (3 ft).

MARINA
Private.

CAUTIONARY NOTES: *Wilson Creek is a windy spot. In a crosswind and sea, the sandbar and off-lying shallow water make entering the marina a challenge. In a crosswind, internal manoeuvring can be quite tricky.*

The beach at Wilson Creek.

Public moorage is not currently available at Wilson Creek. Port Stalashen Marina, the only all-weather protection between Gibsons and Merry Island, is private. If you need to pick up provisions at the IGA or Canadian Tire, Wilson Creek is accessible by foot or short bus trip from nearby Selma Park and Davis Bay. A laundromat at WILSON CREEK CAMPGROUND (4314 Sunshine Coast Highway) is open year-round.

Morning departure.

SELMA PARK

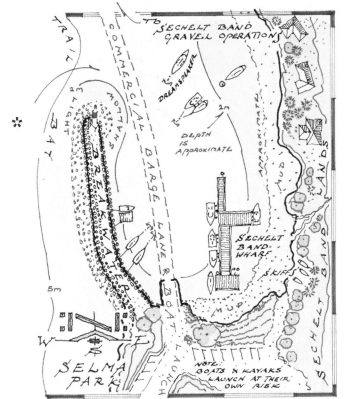

Not to scale. Not to be used for navigation.

CHARTS 3512. 3311, Sheet 3

APPROACH
From the SW. The industrial in-water structures of the gravel operation are conspicuous. Enter by rounding the starboard (red) lighted aid on the tip of the breakwater.

ANCHOR
Temporary anchorage E of the commercial barge lane. Good protection from the SE and NW.

MARINA
The wharf belongs to the Sechelt Band and is private.

BOAT LAUNCH
A sign indicates "launch at your own risk" and belongs to the Sechelt Band.
Note: Local boats stern-tie to the breakwater, which is not recommended. This anchorage is useful as a temporary day or emergency stop only.

DAVIS BAY COMMUNITY

CHARTS 3512. 3311, Sheet 3

APPROACH
From the W, after giving the Chapman Creek delta to the E of Mission Point a wide berth.

ANCHOR
Temporary anchorage, parallel to the beach. Depths 5 m (16 ft) plus. Holding good in sand.

PUBLIC WHARF
The old steamship wharf has no small craft landing facility.

Note: A strong southeasterly wind and accompanying seas die off at Davis Bay, which is somewhat protected by Mission Point. However, a strong northwesterly creates exciting surfing conditions (for local boogie boarders only!).

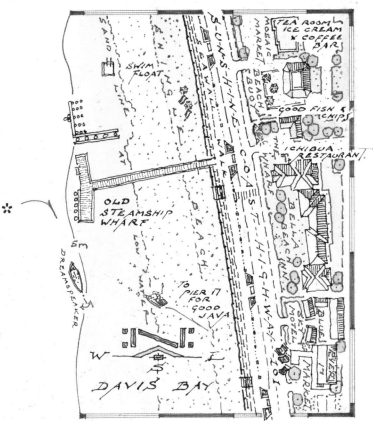

Not to scale. Not to be used for navigation.

6.5 SECHELT VILLAGE

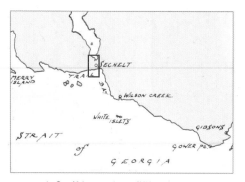

✳ 49°28.0'N   123°45.3'W

CHARTS 3512. 3311, Sheet 3

APPROACH
Only recommended on a calm day. The Maritime Gateway Pier and mid-rise condominiums to the W are the most conspicuous landmarks.

ANCHOR
Parallel to the beach. Best between Ocean and Trail Avenues. Depths 5 m (16 ft) plus. Good holding in sand and shingle.

PUBLIC WHARF
The Gateway Pier has no small craft facilities and dinghies should be pulled up on the beach.

Note: Even when the Strait of Georgia is glassy calm, the surge and wake from passing boats makes this anchorage a very temporary stop.

One of many Sechelt totem poles.

Note: From April to October a superb farmers market and craft fair takes place in the RAVEN'S CRY *parking lot (Saturdays 8:30 a.m.–1 p.m.).*

Nestled on a narrow strip of land between Georgia Strait and southern Sechelt Inlet lies the colourful Village of Sechelt, "The Land Between Two Waters," on an isthmus only a kilometer wide at the centre, this fascinating destination has an extensive shoreline, but there is no easy protected anchorage for the recreational boater from Trail Bay. On a rare calm day it is fun to anchor off the beach and take the dinghy ashore, as in the early pioneering days. A comfortable alternative is the affordable bus trip from Gibsons (see 6.1, page 70) or Secret Cove (7.9, page 88). The village is also an easy walk from Porpoise Bay, Sechelt Inlet (10.11, page 133), but you have to get your boat there first!

An enjoyable day exploring Sechelt could start with a stroll along the charming Waterfront Boulevard, stopping off at the Maritime Gateway Pier before heading to PEBBLES RESTAURANT overlooking the Strait of Georgia. The heritage Rockwood Lodge and Gardens, famous for hosting the Annual Festival of the Written Arts, has beautiful grounds with flowers and trees in bloom year-round. Then on to the unique red-cedar log building that houses the Sunshine Coast Arts Centre and its rotating display of fine local and regional art.

The pioneering Sechelt Indian Band have worked long and hard to attain political autonomy. In May 1986 the *Shishalh* became a self-governing body with all the rights of any other Canadian municipality, the first in this country. The best way to learn more about their rich history and culture is to explore the *hewhiwus* (house of chiefs) and the *tems swiya* (our world) museum that presents a comprehensive collection chronicling the heritage of the Shishalh Nation. The band has a long tradition of carving and fine totem poles can be seen on their lands and in prominent spots throughout the village. The popular RAVEN'S CRY THEATRE hosts cultural activities and a movie theatre, and the TSAIN-KO GIFT SHOP has a great selection of art and books. For cultural guided tours call 604-885-4592.

DAPHNE'S serves good Greek fare and the OLD BOOT offers Italian food, including a delicious meatball sandwich big enough for two.Visit GALIANO MARKET for provisions, SECHELT FISH MARKET for the catch of the day and WHEATBERRIES for coffee and fresh baking. TALEWIND BOOKS on Trail Avenue has a great selection of books and guides. TRAIL BAY MALL includes a grocery store, drugstore and a B.C. Liquor Store.

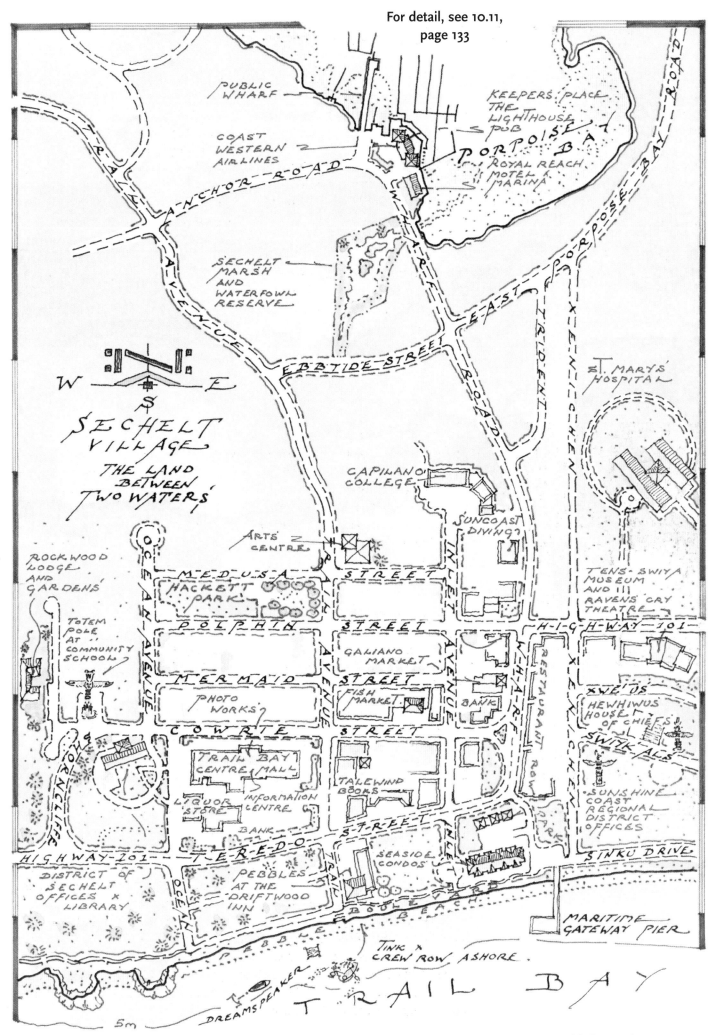

PUBLIC WHARF

COAST WESTERN AIRLINES

ANCHOR ROAD

AVENUE

SECHELT MARSH AND WATERFOWL RESERVE

EBBTIDE STREET

KEEPERS PLACE
THE LIGHTHOUSE PUB

PORPOISE BAY

ROYAL REACH MOTEL & MARINA

WHARF ROAD

EAST PORPOISE BAY ROAD

TRIDENT ROAD

XENICHEN

ST. MARY'S HOSPITAL

W E
S

SECHELT VILLAGE
THE LAND BETWEEN TWO WATERS

ARTS CENTRE

CAPILANO COLLEGE

SUNCOAST DIVING?

ROCKWOOD LODGE AND GARDENS

TOTEM POLE AT COMMUNITY SCHOOL

MEDUSA STREET

HACKETT PARK

DOLPHIN STREET

MERMAID STREET

PHOTO WORKS?

COWRIE STREET

TRAIL BAY CENTRE MALL

LIQUOR STORE

INFORMATION CENTRE

BANK

TEREDO STREET

OCEAN AVENUE

AVENUE

GALIANO MARKET

FISH MARKET

BANK

TALEWIND BOOKS

SEASIDE CONDOS

INLET AVENUE

WHARF AVENUE

RESTAURANT ROW

XENICHEN

H-I-G-H-W-A-Y - 101

TENS SWIYA MUSEUM AND RAVENS CRY THEATRE

XWE'US
HEWHIWUS HOUSE OF CHIEFS

SWIXA ALS

SUNSHINE COAST REGIONAL DISTRICT OFFICES

SINKU DRIVE

MARITIME GATEWAY PIER

HIGHWAY 201

DISTRICT OF SECHELT OFFICES & LIBRARY

ORNCLIFFE AVENUE

PEBBLES AT THE DRIFTWOOD INN

BOULEVARD

PEBBLE BEACH

TINK & CREW ROW ASHORE.

DREAMSPEAKER

T R A I L   B A Y

5m

6.6 SARGEANT BAY

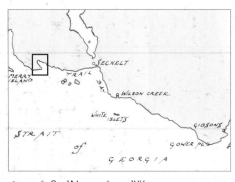

✽ 49°28.2'N 123°51.0'W

Note: Overnight anchorage in a northwesterly is fine. If there is any hint of a switch to the S, SE or E this is not the place to be.

CHARTS 3512. 3311, Sheet 3

APPROACH

From the E, in settled weather and northwesterly winds. The "Mighty Boulder" is the most conspicuous landmark.

ANCHOR
To the S of the "Mighty Boulder." Good protection from the NW. Depths 3–8 m (10–27 ft). Holding good in sand and mud.

Dreamspeaker *and company.*

Sargeant Bay, just SE of Reception Point, is a truly idyllic anchorage when the weather is on your side. Mounds of sun-dried driftwood and a bird sanctuary back the crescent-shaped sand and shingle beach. A large sunbathing rock just off the beach invites you to dive into the crystal-clear water. Although the "Mighty Boulder" looks tempting to explore, it is unfortunately private.

Twelve hectares (30 acres) of land around Sargeant Bay have become a provincial park and bird sanctuary, preserving the largest area of marsh and meadowland on the Sunshine Coast and providing habitat for a variety of bird and animal life. The uplands area is criss-crossed with deer trails and contains marshes filled with wildflowers in the summer months.

A salmon-bearing creek runs along one side of the park and you can visit the fish ladder and beaver pond before setting off on a vigorous hike to Triangle Lake where you will find lily-pad ponds, huge yellow arum (large skunk cabbage), waterfowl and other marshy delights. The Trout Lake Trail offers magnificent views and joins the Triangle Lake Trail at the 2.4 km (1.5 mile) mark.

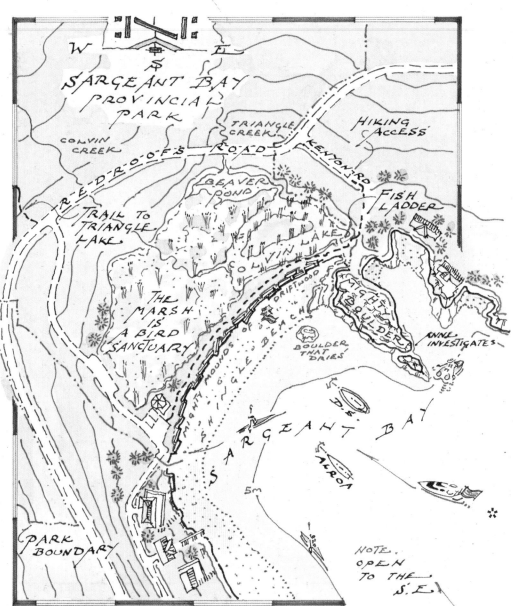

Not to scale. Not to be used for navigation.

Chapter 7

WELCOME
PASSAGE

The great anchor in Priestland Cove, see 7.3 page 82.

Halfmoon Bay general store.

Chapter 7
WELCOME PASSAGE

TIDES
Canadian Tide and Current Tables, Volume 5
Reference Port: Point Atkinson
Secondary Ports: Halfmoon Bay and Secret Cove

CURRENTS
The is no specific reference or secondary station; however, currents flood N and ebb S at up to 3 knots through the constriction of Welcome Passage.

WEATHER
Area: Strait of Georgia (North of Nanaimo)
Reporting Station: Merry Island

Note: Northwesterlies and especially southeasterlies tend to funnel through the Welcome Passage gap where winds can accelerate beyond their forecast strength.

CAUTIONARY NOTES: *Be aware of the extent of Tattenham Ledge, especially on a flooding current, as the tide has a diagonal westerly set and boats big and small have inadvertently drifted onto the ledge with disastrous results.*

Welcome Passage is a ribbon of water that separates Sechelt Peninsula on the B.C. mainland from South Thormanby Island. Although it is often very busy with commercial traffic, it is truly a welcome sight, especially when the wind and sea are playing up. There is no shelter in the passage itself, but protected anchorage and moorage facilities abound in adjacent waters.

Little known Simpson Marine Park extends over 460 hectares (1,150 acres) on South Thormanby Island and includes 155-m (508-ft) Spy Glass Hill, a number of headlands with fine views of Welcome Passage and the Strait of Georgia, and 8 km (5 miles) of bays, coves and bites. Be sure to pop into "Skinny Cove" and "Miss Piggy Bay" to explore the unique rock formations and visit the old homestead, orchard and freshwater lake bustling with bird life.

Pick up a fresh loaf of homemade bread, some free-range eggs and a bottle of wine at the general store in Halfmoon Bay, then head into the hidden tranquility of Frenchmans Cove. A few days can be spent digging clams, picking oysters, swimming in the small lagoon and exploring the shallow inlet on a flooding tide.

The all-weather anchorage in Smuggler Cove Marine Park is a favourite with boaters transiting the windy portion of this coastline. With three cosy basins, stunning sunset views and a maze of nooks and crannies to explore, it provides much more than shelter from the storm. Once the daytrippers have left you can explore the cove's delights and enjoy the peace and harmony of nature at its best.

Buccaneer Bay Marine Park, just across the way from Smuggler Cove, is the perfect picnic spot if you are planning a day at the beach. An idyllic hectare of soft white sand, tidal pools, warm-water swimming in the "lagoon" and a finger of grass for camping make Grassy Point a small patch of paradise well worth investigating. The nearby Surrey Islands and Water Bay provide convenient shelter from SE winds should one suddenly spring up.

Ample moorage facilities, marine services, fuel and protected anchorage are available in popular Secret Cove. The store at SECRET COVE MARINA stocks all the essentials and includes a B.C. Liquor Store outlet, while BUCCANEER BAY MARINA offers excellent marine repair facilities. THE UPPER DECK CAFÉ and JOLLY ROGER PUB AND RESTAURANT offer waterfront views and a mix of West Coast and traditional dishes.

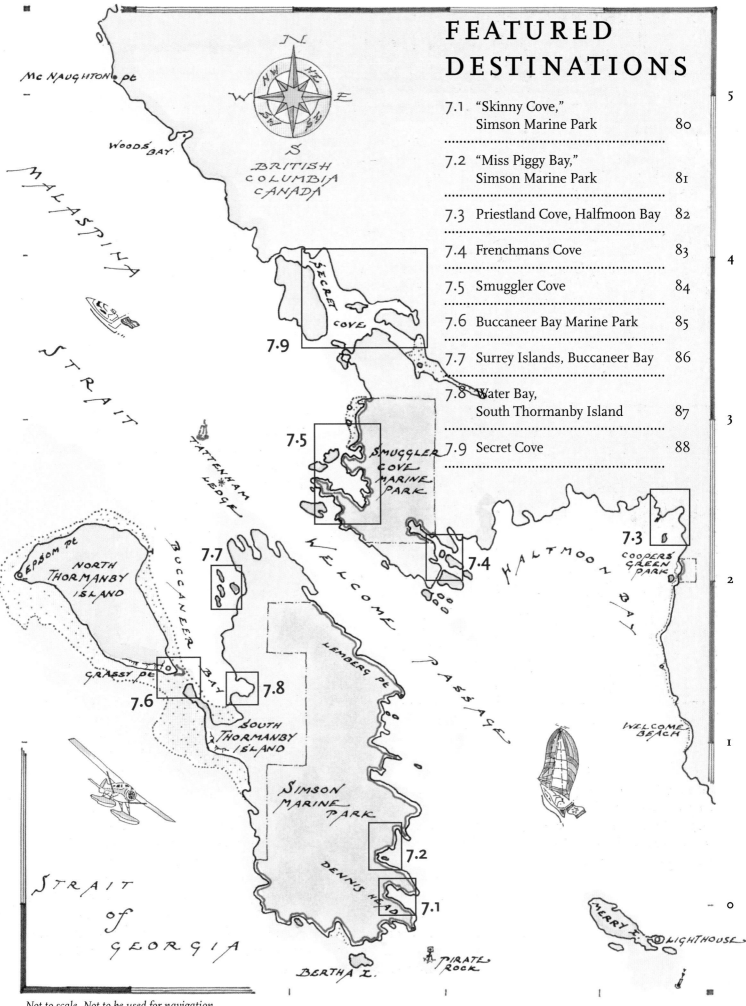

FEATURED DESTINATIONS

Not to scale. Not to be used for navigation.

7.1 "SKINNY COVE," SIMSON MARINE PARK

❋ 49°28.2'N 123°57.0'W

CHARTS 3535. 3311, Sheet 3

APPROACH
"Skinny Cove" lies N of Pirate Rock and Dennis Head on South Thormanby Island. The entrance is open without obstructions.

ANCHOR
At the head of the cove. There is room for 3 to 4 boats with good protection from the NW, though the cove is entirely open to the SE. Depths 3–6 m (10–20 ft), holding good in mud.

Meleet, *a junk-rigged sailboat, meets* Dreamspeaker.

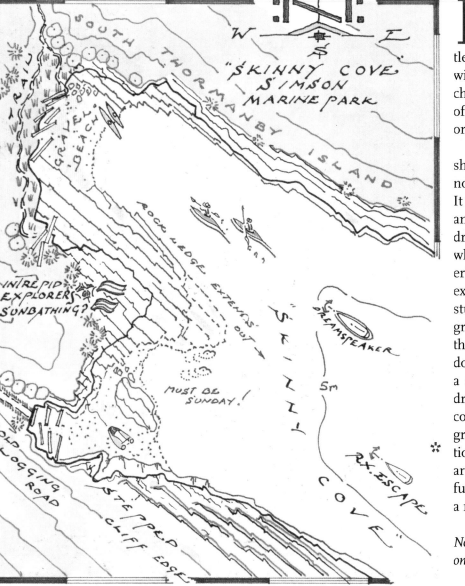

Not to scale. Not to be used for navigation.

In high-pressure, settled weather or if a northwesterly is forecast, take some time to investigate little-known Simson Marine Park. You will be pleasantly surprised to find two charming anchorages and a multitude of hideaways to be explored by dinghy or kayak.

In keeping with its topographical shape, we named this intimate bay north of Pirate Rock "Skinny Cove." It is the best protected of the two anchorages and a peaceful spot to drop your hook. The windswept cliffs which are open to winter southeasterlies are fascinating to climb and explore. A thin layer of soil supports stunted arbutus and pine trees that grow horizontally along the rocks, their roots clinging to anything that doesn't move. At the head of the cove a small gravel beach piled high with driftwood and upturned tree trunks connects to a rocky ledge of flat black granite. These unique rock formations extend well into the cove and are perfect for spreading out a colourful towel and enjoying the sunshine, a refreshing swim or a good book.

Note: Logging debris may be found lurking on the muddy bottom

"MISS PIGGY BAY," SIMSON MARINE PARK

The park is good kayaking territory.

CHARTS 3535. 3311, Sheet 3

APPROACH
The parks sign on the bluff is the most conspicuous landmark. Follow the southern shoreline into the bay.

ANCHORAGE
Good temporary anchorage for park exploration. The bay is open except to the NW. Depths 5 m (16 ft) plus, holding fair in shingle and mud.

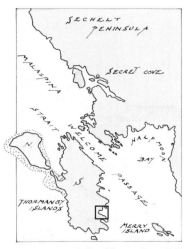

✿ 49°28.4'N   123°57.0'W

The graffiti on the rocks above the entrance clearly name this "Miss Piggy Bay." Known locally as Farm Bay, it is more a cosy cove than a real bay and offers many surprises.

From the small gravel beach a walk through the cut will take you within sight of an old homestead in a magical setting: apple trees laden with fruit stand in a grassy meadow beside a freshwater lake bustling with bird life. We saw deer feasting on the fallen apples and the afternoon sun lit up the stage as we lay on the grass. Thanks to the generosity of Calvert Simson and his pioneering family, who donated the land to the province in 1983, all can now enjoy this wonderful marine park and its many hidden secrets. The island is criss-crossed with logging roads and the chiselled tree stumps are evidence of the industrious resident beaver colony. A short walk along one of the roads leading from the homestead will take you through a cool forest to the delights of "Skinny Cove" (see 7.1, page 80).

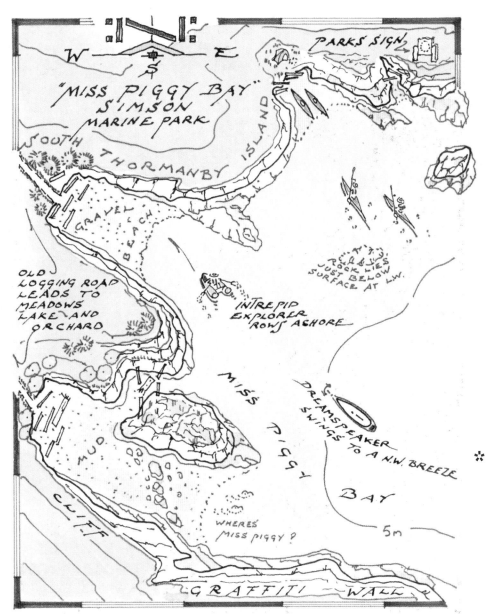

Not to scale. Not to be used for navigation.

Vancouver, Howe Sound & the Sunshine Coast – 81

7.3 PRIESTLAND COVE, HALFMOON BAY

✳ 49°30.5'N 123°55.0'W

CHARTS 3535. 3311, Sheet 3

APPROACH
From the SW. The public wharf, live bait float and Anchor Rocks are all conspicuous.

ANCHOR
Temporary anchorage to the E and W of the wharf head. For more shelter from the SE, tuck in behind the booming area.

PUBLIC WHARF
The float is for short stays and essentially for locals and visitors who need access to the store from the water.

MARINA
Private.

Note: Priestland Cove is the most sheltered area in Halfmoon Bay, with protection from both NW and SE winds.

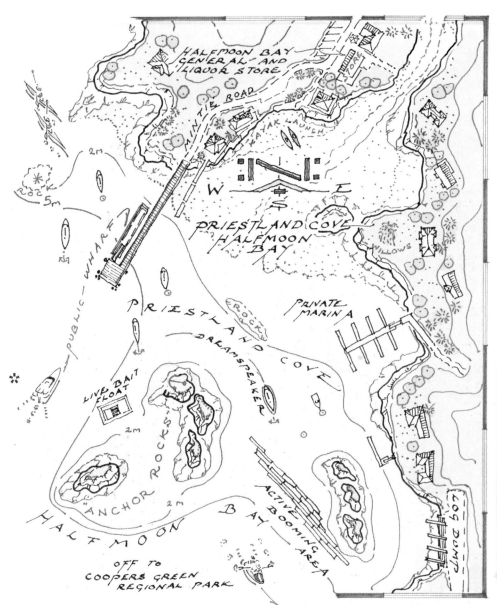

HALFMOON BAY HISTORICAL GENERAL STORE is a little gem in the wilderness — if you are travelling by boat, that is. Not only do they sell fresh homemade bread and free-range eggs, their shelves are also well stocked with basics and local produce. The store operates a B.C. Liquor Store outlet and has a deli and a shaded patio. Ice, bait and tackle are also available; call 604-885-8555.

A short trip from Priestland Cove will bring you to Coopers Green Regional Park which offers enjoyable snorkelling and scuba diving and is clustered with colourful summer cabins and cottages.

The Halfmoon Bay public wharf.

FRENCHMANS COVE

CHARTS 3535. 3311, Sheet 3

APPROACH
With caution and at LW. The run-in is best along the edge of "Mistress III Island." The boulder that guards the entrance will become evident. The minimum depth is 1.8 m (5 ft) — favour the boulder side.

ANCHOR
As indicated in the shoreline plan, with a stern line ashore. There is very limited room to swing. Depths of 2–3 m (6–10 ft), holding good in mud and shell. The cove is very sheltered from the NW and offers fair shelter from the SE; however, the wind does tend to funnel through the anchorage.

Note: The rustic beachcombers' float is occasionally used by local and visiting boats and the log boom is active on a small scale.

❋ 49°30.1'N 123°56.5'W

Reputed to be one of the tightest coves on the coast, Frenchmans Cove requires respect, good anchoring skills and a taught stern line, as swinging is very restricted. "Mistress Islands I & II" are recreational reserves. "Mistress Island III" and the western shoreline are private. Oysters can be gathered on the gravel beach and the little lagoon provides blissful warm-water swimming on a rising tide.

The long, narrow inlet behind the islands dries completely. It's worth packing a picnic and taking advantage of the flooding tide to the head of the inlet. In the quiet of the evening, this small slice of Eden comes alive with the snorting and splashing of seals at play on the nearby islets.

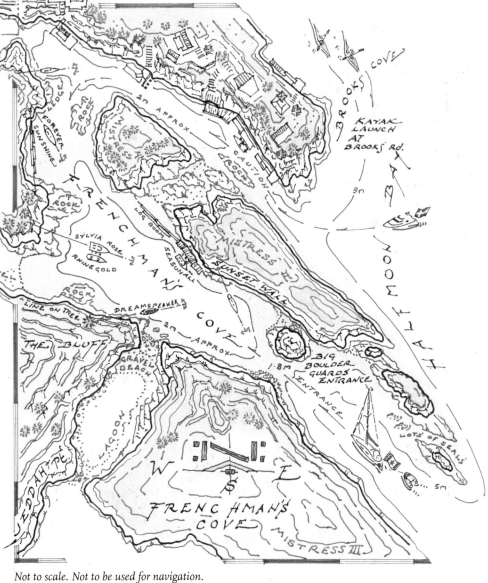

A big boulder guards the entrance.

Not to scale. Not to be used for navigation.

7.5 SMUGGLER COVE

✤ 49°30.9'N 123°58.3'W

Summer evening in Smuggler is as good as it gets.

A late arrival negotiates the entrance.

*Cool drink in hand, a couple celebrates another
glorious day.*

A maze of basins, nooks and crannies awaits discovery in this protected, all-weather anchorage. With its magnificent surroundings and abundant wildlife, Smuggler Cove Marine Park provides boaters with a quiet weekend getaway, shelter from the storm and an incentive to relax.

After rounding Grant Island, it is easy to miss the narrow entrance to the cove which has reefs extending from both sides, narrowing the passage to less than 15 m (50 ft) — a little intimidating the first time around. Once inside, the cove opens up to a choice of three cosy basins.

Although Smuggler Cove is crowded in the summer, boaters will often anchor overnight, then hop off the following day to visit the beaches at Buccaneer Bay or move on. With paradise to yourself, you can take a leisurely hike, pick oysters or just laze in the warm tidal lagoon off Isle Capri enjoying the solitude. As late afternoon approaches, boats begin to stream in while you lie back in the cockpit, cool drink in hand, to witness a display of anchoring techniques. This is far more entertaining than TV.

There are many trails criss-crossing the park. From the south basin you can continue south to Wilbraham Point overlooking Welcome Passage or west along the interpretive trail to the remarkable viewing and fishing rocks overlooking the cove's entrance. The eastern route takes you along a maintained trail bordered by marshland and overhung with leafy shade to Brooks Road. To explore further, continue down to Brooks Cove, then turn right and follow Shermin Lane to a section of park looking down on beautiful Frenchmans Cove (see 7.4, page 83). Picnicking on the mossy ledges allows a bird's-eye view of this unique hideaway.

Early evening is a lovely time to take a gentle row around the cove to meet your neighbours and the local wildlife. The two quaint cottages on the private islands add a certain domestic charm to the setting, a far cry from times gone by when this hideout was used as a cache for bootleg liquor and illegal navvies in transit to the U.S. As the sun goes down, watch the local geese, ducks and shorebirds enjoying the last of the daylight. Bald eagles are often seen perched high in the treetops and otter families have been spotted sliding down the grassy slopes before disappearing into the water.

Note: Halfmoon Bay (7.3) and Secret Cove (see 7.9) are easily accessible from Smuggler Cove should you need to provision, shower or eat out.

CHARTS 3535. 3311, Sheet 3

APPROACH slowly and with caution — preferably at LLW. Favour the Isle Capri shoreline initially, then head straight for "Sunset Bluff" on the shoreline plan.

ANCHOR

As indicated on the shoreline plan with a stern line ashore; there are rings provided. The cove affords good all-weather protection. If anchoring stern-to along the eastern shore, angle the bow of your boat towards the forecast wind direction. Depths 2–4 m (6–13 ft), holding good in sticky mud.

Note: In summer, especially after a small craft warning, the anchorage fills with boats seeking shelter. Don't be tempted to swing, as this restricts anchoring opportunities. Boaters should be aware of the shallow areas in the cove, especially on a large tide.

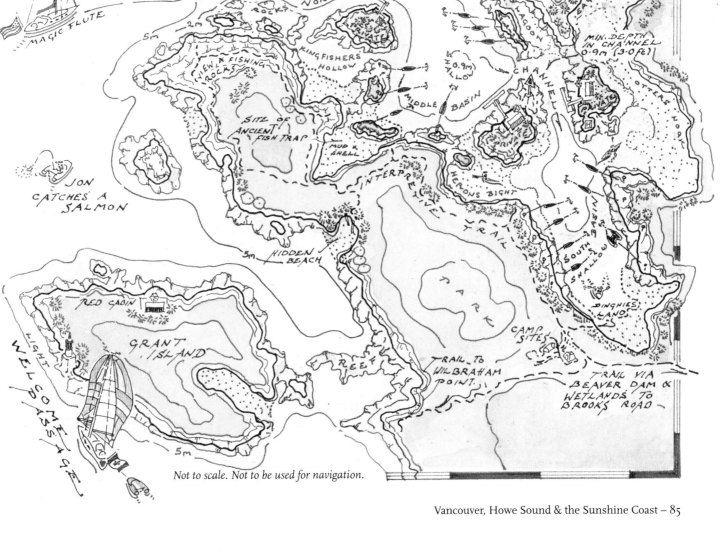

Not to scale. Not to be used for navigation.

7.6 BUCCANEER BAY MARINE PARK

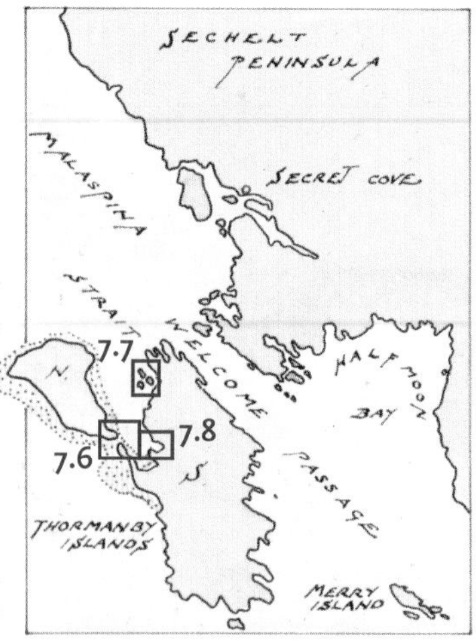

✲ 49°29.8'N 123°59.3'W

CHARTS 3535. 3311, Sheet 3

APPROACH
Within Buccaneer Bay, head for the gap between North and South Thormanby islands. Beware of the steep drop-off as you near the shore.

ANCHOR
Off the beach. Depths 5–10 m (16–33 ft), holding good in sand. The bay is open to the NW but offers excellent shelter from southeasterlies.

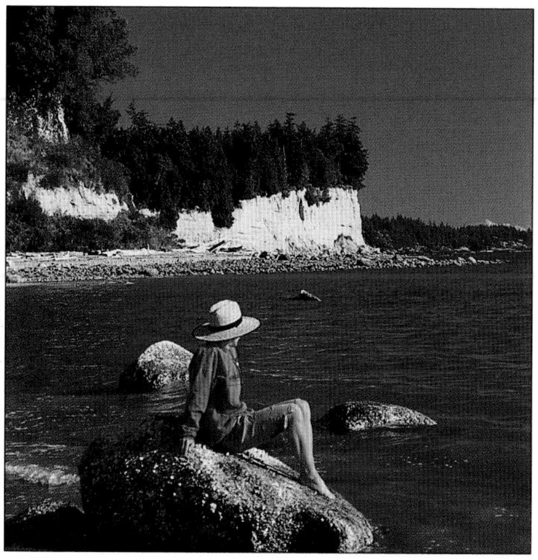

Anne against the landmark sandstone cliffs.

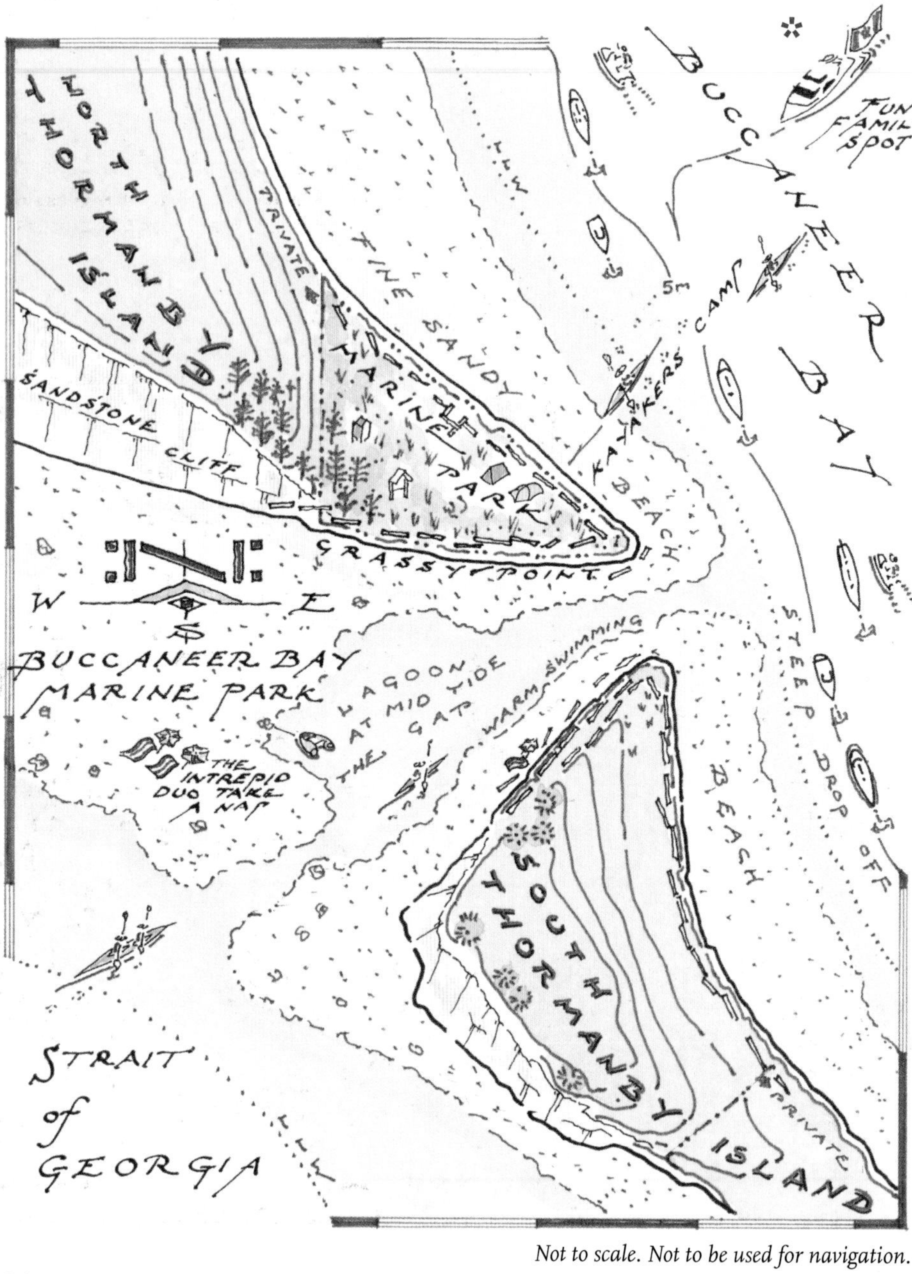

Not to scale. Not to be used for navigation.

Buccaneer Bay Marine Park on North Thormanby Island offers an idyllic hectare of white sandy beach and a campsite on Grassy Point, which extends into the gap between North and South Thormanby islands.

Popular with families in the summer months, the bay is a perfect picnic stop, and the steep drop-off makes anchoring off the sandy beach easy. The gap floods at HW, but mid-tide provides blissful warm-water swimming in the "lagoon" that forms in the gap. Sandstone cliffs back the park and the beaches abound with sun-baked driftwood that provides comfortable backrests for reading or napping. The park boundary is on the southern tip of North Thormanby and the surrounding private properties should be respected. The bay is also home to many seabirds and a vocal colony of seals, and according to the *B.C. Marine Parks Guide,* sea lions sometimes frequent the beaches. Be warned that in the busy summer months Buccaneer Bay traffic includes runabouts, water skiers, personal watercraft and float planes.

Note: Deep in Buccaneer Bay, off Gill Beach, good shelter, good holding and plenty of swinging room are available to survive the strongest of southeasterly winds.

CHARTS 3535. 3311, Sheet 3

APPROACH
With caution, to both anchorages A and B.

ANCHOR
"A" provides good shelter from the SE and fair protection from the NW.
"B" gives good shelter from the SE but is open to the NW.
Depths 5–10m (16–33 ft), holding fair over a rocky bottom.

The lands around the Surrey Islands are private but the two small beaches on the eastern shoreline make convenient picnic spots. The wildlife here is plentiful and the playful seals and otter families are fascinating to watch on a quiet dinghy row around the islands.

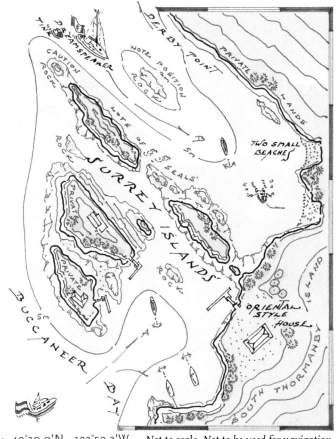

✳ 49°30.0'N 123°59.3'W *Not to scale. Not to be used for navigation.*

WATER BAY, SOUTH THORMANBY ISLAND 7.8

CHARTS 3535. 3311, Sheet 3

APPROACH
From Buccaneer Bay, a port beacon sits on the western edge of a big rock.

ANCHOR
West off the private marina and south of the big rock. Good shelter from the SE. Depths 5–10m (16–33 ft), holding fair over a varied bottom.

Water Bay offers excellent shelter from SE gales. Once at anchor, the commotion swirling in the treetops is hardly audible, although an occasional gust will find its way into the bay. The marina and surrounding land are private.

✳ 49°29.6'N 123°59.1'W *Not to scale. Not to be used for navigation.*

7.9   SECRET COVE

✳ 49°31.6'N   123°58.2'W

Approaching the marina, store and fuel float.

A catboat sails within the harbour.

In the busy summer months a steady stream of boats enter and exit the gap between Turnagain and Jack Tolmie islands, a sure sign of activity within. Once the marked rock has been safely navigated and the gap negotiated, hidden Secret Cove comes clearly into view. This spacious bay is spread out into three main fingers and resembles a small harbour, with all the facilities — ample moorage, excellent marine services, two fuel docks and good all-weather protection — should you choose to anchor.

Fuel and moorage can be found at SECRET COVE MARINA and their well-stocked store offers a good selection of boating essentials and provisions including ice, books, charts, boating guides, marine supplies and fishing tackle. Cold beer and wine can be purchased through their B.C. Liquor Store outlet. Their shower facilities are well serviced and the hot water supply ample. Breakfast, lunch and dinner with a view are available at the marina's UPPER DECK CAFÉ while the outdoor patio is a pleasant spot to sit with a drink while enjoying the entertaining dockside and boating activities.

BUCCANEER MARINA is a well-maintained, family-operated business that includes a fuel dock, busy boat launch, small store and limited moorage. It is known for its excellent marine repair facilities, with local mechanics on call seven days a week in case of more serious problems. It is the only facility to carry propane.

THE JOLLY ROGER runs a popular waterfront pub and dining room open seven days a week during the summer months. It serves traditional pub fare and its restaurant is noted for its well-priced steak and seafood dishes. Limited moorage is also available.

When anchoring in the west finger of Secret Cove, keep in mind that a clear channel should be kept for boat and float plane access to SECRET COVE MARINA and fuel dock. The upside is a gorgeous sunrise. Alternatively, drop your hook behind Jack Tolmie Island for grand sunset views. Should you need to get away from it all, anchor deep in the southeast finger and relax with a gentle row in the shallows to drift with the seals and birds.

Note: Secret Cove is a busy harbour. Leave channels to all marinas and fuel floats clear.

CHARTS 3535. 3311, Sheet 3

APPROACH
From the S. The lighted starboard beacon atop the rock within the gap and between Jack Tolmie and Turnagain islands forms a recognizable profile.

ANCHOR
Secret Cove offers good all-weather protection in the three main locations indicated. Holding good in mud, though some logging debris remains on the bottom.

PUBLIC WHARF
Used mainly by local boats.

MARINA
SECRET COVE MARINA (604-885-3533) offers extensive visitor moorage and is a full service marina. BBX wireless internet available. BUCCANEER MARINA AND RESORT (604-885-7888) and THE JOLLY ROGER (604-885-7860) have limited visitor moorage; call ahead to determine availability.

FUEL
Fuel floats at both SECRET COVE and BUCCANEER MARINAS. Propane at BUCCANEER MARINA.

BOAT LAUNCH
Private at BUCCANEER MARINA.

Good sunset views.

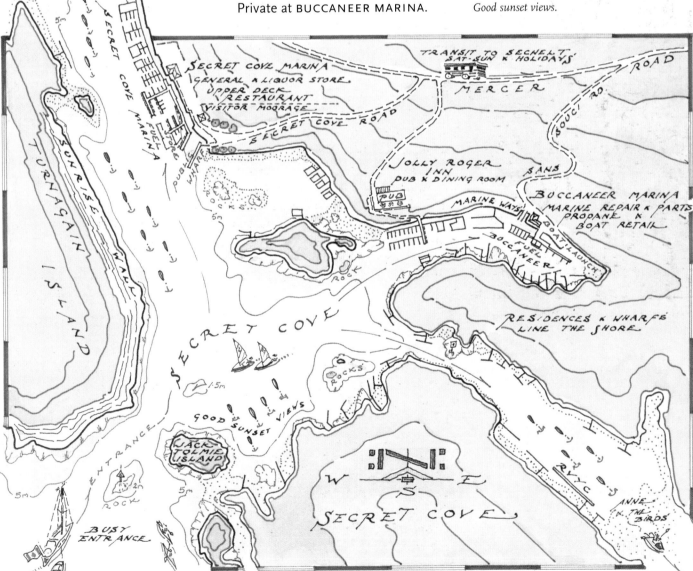

Not to scale. Not to be used for navigation.

Chapter 8

McNAUGHTON POINT TO PENDER HARBOUR

Dreamspeaker joins the work boats at Hospital Bay public wharf, see 8.6, page 100.

The lookout pavilion in Madeira Park.

Chapter 8
McNAUGHTON POINT
TO PENDER HARBOUR

TIDES
Canadian Tide and Current Tables,
Volume 5

Reference Port: Point Atkinson
Secondary Port: Irvines Landing and
Pender Harbour

CURRENTS
Note: On a large tide a strong tidal
current with overfalls occurs on both
the flood and the ebb in the passage
leading to Gunboat Bay.

WEATHER
Pender Harbour lies approximately
midway between the reporting
stations of Merry Island and Grief
Point. The weather is predominantly
as forecast "for the Strait of Georgia,
North of Nanaimo." Strong NW
winds over a flooding current and
strong SE winds over an ebbing
current will kick up short, choppy
seas in Malaspina Strait.

CAUTIONARY NOTES: *The harbour is*
largely protected from the NW. It also
offers good protection from the S,
although during strong to gale-force SE
winds, unexpected squalls race through
the various bays, coves and passages.
Boats at anchor may experience strong
wind shifts and exaggerated swinging.
Ensure that the anchor is well set and
the boat has good clearance to swing.
Avoid using excessive scope.

Pender Harbour is central to this chapter and provides a welcome respite from the otherwise exposed coastline that extends from McNaughton Point in the S to the entrance of Agamemnon Channel in the N. Strong southeasterly and northwesterly winds in Malaspina Strait regularly lash this portion of the shoreline year round.

Just before the shelter of Pender Harbour, a surprise anchorage and marina, backed by a sandy beach, lies hidden behind Harness and Hurrens islands. N of Edgecombe Island lies the entrance to Bargain Bay. Good anchorage can be found at the head of the bay.

Pender Harbour lies in the NW corner of the Sechelt Peninsula. Tucked below magnificent Mount Daniel and protected from the seas in Malaspina Strait by Francis Peninsula, it offers the only completely sheltered anchorage on this portion of the coast and moorage facilities abound.

The boating season begins with the Pender Harbour May Day celebrations. Hospital Bay Days are held every August to celebrate the community's historical heritage and in mid-September the Pender Harbour Music Society hosts a jazz weekend with excellent live music to conclude the summer season.

The two major communities of Pender Harbour are Garden Bay and Madeira Park. Both are fascinating to explore and offer insights into the harbour's intriguing history as well as providing excellent provisioning and dining opportunities.

Four prominent and majestic landmarks — Pender Hill, Harbour Peak, Cecil Hill and, tallest of all, Mount Daniel — surround Pender Harbour. The newly acquired (2001) Francis Point Marine Park is ideal for hiking, picnicking, camping and viewing the abundant wildlife.

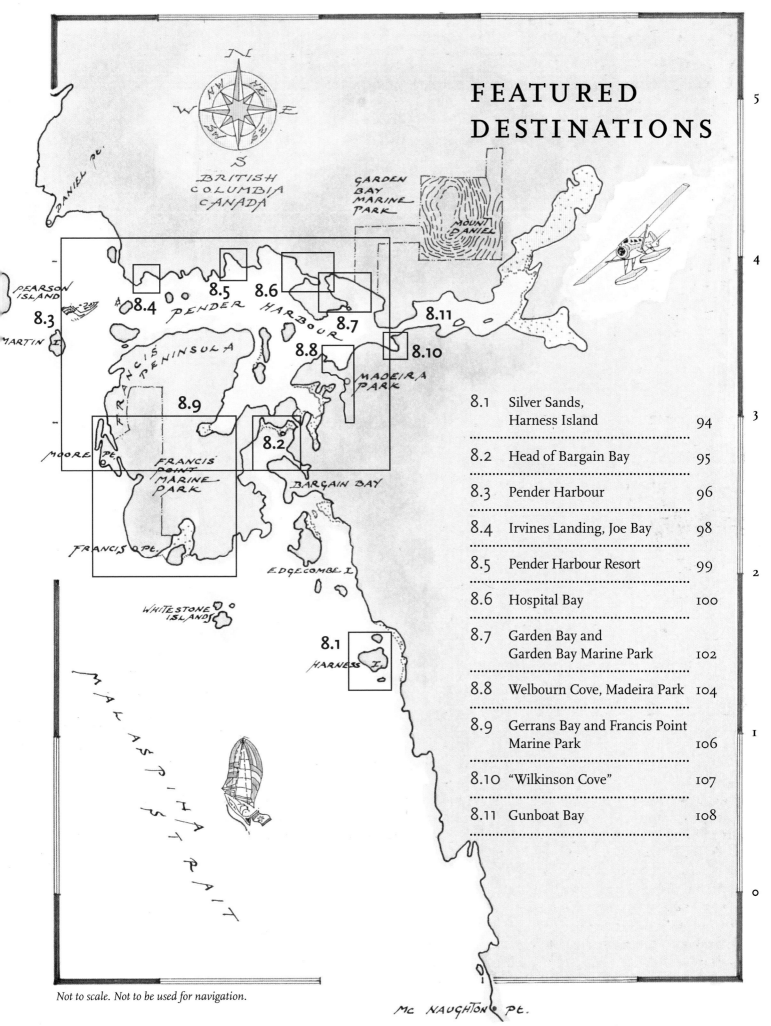

FEATURED DESTINATIONS

Not to scale. Not to be used for navigation.

8.1 SILVER SANDS, HARNESS ISLAND

✱ 49°35.4'N 124°01.4'W

CHARTS 3512. 3311, Sheet 3

APPROACH
From the SW, in the centre channel between Harness Island and the rocks to the S.

ANCHOR
In the pool formed by the mainland, Hurrens Island and Harness Island. Reasonable protection from moderate SE and NW winds. Depth 4–5 m (13–16 ft), holding fair in mud and shingle.

MARINA
Private.

BOAT LAUNCH
Private, at marina.

Note: The anchorage becomes uncomfortable if a strong NW or SE wind gets up.

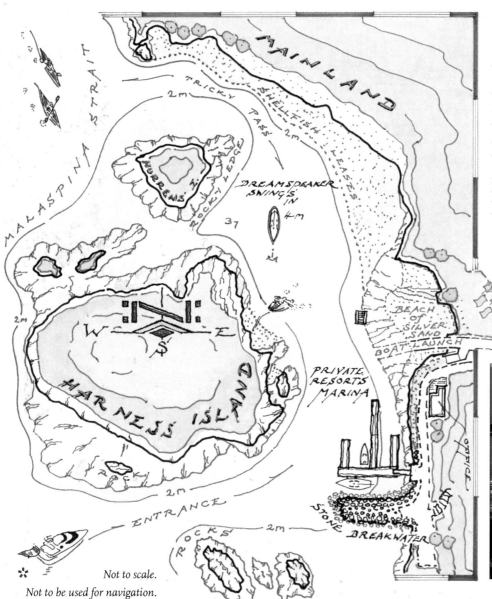

✱ *Not to scale.*
Not to be used for navigation.

Hidden behind Harness and Hurrens islands is a surprise, cosy anchorage and marina backed by a small silver-sand beach. Although the islands are Crown land and designated as a recreational reserve, the undergrowth is very dense, making them difficult to explore on foot. The best way to investigate the shoreline nooks and crannies is by dinghy or kayak, making sure that you don't disturb the shellfish leases.

The crew checks out the silver sand.

HEAD OF BARGAIN BAY

CHARTS 3535. 3311, Sheet 3 and 4

Notes: Check your charts for the position of two isolated rocks in the entrance; there is ample water and room between them.

APPROACH
From the S, leaving Edgecombe Island to the E. Stay in deep water up to the head of Bargain Bay.

ANCHOR
S of the rocky fringe. Good protection from the NW and reasonable protection from moderate SE winds. Depths 5–7 m (16–23 ft), holding fair over rock and mud.

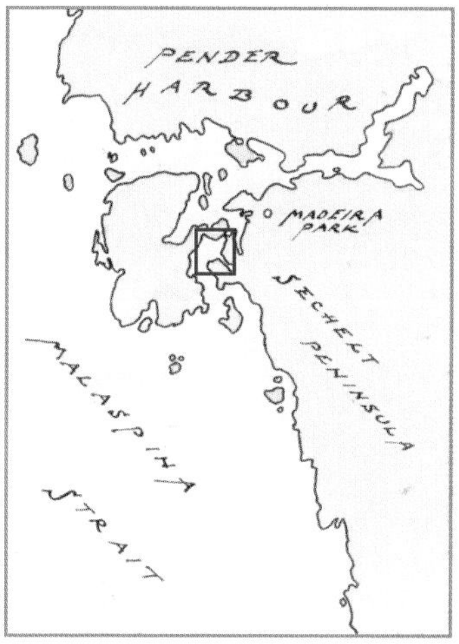

✣ 49°36.2'N 124°02.2'W
(Abeam of Edgecombe Island)

Bargain Bay is a pleasant anchorage with excellent possibilities for dinghy or kayak exploration. At HW, Bargain Narrows will transport you under the bridge and into Pender Harbour for a few fun hours of discovery. Alternatively, row into the quiet of "Oyster Lagoon" (local name) and relax with the wildlife. Road access to Whiskey Slough and Francis Point Marine Park is possible from the head of Bargain Bay, along Francis Peninsula Road. The bay is a quiet anchorage for the most part, although there is occasional vehicular disturbance from the road.

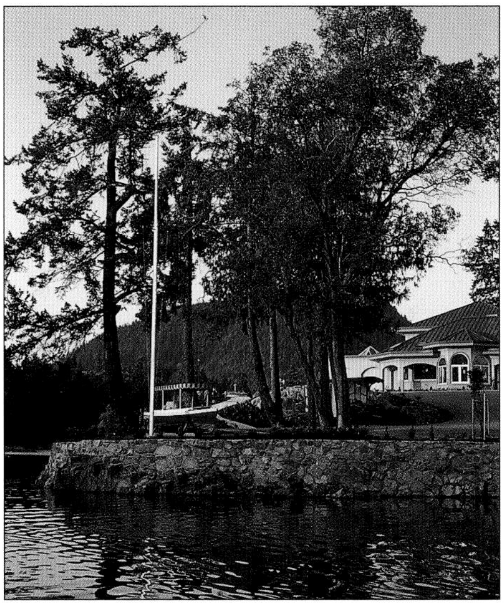

A gem in Bargain Narrows.

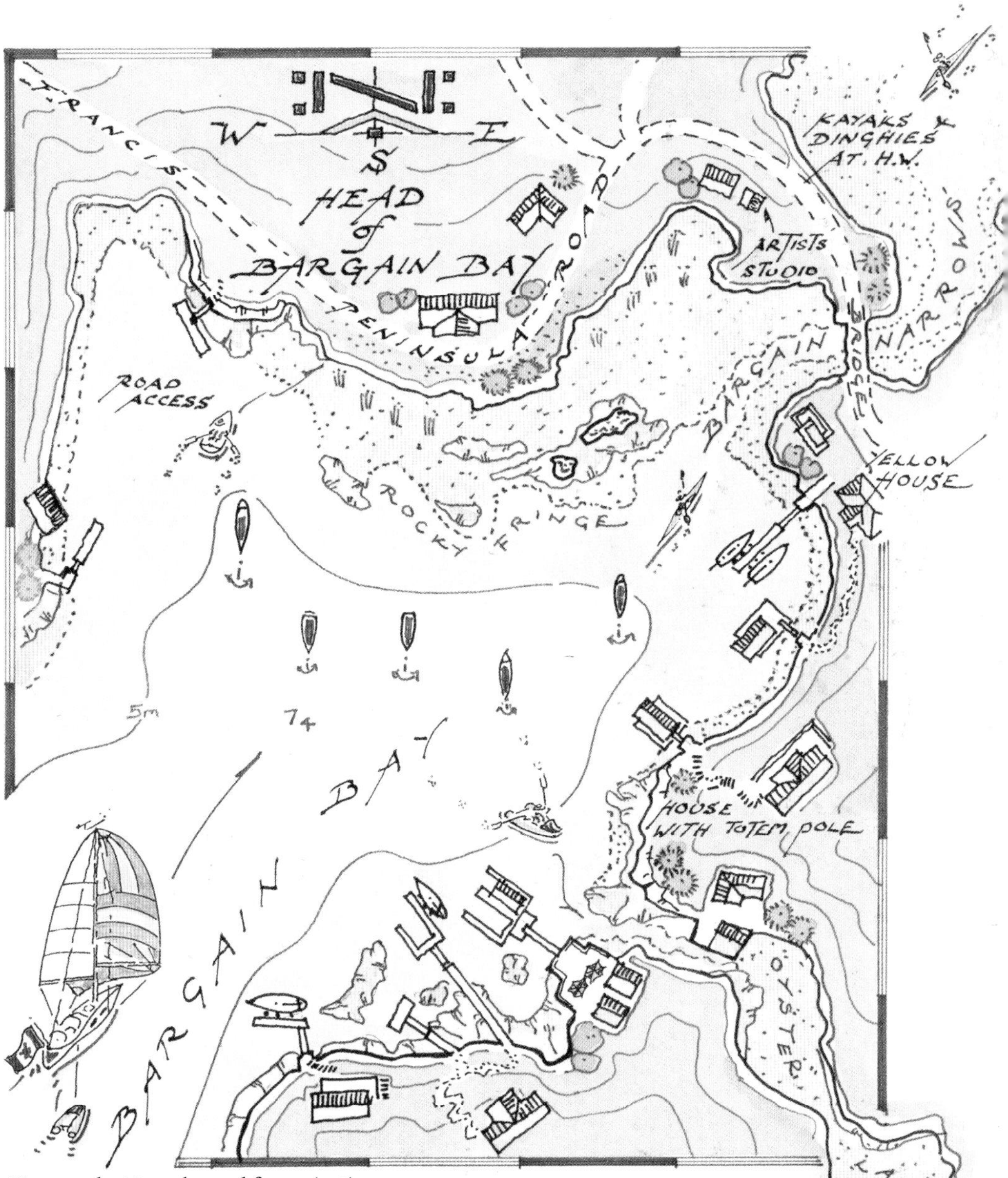

Not to scale. Not to be used for navigation.

8.3 PENDER HARBOUR

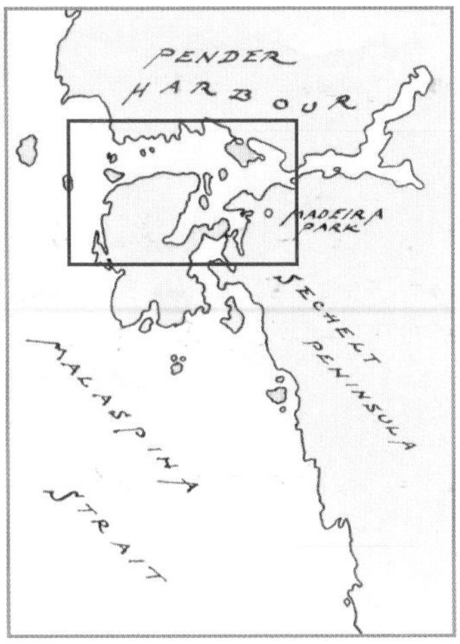

✲ 49°37.8'N 124°03.8'W

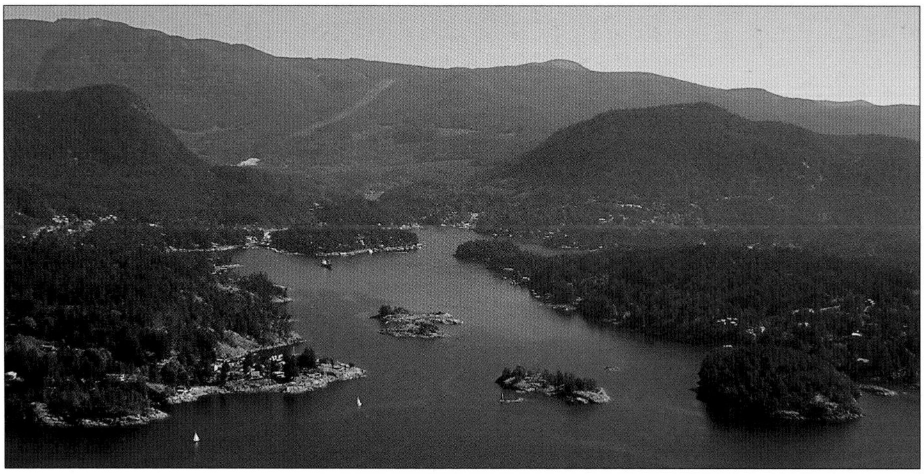

The entrance to Pender Harbour, the Venice of the Sunshine Coast.

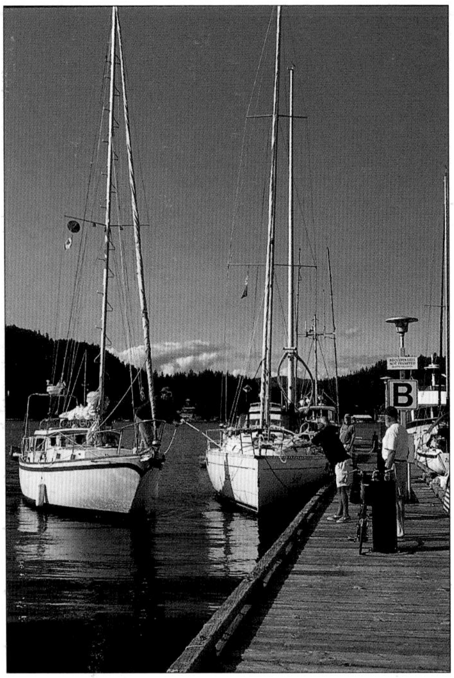

Dockside welcome, Madeira Park.

Tucked behind Francis Peninsula about midway between Welcome Passage and Grief Point is the largest all-weather anchorage on the Sunshine Coast. Sheltered from the winds and seas of the Malaspina Strait, Pender Harbour is the primary recreational boating centre for visitor moorage and fuel and repair facilities, and is popular in the busy summer months with boaters cruising N to Princess Louisa Inlet and Desolation Sound.

Once known as the Venice of the Sunshine Coast, Pender Harbour is made up of a spectacular maze of islands, nooks and crannies and is a delightful destination to explore in its own right. The harbour is only 2.4 km (1.5 miles) long, but all the twists and turns add up to a total of 165 km (102 miles) of shoreline. In the early part of the century, the Pender population did everything by boat, from shopping and visiting friends to going to school and church. The community is still laid out around the harbour, with docks in front of every waterfront home. Visitors can use a water taxi to tour the harbour, provision or dine out, as they will pick you up from the wharf or your boat.

Provisions can be found at Madeira Park and Hospital Bay. The GARDEN BAY HOTEL is actually a cheerful pub and restaurant with a wide selection of dishes.

There is ample anchorage off Garden Bay Marine Park, which has a circular trail and a picnic terrace. For the more energetic, the reward for the vigorous hike to the top of Mount Daniel is an amazing view and the chance to freshen up in the waters of Garden Bay Lake on your way down. Francis Point Marine Park can be accessed from Whiskey Slough public wharf in Gerrans Bay. This newly aquired West Coast treasure is wonderful to explore by kayak or small craft or by hiking the trails to view the abundant wildlife and old-growth trees.

Note: There is a 7-knot speed limit in Pender Harbour for all boats. The harbour is also a no-sewage-discharge zone and boaters are required to use the pump-out station or holding tanks at all times.

CHARTS 3535. 3311, Sheet 4

APPROACH
From the W. The harbour may be entered either to the N or S of Williams Island. Pender Harbour light (red) is on a reef N of Williams Island.

ANCHOR
Hospital Bay and Garden Bay are the popular anchorages, but Gerrans Bay offers the best protection in a strong southeasterly. Holding generally good in mud although in the summer the bottom becomes loose in Garden Bay and anchors may drag.

PUBLIC WHARVES
At Madeira Park, Hospital Bay and Whiskey Slough, in the SE corner of Gerrans Bay.

MARINAS
The following marinas have visitor moorage:

FUEL

BOAT REPAIR
MADEIRA MARINA — 604-883-2266.
GARDEN BAY MARINE SERVICES LTD., "SINCLAIR BAY" — 604-883-2367.

PUMP-OUT
At the Madeira Park public wharf.

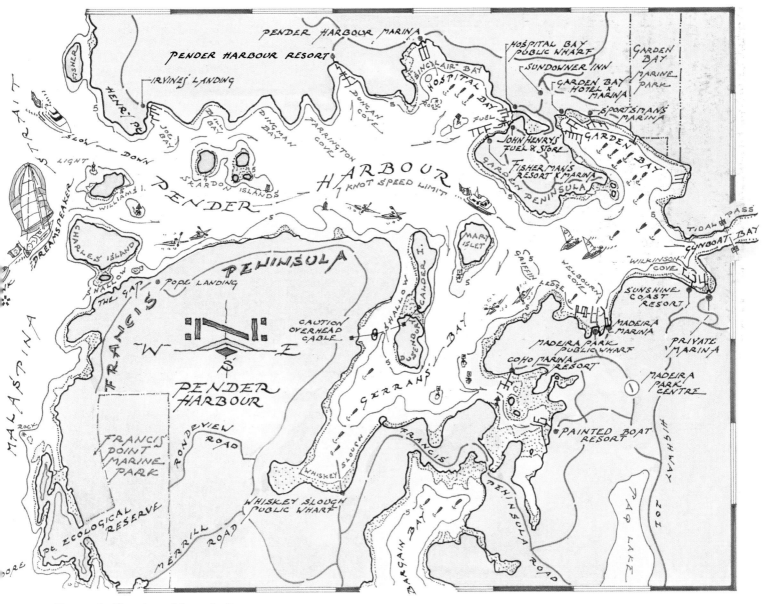

Not to scale. Not to be used for navigation.

8.4 IRVINES LANDING, JOE BAY

CHARTS 3535. 3311, Sheet 4

APPROACH
From the S. Joe Bay is E of Henry
Point.

MARINA
Private.

BOAT LAUNCH
Private.

FUEL
No fuel available.

✽ 49°37.9'N   124°03.3'W

Henry Point and the Landing.

Historic Irvines Landing was named for Charlie Irvine, who lived there in the late 1880s. Irvines was Pender Harbour's original town centre. It supported a post office, general store and hotel owned by the legendary Portuguese Joe Gonzalves after whom Joe Bay is named, and by the 1920s it was a popular social spot on the days the Union Steamship called in to deliver mail, provisions and passengers on its regular route from Vancouver. The old marina site was awaiting redevelopment in 2007. The former pub, marina, fuel dock and laundry facilities were closed.

PENDER HARBOUR RESORT

CHARTS 3535. 3311, Sheet 4

Approach
From the S. The marina takes up the eastern portion of the cove.

ANCHOR
Anchoring is not recommended due to the high level of water activity from the resort.

MARINA
The resort's marina has extensive moorage and ample space for visitors; call 604-883-2424. Wireless intenet available.

BOAT LAUNCH
Private, at the resort.

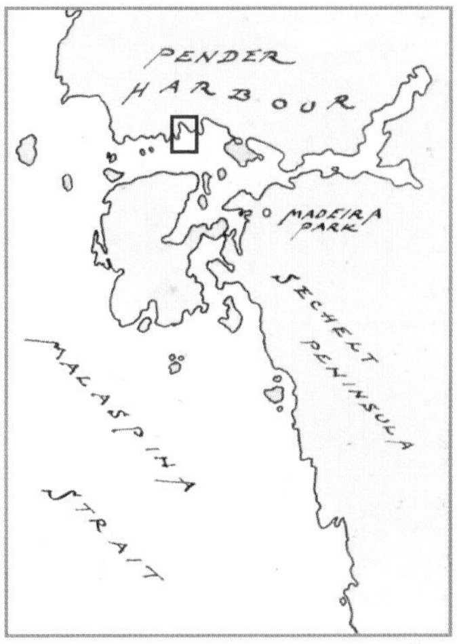

✲ 49°37.9'N 124°02.5'W

The sport fishing enthusiast will feel at home at this family resort, originally known as DUNCAN COVE RESORT, which offers camping facilities, RV sites and self-catering cabins. It also offers overnight visitor moorage and boaters are welcome to use the pool, spa and shower and laundry facilities. A charming gazebo overlooks the marina S to Madeira Park and is a lovely spot to relax and picnic alfresco. A mini-store in the resort office carries ice, pop, juice, ice cream, bread and fishing tackle.

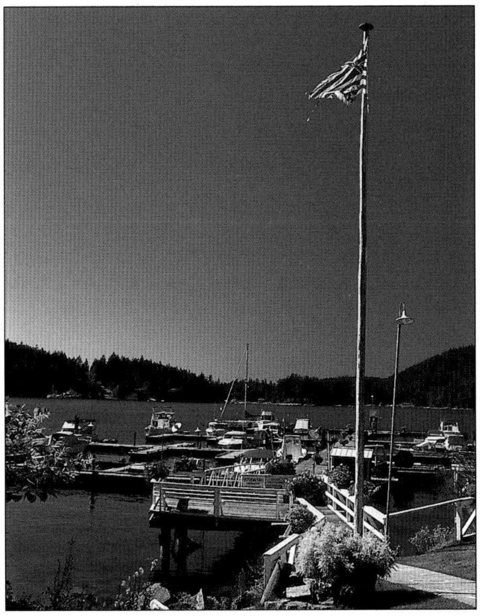

A delightful family affair.

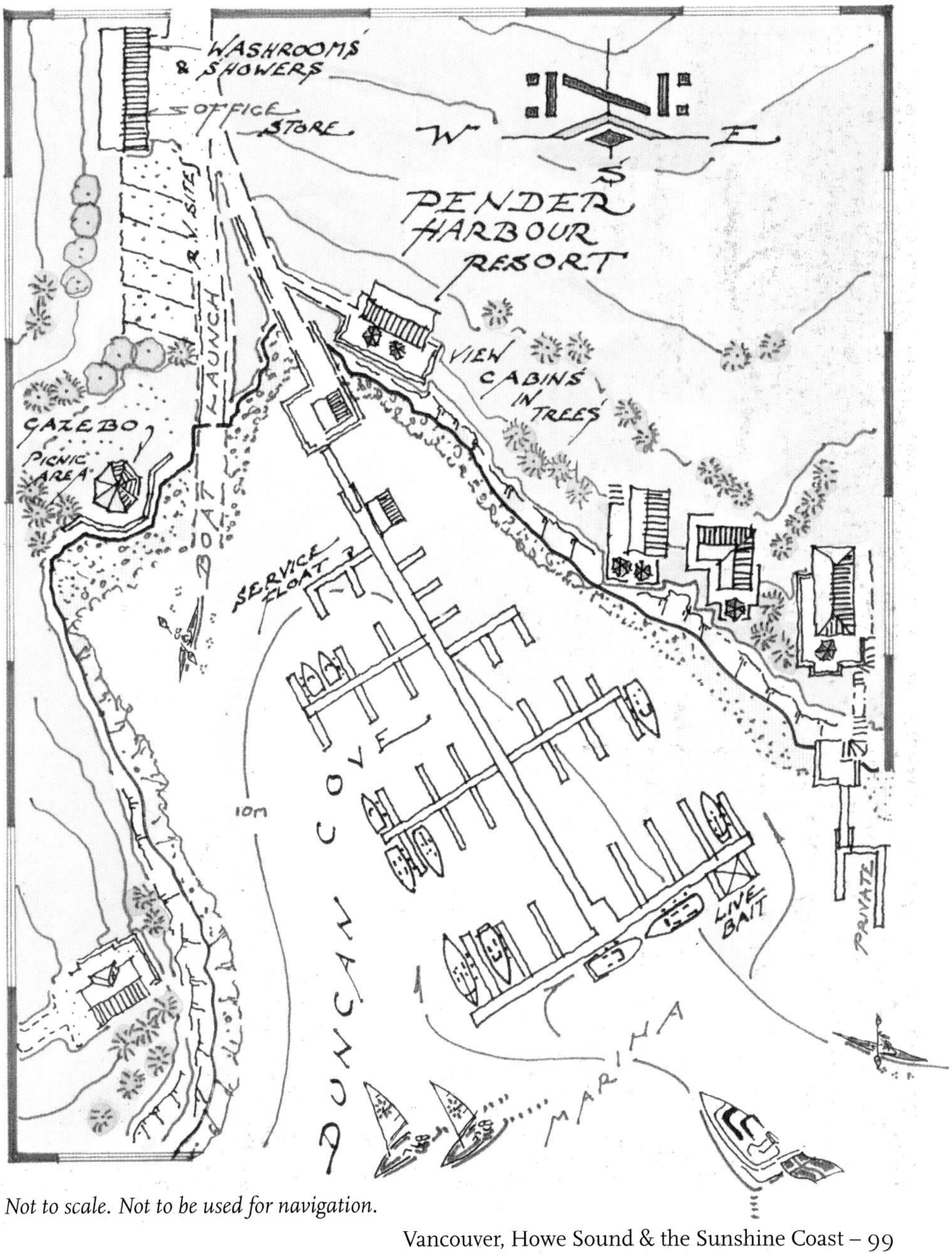

Not to scale. Not to be used for navigation.

8.6 HOSPITAL BAY

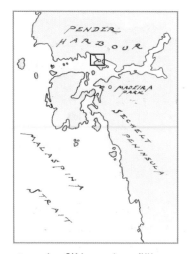

⚜ 49°37.8'N   124°02.3'W

Approaching John Henry's fuel float, Fisherman's Marina to starboard.

The Hospital Bay public wharf.

This yellow biplane is an N3N-3, and still flies.

The "Community of Garden Bay" includes Hospital Bay, Duncan Cove, Garden Bay Lake and "Sinclair Bay." Hospital Bay took its name from St. Mary's Hospital and Chapel, which used to overlook the bay. The easiest way to familiarize yourself with the "downtown core" is to take a circular tour from the public dock, beginning with the historic SUNDOWNER INN, a former lodge and restaurant closed at time of writing. This landmark was constructed by the Columbia Coast Mission as a community hospital in 1930. The hospital is fondly remembered by the many local residents who were born in its maternity ward, baptized there, and married in its chapel.

The tour then continues with a stroll along Lyons' Road, taking you to the GARDEN BAY HOTEL AND MARINA — not actually a hotel at all, but a cheerful pub and restaurant with a wide selection of dishes (see page 102).

A short trail leads S from the back of the hotel along the forested shoreline to the nearby ROYAL VANCOUVER YACHT CLUB outstation. Continue around to JOHN HENRY'S GENERAL STORE AND POST OFFICE, a popular local meeting spot run with gusto; a sign reads "Please don't ask for anything specific, this is a general store." Boaters delayed by wind or tide will appreciate that the LIQUOR STORE here remains open seven days a week. They also carry a selection of fresh produce, basic provisions, specialty items such as homemade pickled garlic and marine supplies, propane, books, cruising guides and charts. Their fuel dock is busy, friendly and well run.

The efficiently run FISHERMAN'S RESORT AND MARINA is a neat and tidy complex. Hanging baskets overflowing with flowers line the docks and inviting picnic tables wait nearby in the shade. The resort has shower and laundry facilities, plus waterfront cottages and RV sites.

CHARTS 3535. 3311, Sheet 4.

APPROACH
From the SW. There is deep water between FISHERMAN'S MARINA and the day beacon. Alternatively, leave the day beacon to the S.

ANCHOR
As indicated in the shoreline plan. Be sure to keep a clear channel open to the marina, fuel dock and public wharf. Depth 5–12 m (16–39 ft), holding good in mud.

PUBLIC WHARF
Located below the SUNDOWNER INN, which generally has ample visitor moorage.

MARINA
FISHERMAN'S RESORT AND MARINA has extensive, well-maintained floats and is popular in the summer; reservations are recommended (604-883-2336). BBX wireless internet available.

FUEL
At JOHN HENRY'S FUEL DOCK, where propane is also available. Temporary moorage available for patrons of JOHN HENRY'S GENERAL STORE; call 604-883-2253. BBX wireless internet available.

BOAT LAUNCH
Private, at the marina.

Note: Pender Harbour is a float plane operations zone and the designated float at fisherman's marina is used regularly in the summer months.

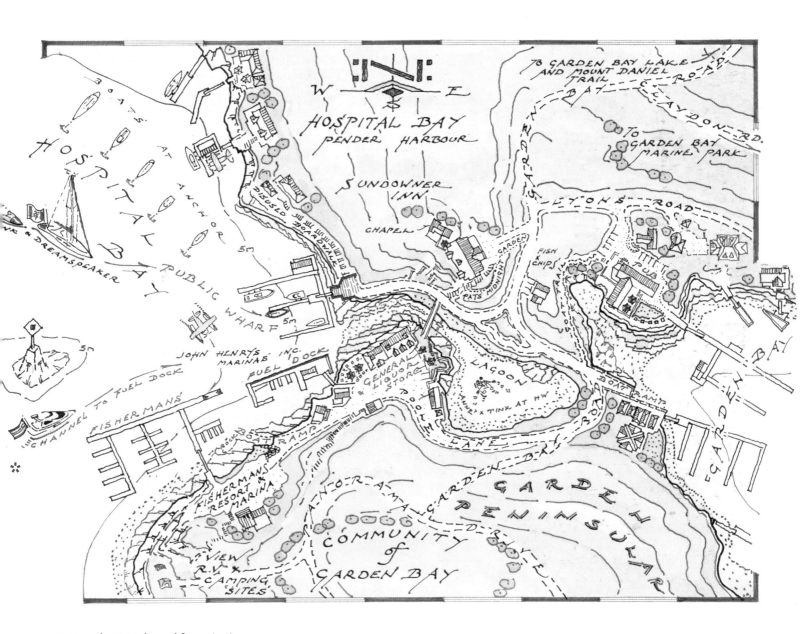

Not to scale. Not to be used for navigation.

8.7 GARDEN BAY AND GARDEN BAY MARINE PARK

49°37.7N 124°01.3W

Garden Bay to Hospital Bay, from Mount Daniel.

Evening in the bay.

The morning after.

On the N shore of Pender Harbour, popular Garden Bay offers ample moorage at two friendly marinas. The anchorage off Garden Bay Marine Park can accommodate numerous boats in the busy months, especially when boaters think ahead and tie stern-to the park's shoreline. There is a 7-knot speed limit for all boats, and residents with private floats off Garden Peninsula really appreciate boaters slowing down to a wake-free speed.

THE GARDEN BAY HOTEL AND MARINA provides power and water on its docks, but no shower or laundry facilities are available. The hotel is actually not a hotel but a cheerful, smoke-free pub and restaurant with a wide selection of dishes and a great view of Mount Daniel. A stone's throw away, SPORTSMAN'S MARINA offers shower and laundry facilities and ice. As the marinas are close together, boaters can combine the various facilities — feel free to shower, throw in the laundry and relax at the pub during the drying cycle.

Garden Bay Marine Park has a designated dinghy dock with access to a 500–m (quarter-mile) circular trail that leads to a lovely picnic terrace and up to Claydon Road. From here the energetic can continue along Garden Bay Road to the Mount Daniel trail. Described as intermediate to advanced, this strenuous trail winds its way unrelentingly to the summit, a 1.5-hour hike. Allow extra time for sightseeing, picnicking and recovery — the payoff is the amazing view from the top. Here you may also find "moon rings," artefacts of a Native rite of passage for girls reaching puberty. Directly below are Katherine Lake, Mixal Lake and Garden Bay Lake, which provide blissful freshwater bathing on your journey back. A lift from a kind local to the start of the trail may prove prudent for those with less time on their hands.

For an unforgettable meal, treat yourself to dinner at the family-run RUBY LAKE RESORT (see page 116).

Note: As the anchorage is very popular in summer, the mud bottom is well churned and boats have been known to drag their anchors. Make sure the hook is well set and avoid using excessive scope as swinging room is limited.

CHARTS 3535. 3311, Sheet 4

APPROACH
From the S by rounding the two rock islets off the eastern tip of Garden Peninsula.

ANCHOR
Towards the northern shoreline. Be sure to leave a clear channel off Garden Peninsula for boats heading to the numerous private docks and marinas. Anchor stern-to the marine park shoreline if swinging room is limited. Depths 3–9 m (10–29 ft), holding fair in mud.

MARINAS
Extensive marina facilities are available at the GARDEN BAY HOTEL AND MARINA (604-883-2674, BBX wireless internet available) and limited facilities at SPORTSMAN'S MARINA (604-883-2479). Book ahead in summer.
ROYAL VANCOUVER YACHT CLUB. Reciprocity only. BBX wireless internet available.

FUEL
No fuel float available.

BOAT LAUNCH
Private, at the ROYAL VANCOUVER YACHT CLUB.

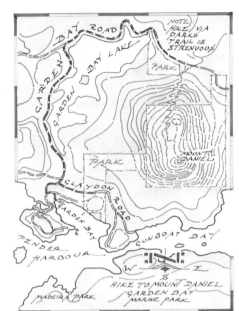

The route to the hike to Mount Daniel.

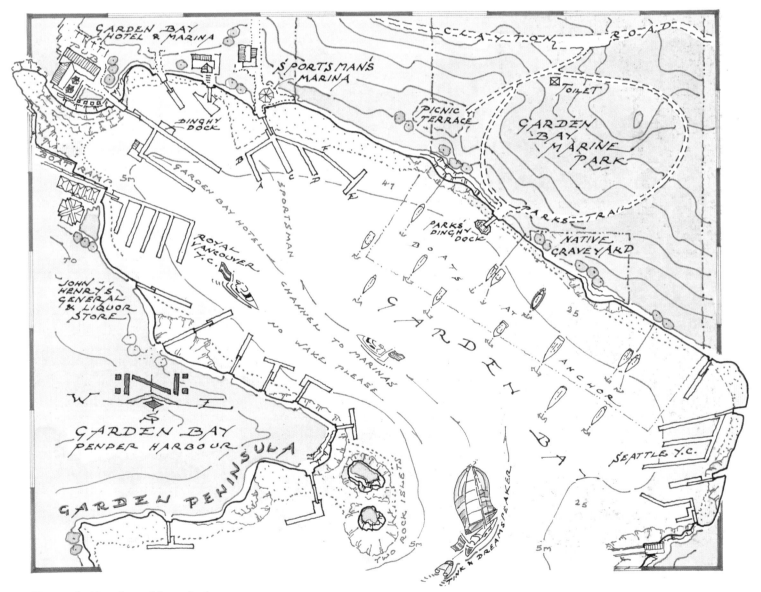

Not to scale. Not to be used for navigation.

8.8 WELBOURN COVE, MADEIRA PARK

✼ 49°37.5'N   124°01.5'W

Approaching the public wharf.

A fishing boat on the ways.

New Seafarer Millenium Park.

The joys of cruising are many and it's a real treat to arrive at a new destination with time to discover what it has to offer. The sociable public wharf in Welbourn Cove is one such place and Madeira Park is a community worth exploring. At the head of the public wharf is the neatly landscaped Seafarer Millennium Park, complete with boardwalk, lookout turret, gift store and umbrella-equipped picnic tables. The wharf is a favourite rendezvous for visiting boats and a great place to catch up on local news. Fresh tuna or halibut can often be purchased right off the fishing boats and the SLO-CAT will ferry you to a number of harbour destinations.

The wharf office is run by friendly staff who take pride in their new facilities and although the showers may seem a little pricey, they deliver in quality and quantity. A short walk along Madeira Park Road takes you past the historic music school and library complex, set within a tiny regional park, which also houses a small art gallery and a preschool.

Farther on you'll discover a cosy coffee shop/art studio. A rendezvous frequented by locals, it serves delicious sandwiches, baked goods and coffee.

At the heart of Madeira Park is a cluster of shops and services including OAK TREE MARKET, a gift store, a B.C. Liquor Store, MARINA PHARMACY and a well-stocked IGA which sells hardware, magazines, books and cruising guides as well as groceries, and will even loan its trolleys to transport your provisions to the dock. Pay a visit to MONACLE STAINED GLASS just off Madeira Park Road, owned and operated by Gord Wenman.

Don't miss the famed burgers and chips at the colourful stand beside the community hall. For second-hand books and assorted paraphernalia, visit the BARGAIN BARN and have fun sorting through the shelves and boxes. The post office and the KNITTING ZEN store can be found on Gonzales Road.

CHARTS 3335. 3313, Sheet 4

APPROACH
From the N. The marina, public wharf and private boat sheds are a conspicuous mass.

ANCHOR
W of the submarine cable in depths of 5–10 m (16–33 ft). Holding good in mud and shingle.

PUBLIC WHARF
Extensive recreational craft moorage on the western float; call 604-883-2234 or tune in to VHF 9. A dinghy dock is designated for boaters visiting or provisioning in Madeira Park.

MARINA
MADEIRA MARINA has no visitor moorage; however their marine repair facilities are extensive and include a marine way; call 604-883-2266.

BOAT LAUNCH
Public, adjacent to the public wharf.

Note: Anchorage is possible E of the submarine cable, although this is a heavy traffic zone and float planes are frequent visitors to the public wharf.

WELBOURN COVE

DREAMSPEAKER AT ANCHOR

PRIVATE

5m

5m

ANNE RETURNS FROM A PROVISIONING VISIT

PUBLIC WHARF

MADEIRA MARINA

MARINE WAY

WATER TAXI

DINGHY DOCK

BOAT LAUNCH

SUBMARINE CABLE

TURRETED LOOKOUT

NEW SEAFARER MILLENNIUM PARK

DOCK OFFICE & SHOWERS

TO THE POST OFFICE

MUSIC SCHOOL

LIBRARY

ART GALLERY

PLAYSCHOOL

TOTEM POLE

GONZALES ROAD

SCHOOL

SCHOOL PLAYING FIELD

WELBOURN COVE
MADEIRA PARK
PENDER HARBOUR

MADEIRA PARK ROAD

MADEIRA CENTRE

BLACKBERRIES

1: VISITOR CENTRE
2: COMMUNITY HALL
3: BARGAIN BARN
4: HAMBURGER STAND
5: COFFEE SHOP / ART GALLERY
6: MARINA PHARMACY
7: CREDIT UNION
8: IGA
9: OAK TREE MARKET
10: GIFT SHOP
11: MONACLE / STAIN GLASS
12: JAVA DOCKS

Not to scale. Not to be used for navigation.

8.9 GERRANS BAY AND FRANCIS POINT MARINE PARK

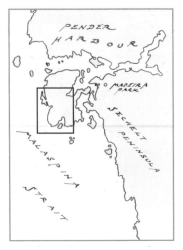

✳ 49°37.2'N 124°02.4'W

CHARTS 3535. 3311, Sheet 4

APPROACH
Gerrans Bay: from within Pender Harbour, see page 96.

ANCHOR
To the N of the public wharf. Excellent protection, especially from strong SE winds. Depths 2.5–8 m (8–26 ft), holding good in mud.

PUBLIC WHARF
The twin floats at Whiskey Slough are

frequented by local boaters although there is usually room for visitors.

The view from Middle Bay to Francis Bay.

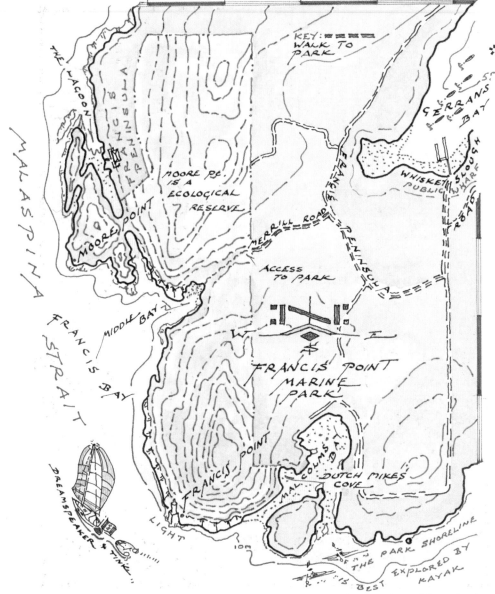

Not to scale. Not to be used for navigation.

Gerrans Bay offers access to Whiskey Slough public wharf and the newly acquired Francis Point Marine Park (2001), a pristine example of Canada's endangered ecosystems. This 9-hectare (22-acre) coastal treasure is ideal for hiking, picnicking, camping and viewing wildlife. The point's forested uplands feature old-growth Douglas fir and western red cedar and the rocky headlands offer breathtaking vistas up and down Malaspina Strait. Moore Point is slated to become an ecological reserve.

Access to the park commences at the end of Merrill Road. A short trail to Middle Bay allows visitors to portage kayaks and small craft so they can explore the Malaspina Strait shoreline.

Note: Tie dinghies at the foot of the wharf head, as moorage space at the public wharf is limited.

"WILKINSON COVE"

CHARTS 3335. 3313, Sheet 4

APPROACH
From the NW. The two marinas and numerous private floats resemble a maze from the water; proceed with caution parallel to the NE shore.

MARINAS
SUNSHINE COAST RESORT AND MARINA (604-883-9177) has visitor moorage. Wireless internet service is available.

✿ 49°37.55'N 124°01.2'W

This convenient moorage is in a quiet cove with "downtown" Madeira Park just a 10-minute walk away (see page 104). sunshine coast marina provides laundry and shower facilities and cable tv hookup on some floats.

The understated tranquillity of a Sunshine Coast marina.

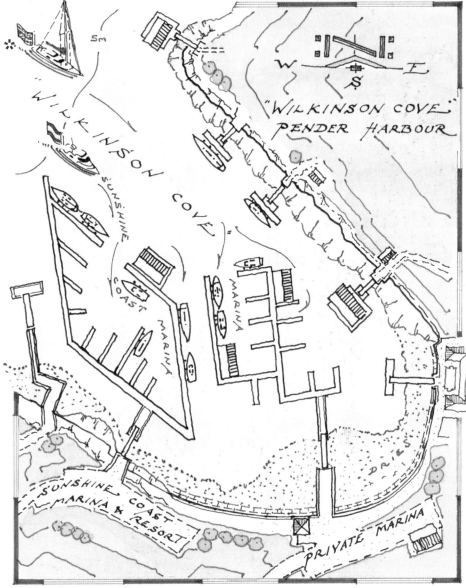

Not to scale. Not to be used for navigation.

8.11 GUNBOAT BAY

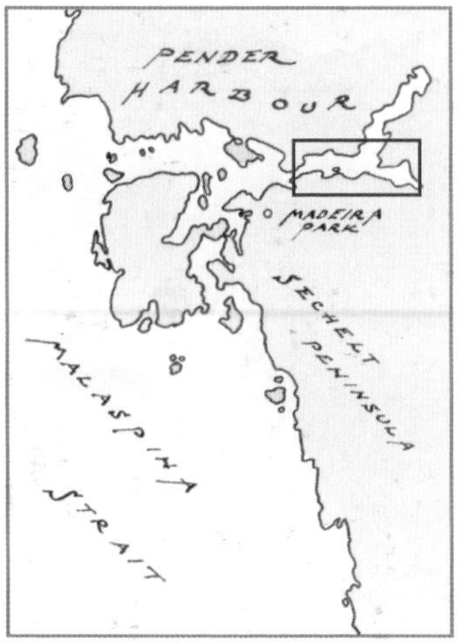

✲ 49°37.55'N 124°01.2'W

CHARTS 3535. 3311, Sheet 4

APPROACH

Best at HW. Enter through "Gunboat Passage" (local name), a narrow channel that has a least depth of 0.7 m (2 ft). A rock lies in the entrance, close to the N shore, and dries 1.1 m (4 ft).

ANCHOR

E or W of the submarine cable. Note that half of Gunboat Bay dries at LW.

Depths 5–10 m (16–33 ft), holding good in mud

Note: There is a minimum clearance of 32 m (105 ft) under the hydro cable. Strong tidal currents with overfalls occur between HW and LW. On a large tide the current can run 4–6 knots; there are no official current stations or recordings.

The view from Mount Daniel.

Visiting boaters are often hesitant to explore Gunboat Bay via the narrow passage, as it is shallow and white water can often be seen rushing between the steep sides. However at high slack water all is calm and once inside, this protected, tranquil anchorage becomes an undisturbed hideaway where a blissful few days can be spent lazing in the cockpit, communing with nature and investigating Oyster Bay, a wide shallow arm that almost dries out at LW. A channel, navigable by dinghy or kayak, leads you through the peaceful tidal flats and past oyster beds to the salt marshes at the head of the bay.

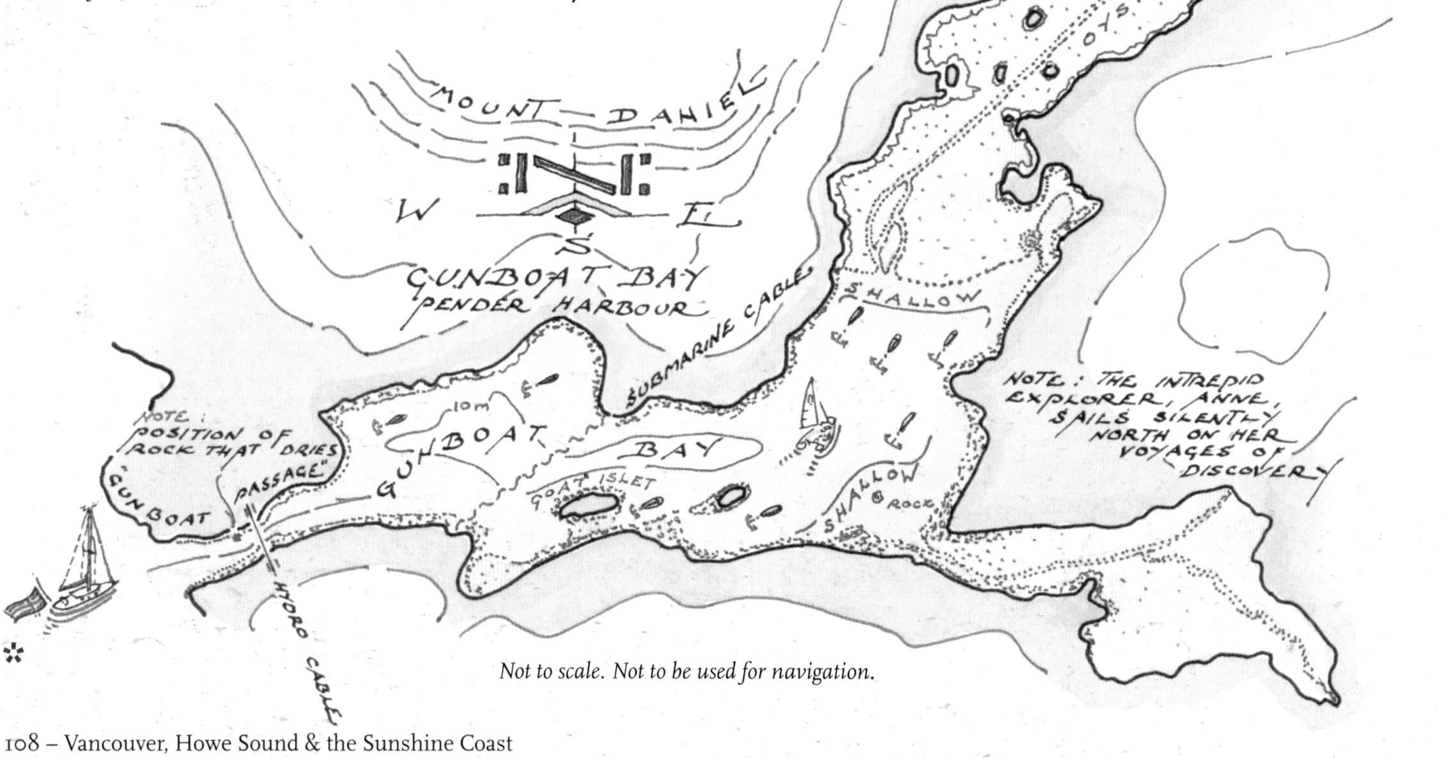

Not to scale. Not to be used for navigation.

Chapter 9

AGAMEMNON CHANNEL TO SKOOKUMCHUK NARROWS

The Queen of Tsawwassen steams past Agamemnon Bay.

Whitewater and nerves of steel, Sechelt Rapids.

Chapter 9

AGAMEMNON CHANNEL TO SKOOKUMCHUK NARROWS

TIDES
Canadian Tide and Current Tables, Volume 5
Reference Port: Point Atkinson
Secondary Ports: Irvines Landing and Egmont

CURRENTS
Note: Tidal streams in Skookumchuck Narrows run up to 4–6 knots on a large tide, producing significant back eddies along the southern shore.

WEATHER
Note: Winds in Agamemnon Channel funnel towards the channel. A southerly or SE wind will blow north-wards while an outflow wind will push south. Skookumchuck Narrows is between wind systems and enjoys light summer breezes.

CAUTIONARY NOTES: *Agamemnon Channel is the preferred water highway for recreational boaters on their annual pilgrimage to Princess Louisa Inlet. The channel is also a busy commercial artery and cruising boaters should keep a constant lookout.*

Agememnon Channel is transformed into a bustling highway in the summer because it provides a direct route from Pender Harbour to the mecca of cruising destinations — Princess Louisa Inlet — and the cruising grounds of Hotham Sound and Sechelt Inlet. This major passageway runs between Sechelt Peninsula and the eastern shoreline of Nelson Island, which offers overnight anchorage in historic Quarry Bay and the quiet, well-protected waters of Green Bay.

On the Sechelt Peninsula side of Agamemnon Channel, Earls Cove serves as a major ferry terminus, linking the peninsula with the upper Sunshine Coast. Unfortunately no facilities are provided for pleasure craft to pick up or drop off family and friends and a trip must be made to Saltery Bay public wharf should you need to make use of the B.C. Ferry services. Just E of Earls Cove a surprise anchorage can be found in Agamemnon Bay; though it is open to occasional ferry wash and the wake of passing boats, it makes for a convenient tea stop or overnight anchorage.

Across from Aagamemnon Bay and just to the N of Nile Point is an enticing two-boat picnic anchorage backed by a narrow tombolo connecting Nelson Island to "Captain Islets" at LW. If you need to refuel and tie up for the night, head over to the EGMONT MARINA AND RESORT at the mouth of Sechelt Inlet in the Skookumchuck Narrows. The marina has a down-home, friendly atmosphere and a lively visitors' dock, and the BACKEDDY PUB serves wonderfully fresh fish and chips.

Just down from the marina lies historic Egmont Village, located on the N shore until 1946, when the local postmaster moved S and took the name with him. The present village in Secret Bay is the perfect place to provision, shower or throw in that last bag of laundry. The bright pink BATHGATE GENERAL STORE AND MARINA is well maintained and run and carries a good selection of basic necessities, including a B.C. Liquor Store outlet.

If you are fortunate enough to be passing through Egmont when a large tide is predicted, don't miss the "Skookumchuck experience." The Sechelt Rapids are rated one of the largest salt-water rapids in the world and held in esteem by local and international surf kayakers.

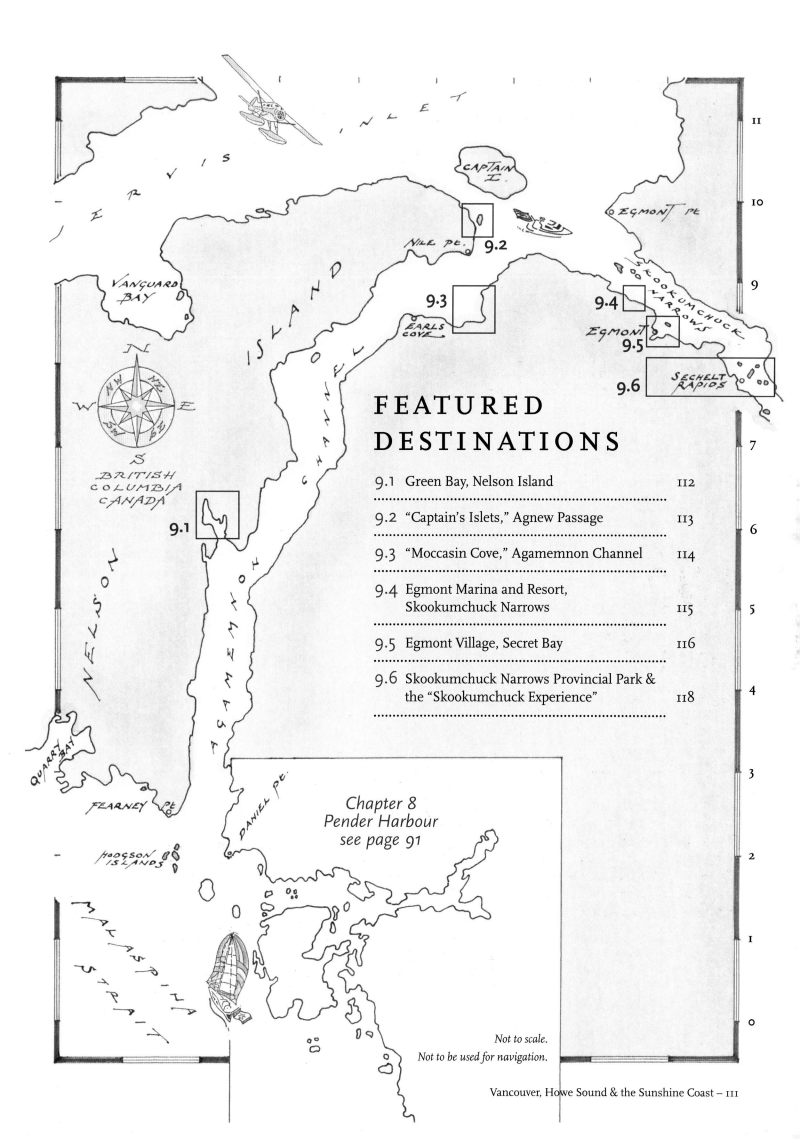

FEATURED DESTINATIONS

Chapter 8
Pender Harbour
see page 91

Not to scale.

Not to be used for navigation.

9.1 GREEN BAY, NELSON ISLAND

49°42.0'N 124°04.5'W

CHARTS 3512. 3312, page 2

APPROACH
From the SE. The bay is the only real indentation on the Nelson Island shoreline.

ANCHOR
Good protection from all quarters excepting the SE, although even strong SE winds and the surge from Agamemnon Channel tend to dissipate deep into the bay.

Anchor as indicated on the shoreline plan, in depths of 10 m (33 ft) plus, holding good over a varied bottom.

Notes: Logging and booming may be active in the bay. There is a dangerous reef marked by two anchored logs.

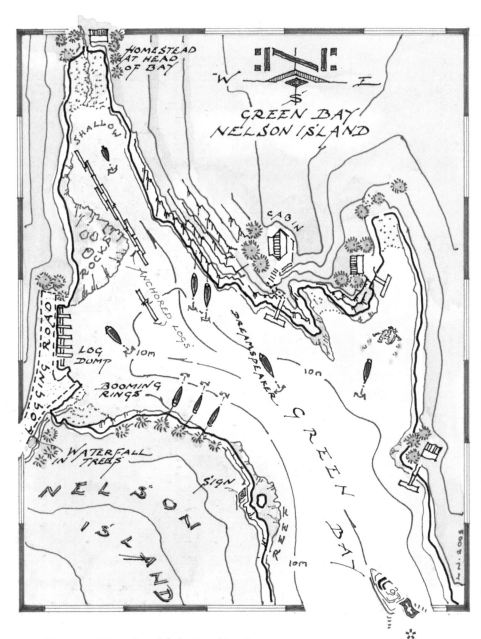

Historic Nelson island has been called "the Gulf Island nobody knows even though it's bigger than Bowen, Gabriola or Lasqueti." The beautiful granite that was shipped to Vancouver to adorn the landmark buildings like the Art Gallery came from the island.

Peaceful Green Bay offers ample protected anchorage. One of the more protected areas is in the westernmost nook with booming rings on the S side, useful for anchoring stern-to. A waterfall provides a soothing backdrop. The northern anchorage, near the shallows, also offers good shelter.

Swinging off the log dump.

"CAPTAIN ISLETS," AGNEW PASSAGE

CHARTS 3512. 3312, pages 2, 3 and 4

APPROACH
From the N out of Agnew Passage. Best investigated at LW.

ANCHOR
Tuck in as far as possible. A long stern line may be advisable. Anchor in depths of 2–5 m (6–16 ft), holding fair over boulders and gravel.

Note: This is a picnic stop, although in settled weather an overnight stay is possible. Anchorage subject to ferry wash.

❀ 49°46.7'N   123°59.5'W

Across from Agamemnon Bay and just N of Nile Point lies an enticing two-boat anchorage with spectacular views and backed by a narrow, pebble-strewn tombolo that connects Nelson Island to "Captain Islets" at LW. Named by us, these islets are a delight to explore and are popular with kayakers who can camp on the soft mossy knoll NE of the tombolo. They also provide reasonable protection from ferry wash and seas generated by up-inlet winds that may curl around through Agnew Passage. An absorbing afternoon could be spent hunting for smooth, rounded pebbles and driftwood.

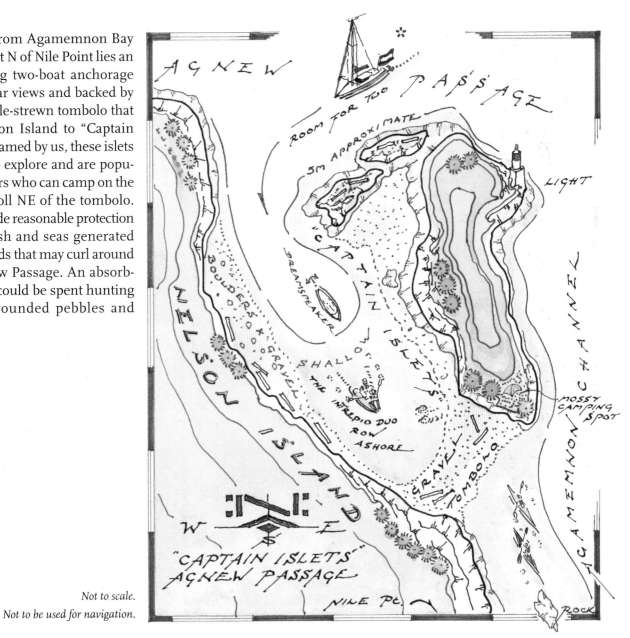

Not to scale.
Not to be used for navigation.

9.3 "MOCCASIN COVE," AGAMEMNON CHANNEL

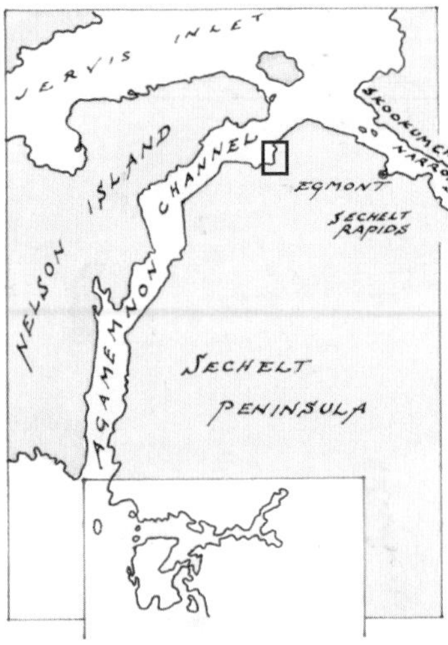

✲ 49°45.3'N 123°59.5'W

CHARTS 3512. 3312, pages 2, 3 and 4.

APPROACH
From the NW, out of Agamemnon Bay. The marina along the NE shore is conspicuous.

ANCHOR
Between the marina and finger-float in 5 m (16 ft) plus. Holding good in gravel.

MARINA
Private, used by THE MOCCASIN VALLEY RESORT.

BOAT LAUNCH
Private, at the resort.

Note: The cove feels a little open but as it lies in a wind shadow it is reasonably protected, although subject to occasional ferry wash.

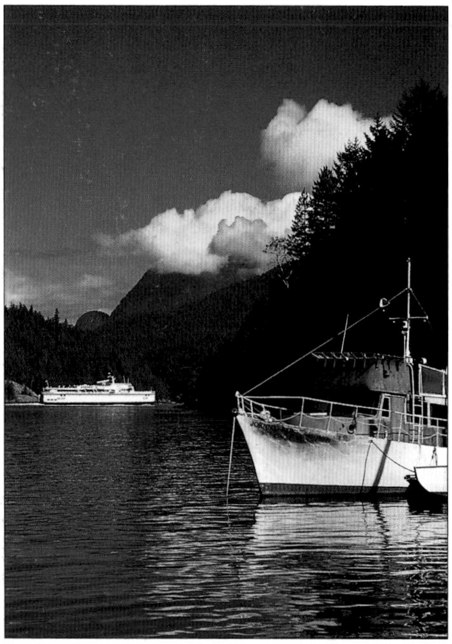

The Johnny Rep *at the marina.*

Just E of Earls Cove is a surprise anchorage in Agamemnon Bay, which we named "Moccasin Cove." This peaceful cove makes for a perfect tea stop or overnight anchorage in settled weather. Nestled in the trees above the curved gravel beach is the MOCCASIN VALLEY RESORT, a laid-back family hideaway just off Highway 101.

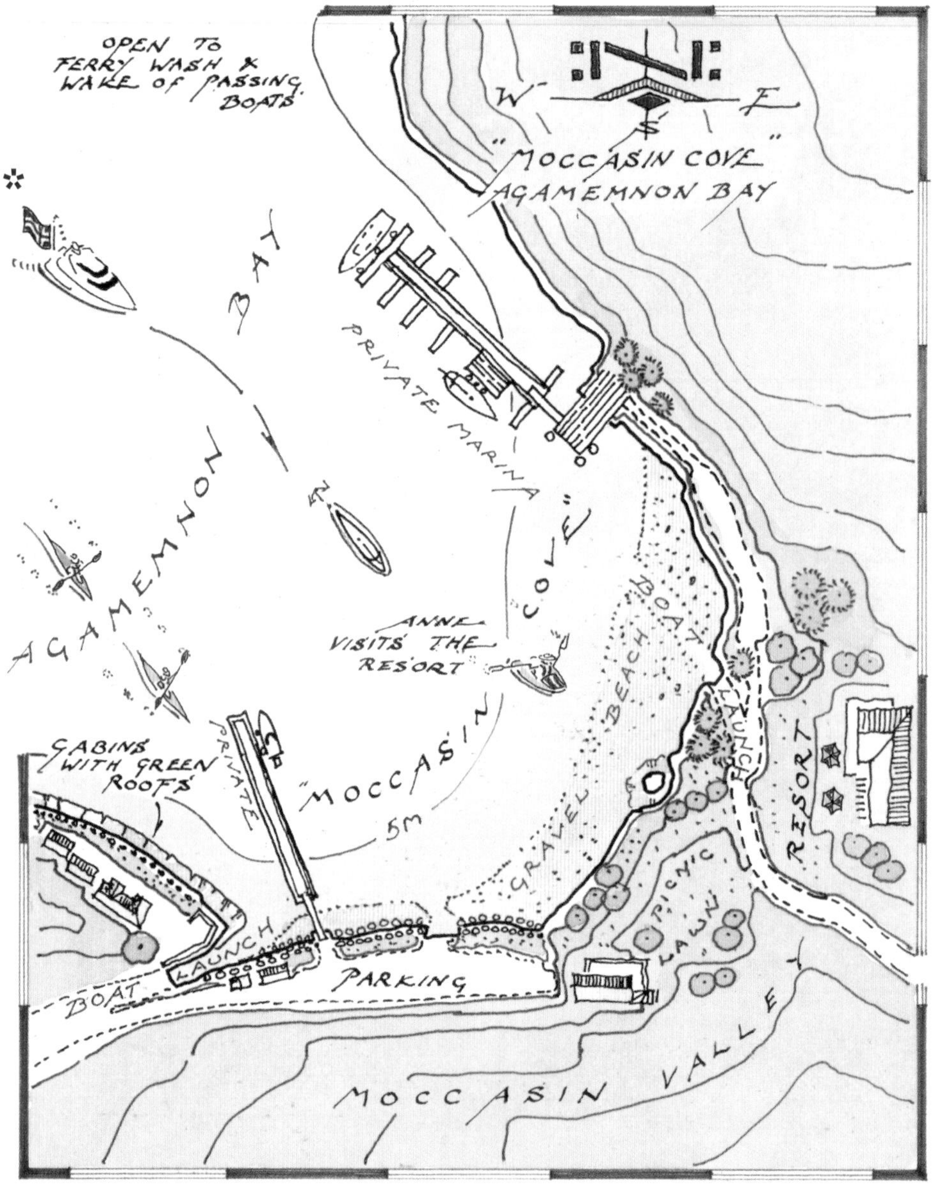

Not to scale. Not to be used for navigation.

EGMONT MARINA AND RESORT, SKOOKUMCHUCK NARROWS

CHARTS 3512. 3312, pages 3 and 4.

APPROACH
The marina lies abeam of the light off the SE tip of the Sutton Islets on the S shore of Sechelt Inlet. The docks and pub are conspicuous.

MARINA
The visitor float and fuel dock lie in deep water on the outside; call ahead for reservations, 604-883-2298 or 1-800-626-0599.

BOAT LAUNCH
Private, at the marina.
Note: Exercise caution while docking, as a strong cross-current from a back eddy can be experienced on a large tide.

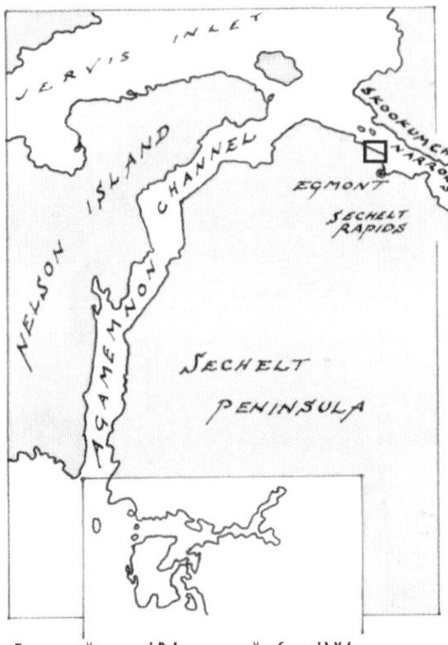

49°45.5'N 123°56.3'W

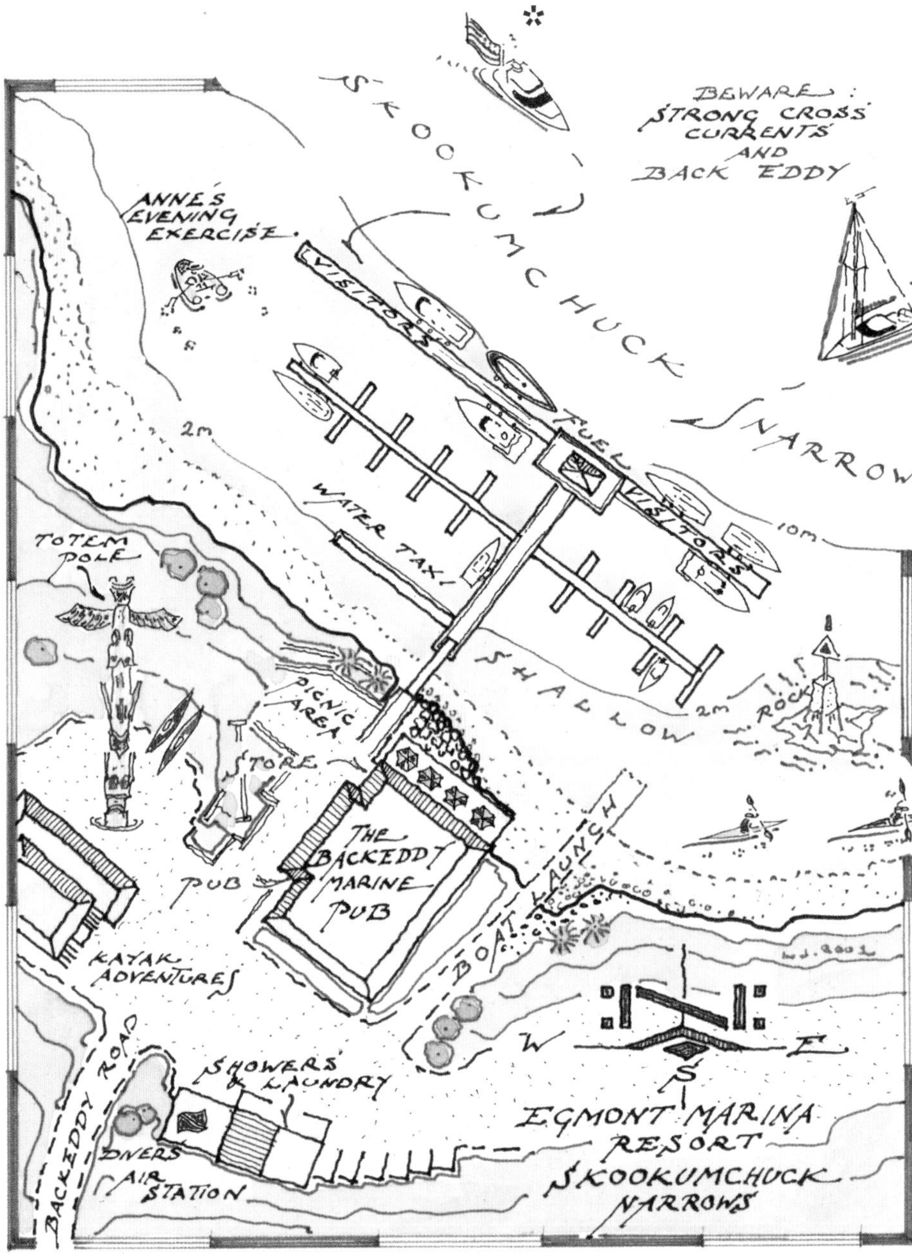

Not to scale. Not to be used for navigation.

Home to the popular BACKEDDY PUB and the Kwatamus Totem Pole, EGMONT MARINA RESORT has a down-home friendly atmosphere and a lively visitors' dock. Shower and laundry facilities are available and the pub's "fresh from the boat" fish and chips (or shrimp and chips in season) are recommended; it also offers the "Skookum Burger," said to be the largest burger on the B.C. coast. Boaters with children enjoy the resort's family restaurant, which serves the same hearty meals as at the pub. The small store stocks basic groceries and cruising guides.

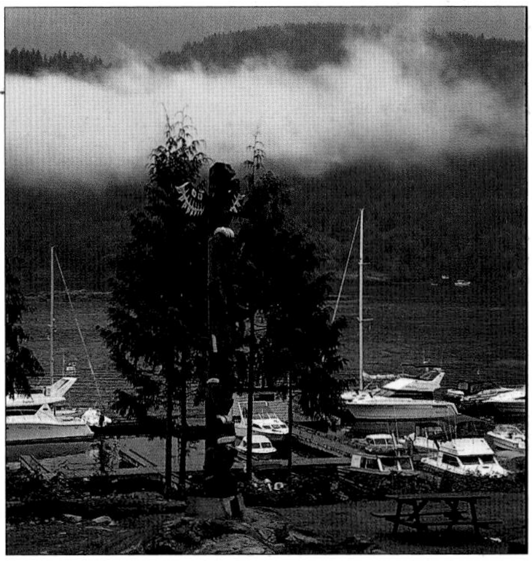

Low cloud hangs over the Skookumchuck Narrows.

❀ 49°45.2'W 123°55.5'W

The approach to Egmont Village public warf.

All trail recommendations are tested and approved by "Sailor" himself.

Until 1946, the community of Egmont was situated near Egmont Point across the narrows from its present position. The story told is that the local postmaster made the decision to move across the water to the S shore, taking the name with him. Old Egmont on the N shore is still an active community, although only accessible by boat.

The present Egmont Village, located in Secret Bay, is the perfect place to provision, take a good shower or do your laundry. The busy public wharf invites neighbourly conversation and social get-togethers and rafting up is common. Bruce Campbell and his four-legged first mate "Sailor" were tied up at the wharf researching suitable pooch-friendly hiking trails in B.C. for their website www.island.net/~bcamp when we visited.

The BATHGATE GENERAL STORE AND MARINA is a well-maintained and efficiently run family business owned and operated by Doug and Vicky Martin since 1988. The well-stocked general store offers a good selection of basics, fresh produce, frozen meat, locally caught fish and prawns, dairy products, ice cream and baked goods. Charts, guidebooks and tide tables are also available along with ice, propane ($10 minimum), fishing equipment and hardware. The store is open from 9 a.m.–6 p.m., seven days a week, as is the government liquor agency.

The village is thick with juicy blackberries in season and a self-conducted berry-picking tour will take you to Egmont Park, just up from the store. Tasty home-made bread is available at the VILLAGE THRIFT STORE on Saturdays and the GREEN ROSETTE carries an excellent selection of baked goods (see page 118).

For an unforgettable meal, treat yourself to dinner at the family-run RUBY LAKE RESORT — highly recommended by many well-known urban restaurateurs. This authentic Italian bistro-style dining room has a cosy ambience and is run by brothers Giorgio and Aldo, a charming duo who have a passion for good food and fresh organic produce. Call 604-883-2269. In their efforts to preserve the Sunshine Coast's wildlife, the family have turned the mini-lake between the restaurant and resort into an enchanting natural garden and reserve that is home to more than 75 species of birds. For more information contact the Iris Griffith Interpretive Centre, 604-883-9201.

Tie your dinghy at West Coast Wilderness Lodge Resort's dock and walk up for a first-class meal or tapas on the deck. Specializing in fresh West Coast cuisine, the lodge's restaurant is open for breakfast, lunch and dinner from 7 a.m–8 p.m., May 1 to September 30. Call 604-883-3667 for more information.

CHARTS 3512. 3312, page 3 and 4.

APPROACH
Secret Bay lies SE of a charted, unnamed and unmarked rocky islet in the Skookumchuck Narrows.

ANCHOR
Anchorage is possible to the E, off the public wharf. Depths, holding and bottom condition unrecorded.

PUBLIC WHARF
This is the primary visitor moorage facility and rafting is the norm.

MARINA
BATHGATE GENERAL STORE AND MARINA has limited overnight visitor moorage; call ahead 604-883-2222.

FUEL
At the marina.

BOAT LAUNCH
Public, NW of the public wharf.

Note: Take care while docking as a strong back eddy swirls counter to the tidal stream in Sechelt Inlet.

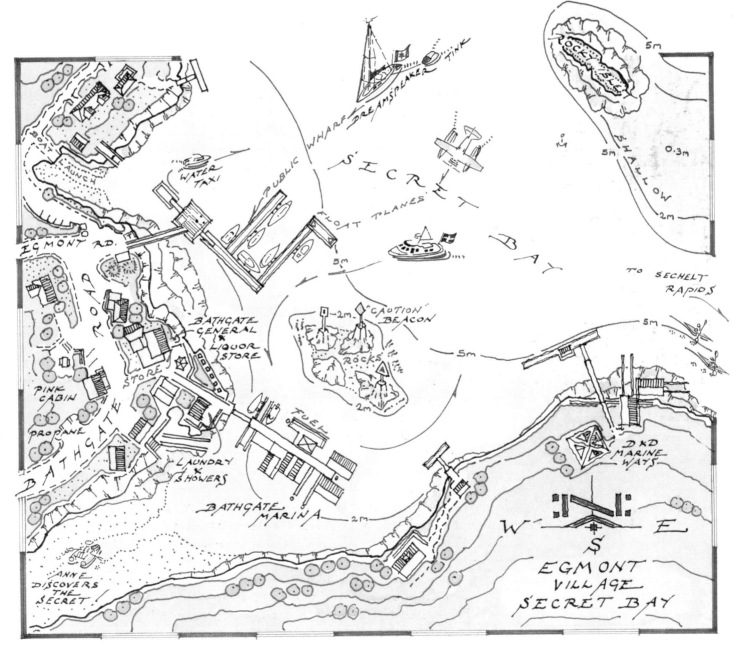

Not to scale. Not to be used for navigation.

9.6 SKOOKUMCHUCK NARROWS PROVINCIAL PARK & THE "SKOOKUMCHUCK EXPERIENCE"

✽ 49°45.5'N 123°56.3'W

CHARTS 3512. 3312, page 4

APPROACH
For information on transiting the Sechelt Rapids see 10.1, page 124

If you are passing through Egmont when a large tide is predicted (anything above a 10 on the flood), don't miss the thrill of viewing the Skookumchuck at close quarters. The Sechelt Rapids are one of the largest salt-water rapids in the world (*skookum* is a Chinook word for "strong" or "power-ful" and *chuck* means "salt water"). The one-hour hike through Skookumchuck Narrows Provincial Park will take you along a well-maintained trail that ambles through a forest of moss-covered cedars and skirts peaceful Brown Lake to North Point. A 10-minute hike down a wind-ing path leads you to Roland Point where a lively assortment of local and international surf kayakers demonstrate extreme skill and daring by riding the huge standing waves on the flooding current off-point. If a large ebb tide is pre-dicted, head for North Point and experience the powerful whirlpools boiling and bubbling a few metres below. Across from the car park the newly developed museum and interpretive centre houses a collection of logging and fishing arti-facts from the historic Egmont community.

Just off the private road leading to the trail, THE GREEN ROSETTE comes as a pleasant surprise. This welcoming bake shop produces a variety of mouth-watering organic baked goods including "very *skookum*" cinnamon buns, peasant bread and whole fruit pies. They also offer a build-your-own picnic lunch. Open 10 a.m.–4 p.m., 7 days a week in July and August or as posted at the public wharf and BACKEDDY PUB.

An unlikely but welcome coffee bake stop.

Not to scale. Not to be used for navigation.

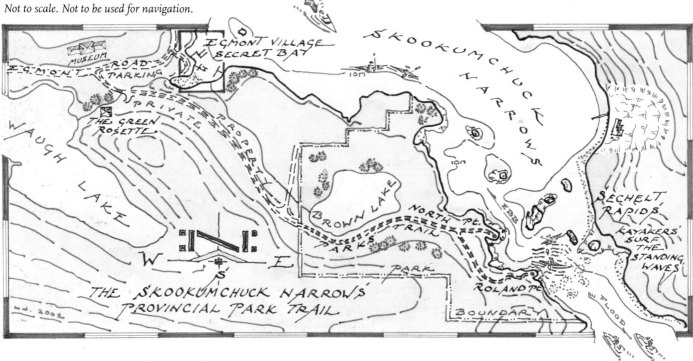

A surf kayaker demonstrates his skill.

Morning tranquillity, a watery maze with many surprises.

Chapter 10

SECHELT INLET

Chapter 10
SECHELT INLET

Misery Falls dwarf Anne and Tink.

TIDES
Canadian Tide and Current Tables,
Volume 5

REFERENCE PORT: POINT
ATKINSON
Secondary Ports: Storm Bay,
Porpoise Bay

CURRENTS
Reference Station: Sechelt Rapids
Secondary Station: Tzoonie Narrows

WEATHER
Note: No specific reporting station
covers this area, so to forecast local
weather, you must extrapolate weather
forecasts for the Strait of Georgia.
Winds tend to be diurnal — inflow,
up-inlet winds in the afternoon and
outflow, down-inlet winds at night.
However, in settled weather the inlet
is glassy smooth at night.

CAUTIONARY NOTES: *In the summer*
Sechelt Inlet enjoys prolonged periods of
light breezy days. However, listen for
strong wind warnings — a strong SE in
the Strait of Georgia will result in a
strong up-inlet wind and an outflow wind
warning covering mainland inlets will lead
to a strong down-inlet wind. Sechelt Inlet
is steep-sided and generally free of isolated
rocks that may impede navigation.
But check your charts: all the destinations
in this chapter have their fair share of
rocks, reefs and ledges, so be warned!

Sechelt Inlet begins at the junction of Agamemnon Channel and Jervis Inlet and heads S/SE for 32 km (20 miles) into the mainland, forming Sechelt Peninsula to the west and connecting with Narrows and Salmon inlets to the east.

Sechelt Inlet has never been a thoroughfare to destinations north, as no one has ever succeeded in building a canal from Trail Bay to Porpoise Bay, although legend has it that the original Sechelt people were the first to try. Once heavily populated by the Tuwanek group, the inlet fell into the hands of eager logging operations, fishing resorts and trial fish farms. Over the years most of these activities have either diminished or disappeared, leaving the quiet and solitude of Sechelt's beautiful deep-water inlets to be explored by kayakers and boaters in search of a little back-water adventuring. Eight rustic but charming pocket parks, accessible only by boat, have been designated as the Sechelt Inlet Marine Recreation Area.

Boaters preparing to access Sechelt Inlet from the N will have to plan ahead, as the only safe way to navigate Skookumchuck Narrows to get beyond the Sechelt Rapids is at slack water. Once through the turbulent waters into the steep-sided inlet you will be awed by the magnificence of the Caren Range rising to the west, with mighty Mount Hallowell standing guard. Amid all this deep water, protected Storm Bay at the entrance to Narrows Inlet makes for a central and convenient anchorage.

On an up-inlet wind it is possible to sail to the head of Narrows Inlet with stunning scenery en route. Tzoonie Narrows Marine Park between Tzoonie Point and the narrows is a delightful spot to drop anchor. Other lovely marine parks include Kunechin Point, Nine Mile Point, Halfway Beach and Piper Point.

Peaceful Salmon Inlet has two natural attractions: powerful Misery Creek, a surprise fall that gushes out into the inlet through a narrow cleft in the sheer rock face, and the magical white sandy beach at Sechelt Creek, a blissful spot for warm-water swimming.

At the head of the Sechelt Inlet it is possible to tie up at Porpoise Bay public wharf and take a stroll into the village of Sechelt, where the pier in Trail Bay offers a glorious view out to the Strait of Georgia.

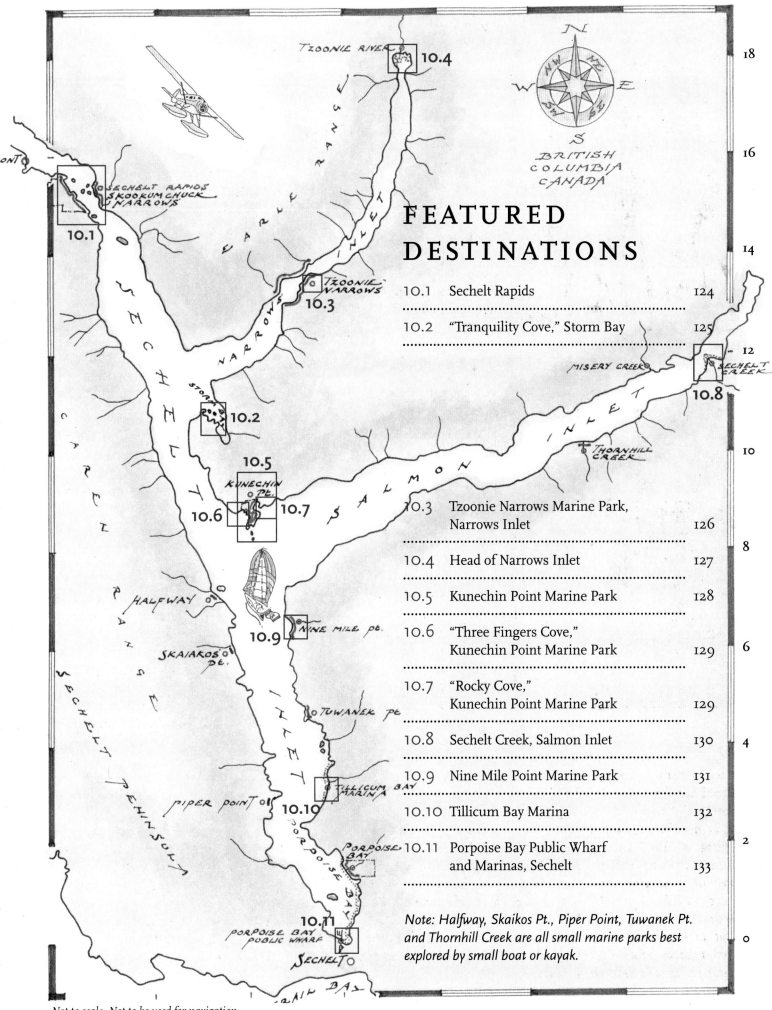

TZOONIE RIVER

10.4

N

BRITISH COLUMBIA CANADA

SECHELT RAPIDS
SKOOKUMCHUCK
NARROWS

10.1

FEATURED DESTINATIONS

TZOONIE
NARROWS

10.3

MISERY CREEK

SECHELT
CREEK

10.8

THORNHILL
CREEK

10.2

SALMON INLET

10.5

KUNECHIN
PT.

10.6   **10.7**

NINE MILE PT.

10.9

HALFWAY

SKAIAKOS PT.

TUWANEK PT.

TILLICUM BAY
MARINA

10.10

PIPER POINT

PORPOISE
BAY

PORPOISE BAY
PUBLIC WHARF

10.11

SECHELT

Note: Halfway, Skaikos Pt., Piper Point, Tuwanek Pt. and Thornhill Creek are all small marine parks best explored by small boat or kayak.

Not to scale. Not to be used for navigation.

10.1 SECHELT RAPIDS

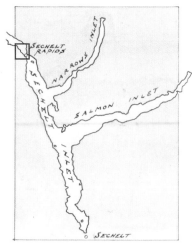

CHARTS 3512. 3312, page 4

APPROACH
From the N passing Boom Islet and the light on Sechelt Islets as indicated on the shoreline plan. Stay well clear of Roland Point.

Note: Transit at slack water. Best when the tide is turning in your favour. For times of slack water see Canadian Tide and Current Tables, Volume 5. Current station, Sechelt Rapids.

Slack at the rapids.

✿ 49°44.9'N 123°54'W

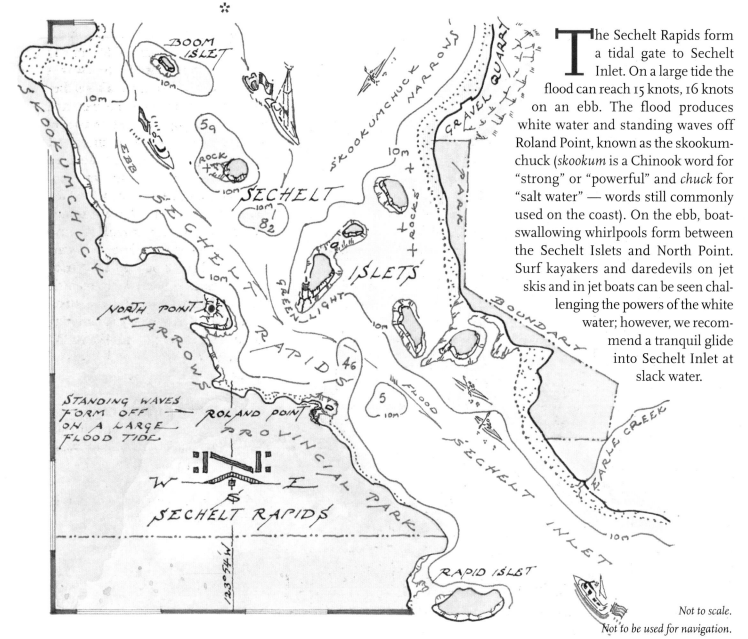

The Sechelt Rapids form a tidal gate to Sechelt Inlet. On a large tide the flood can reach 15 knots, 16 knots on an ebb. The flood produces white water and standing waves off Roland Point, known as the skookum-chuck (*skookum* is a Chinook word for "strong" or "powerful" and *chuck* for "salt water" — words still commonly used on the coast). On the ebb, boat-swallowing whirlpools form between the Sechelt Islets and North Point. Surf kayakers and daredevils on jet skis and in jet boats can be seen challenging the powers of the white water; however, we recommend a tranquil glide into Sechelt Inlet at slack water.

*Not to scale.
Not to be used for navigation.*

The favourite club rendezvous nook.

CHARTS 3512. 3312, page 4

APPROACH
From the NE, "Tranquility Cove" is tucked behind three islets in the NW corner of Storm Bay.

ANCHOR
Stern-to on the W shore, late arrivals swing in the central pool. Depths 2–4 m (6–13 ft). Holding good in sand and mud.

✳ 49°40.0'N   123°49.5'W

Not to scale. Not to be used for navigation.

Once the site of a busy brick factory, protected Storm Bay now provides boaters with a central and convenient all-weather anchorage for exploring the inlets and has become a popular rendezvous spot for those who prefer not to anchor off the pocket parks overnight. Keep an eye out for the boulder-strewn point, well marked by kelp, to the NW of the entrance. Two of the islets are private although the small recreational reserve is easily accessible and favoured by the boat-bound pooch population. A tranquil afternoon can be spent exploring the rocky shorelines and the small lagoon is warm enough for swimming and fun to investigate at HW. At LW clams and oysters are abundant east of the lagoon.

Note: "Tranquility Cove" is the only all-weather anchorage in Sechelt Inlet and becomes quite crowded in summer — be considerate and anchor stern-to if possible. In settled weather, a good anchorage with terrific sunset may be enjoyed at the head of Storm Bay.

10.3 TZOONIE NARROWS MARINE PARK, NARROWS INLET

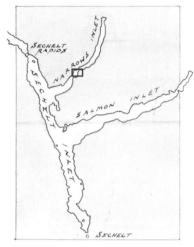

✻ 49°42.4'N 123°47.0'W

CHARTS 3512. 3312, page 4

APPROACH
From the W between "Henry the Whale Islet" and the charted rock to the SW.

ANCHOR
Off the southern shore of Tzoonie Narrows Marine Park in 10–15 m (33–50 ft). Holding fair over a rocky bottom.
Note: Alternative stern-to anchorage is available along the northern shore of Tzoonie Narrows Marine Park.

Luxury camping in the narrows.

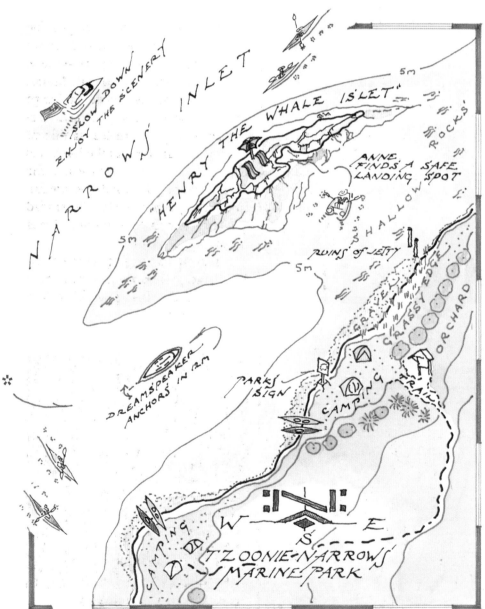

Not to scale. Not to be used for navigation.

Located between Tzoonie Point and the narrows themselves, this kayakers' haven is a delightful little spot to drop anchor and relax. Inspired by Muriel Wylie Blanchet's enchanting story in her classic *The Curve of Time,* "Henry The Whale Islet" (named by us) only takes on a whale-like identity at LW. At HW most of the sunbathing "islet" disappears, leaving an everyday rock in its place — note that shoals on either side of the rock extend out farther than is immediately apparent, at HW. Tzoonie Narrows Marine Park is the largest recreational site in Sechelt Inlet and its 80-hectare (200-acre) parkland snakes along either side of the Tzoonie Narrows. Park campsites are located W of the orchard with flat areas for tents and handy fire rings. The water is warm enough for swimming. In the evening, while toasting your toes around the fire, consider how lucky you are to share in this unique pocket of paradise.

CAUTIONARY NOTE: *Beware of charted rocks to the west, marked by kelp.*

CHARTS 3512. 3312, page 4

APPROACH

From the S. The logging camp is conspicuous on the eastern shoreline.

ANCHOR

W of the active booming area. Stern-to anchorage is also possible off the grassy spot on the western shoreline. Holding is dubious over mud and debris.

Note: Tzoonie Narrows is a tidal rapid that can run up to 4 knots; refer to secondary current station, Tzoonie Narrows, in Canadian Tide and Current Tables, Volume 5. A charted rock lies halfway up Narrows Inlet, towards the SE shore.

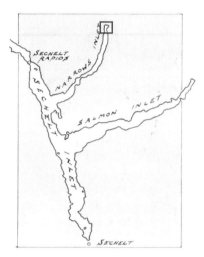

❖ 49°46.9'N 123°44.2'W

Not to scale. Not to be used for navigation.

On an up-inlet wind it is possible to sail to the head of Narrows Inlet. The scenery that awaits is quite stunning, with majestic Mount Drew and the glacier-capped Earl Range to the W. Snow-covered peaks and a cascading waterfall form a magnificent backdrop at the head of the inlet. It is possible to anchor in the bay and the Tzoonie estuary delta and river are fun to explore by dinghy at HW. The shaded grassy spot on the western shoreline is a perfect picnic spot.

In 2002 the logging camp was no longer active and the booming area cleared, making this a peaceful anchorage to explore.

Piles become nurse logs at the inlet's head.

10.5 KUNECHIN POINT MARINE PARK

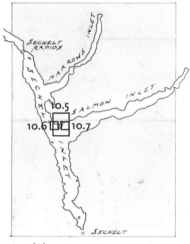

CHARTS 3512. 3312, pages 4 and 5

APPROACH

From Sechelt Inlet. Kunechin Point is at the junction of Sechelt and Salmon inlets. It is conspicuous, a relatively flat peninsula with islets and a light on the southern tip.

Anne takes in the scenery.

✳ (A) 49°37.7'N 123°48.8'W
✳ (B) 49°37.9'N 123°47.7'W

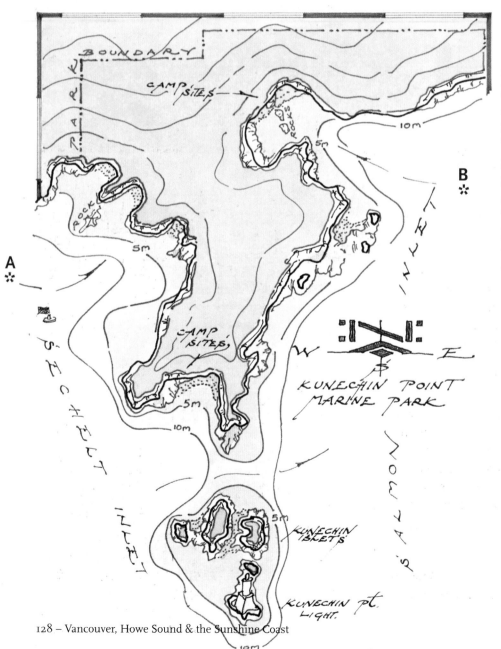

Kunechin Point Marine Park includes the nearby Kunechin Islets and a multitude of ominous off-lying rocks, so keep a sharp lookout when exploring the shoreline. A diving buoy marks the site of the artificial reef created by HMCS *Chaudiere*. The 40-hectare (100-acre) marine park is popular with kayakers thanks to its flat camping sites, creek for fresh water and lovely coves and pocket beaches. The two fair-weather anchorages we highlight are "Three Fingers Cove" on the western shoreline and "Rocky Cove" tucked into the eastern shore.

APPROACH

From the W out of Sechelt Inlet and best at LW. A diving buoy marks the site of the HMCS *Chaudiere* artificial reef.

ANCHOR

With a stern line ashore and the bow pointing S. Reasonable overnight protection is provided in settled weather. Depths of 5–10 m (16–33 ft), holding dubious over weed and rock.

Three small nooks in "Three Fingers Cove" provide stern-to anchorage with great sunset views. In settled weather they are convenient spots to pass the night. The artificial reef just S of the cove is a popular dive site where locals and visitors come to explore the colourful underwater life.

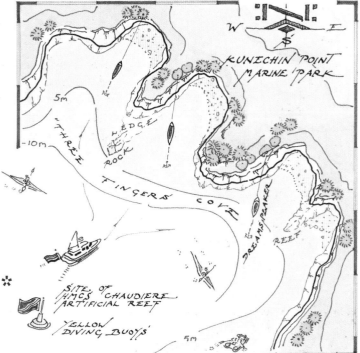

Not to scale. Not to be used for navigation. ✽ 49°237.7'N 123°48.8'W

APPROACH

From the E out of Salmon Inlet and best at LW when the rocks and rocky ledges are apparent.

ANCHOR

A shallow-draft boat can, with caution, tuck well into the cove for a snug night in depths of 1 m (3 ft) plus, moderate holding in mud and weed. Deep keels will need to swing in the mouth or take a stern line ashore. Depths of 2.5–3 m (8–10 ft), holding dubious over rock and weed with reasonable overnight protection in settled weather.

Well known by kayakers touring the inlets, this quiet anchorage makes a pleasant overnight stop in settled weather. When anchoring, be aware of the rock-infested entrance and the gravel beach N of the mouth that dries a good distance offshore at LW. The small gravel beach S of the cove is a delightful spot to enjoy a sunset picnic.

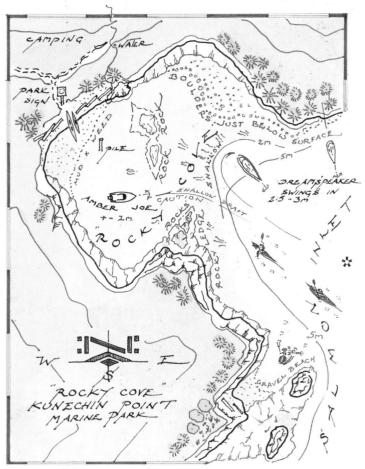

Not to scale.
Not to be used for navigation.

✽ 49°37.9'N 123°47.7'W

10.8 SECHELT CREEK, SALMON INLET

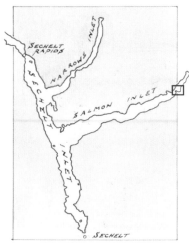

❀ 49°40.8'N 123°33.4'W

CHARTS 3512. 3312, page 5

APPROACH
From the W. Overhead hydro cables with a 30–m (100–ft) minimum clearance cross Salmon Inlet just S of the creek.

ANCHOR
Off the sandbar at LW or on a rising tide. The drop-off is quite steep and one should exercise caution.

Note: Sechelt Creek is not recommended as an overnight stop.

A beach to die for.

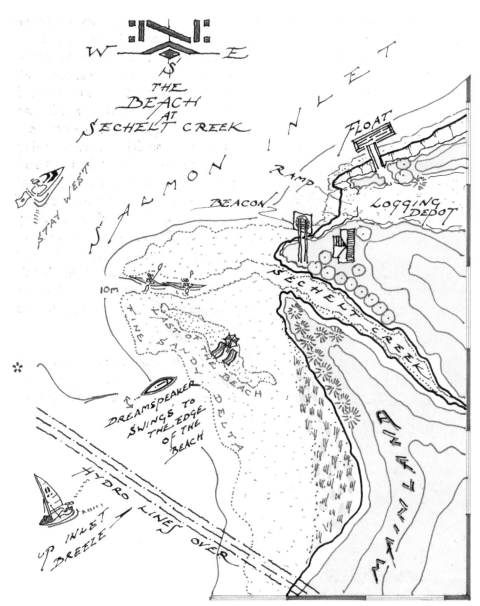

Not to scale. Not to be used for navigation.

A joy to explore, peaceful Salmon Inlet has two entertaining natural attractions. Powerful Misery Creek, on the inlet's northern shore, is a wonderful surprise as it gushes out into the inlet through a narrow cleft in the huge granite slabs of the sheer rock face. In total contrast, gentle Sechelt Creek, on the southern shore, forms a delta with a magical white sandy beach at LW. With its powder-fine, squeaky clean sand flecked with shimmering mica fragments, the beach makes a fine picnic spot when the sun shines; lazing in the clear warm water is a blissful experience. Unfortunately, the best things don't last, and on a rising tide this lovely spot gently melts away.

Note: Safe overnight anchoring is possible in Misery Bay to the NW of Sechelt Creek.

The sunset looking north.

CHARTS 3512. 3312, page 5

APPROACH
From the W, with caution and preferably at LW as the drop-off from the delta beach is very steep.

ANCHOR
Off the marine park sign. Anchor in 15–20 m (50–65 ft) with a taught stern line ashore. Angle the bow S if intending to overnight. No real protection from inclement weather.

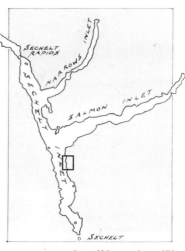

✣ 49°35.4'N 123°47.2W

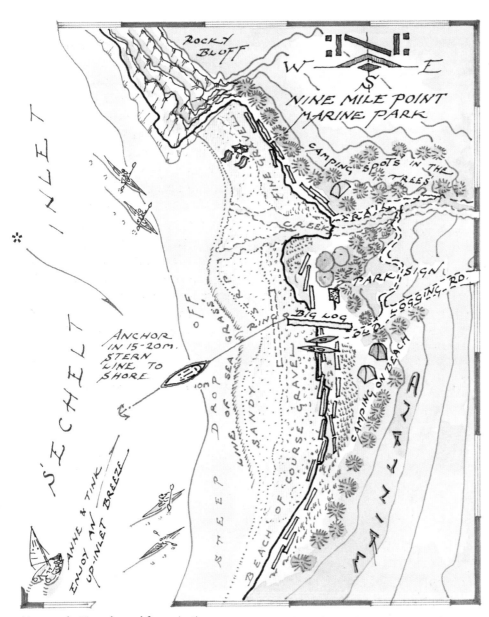

Not to scale. Not to be used for navigation.

The stupendous view from Nine Mile Point Marine Park makes anchoring in deep water off the beach and taking a line ashore well worth the effort. The park is nestled under Mount Richardson and has an ever-ready supply of fresh water from the creek. The delta consists of fine gravel on the N side of the creek and coarse gravel on the S, with a carpet of fine sand leading down to a border of soft seagrass. The beach is backed by a medley of weathered logs and driftwood and kayakers can pitch their tents and set up camp on the beach grass or in the cool of the trees N of the creek. Convenient fire rings are also provided.

Note: In settled weather the up-inlet wind usually dies off in the early evening, leaving the inlet glassy smooth for the night.

10.10 TILLICUM BAY MARINA

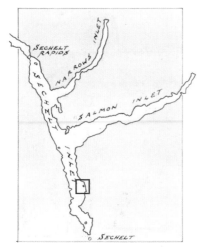

✽ 49°32.1'N 123°46.0'W

CHARTS 3512. 3312, page 5

APPROACH
From the W. A timber jetty lies to the N over marsh and mud flats. Boat masts peeking above the stone breakwater give away the marina's location.

MARINA
TILLICUM BAY MARINA is essentially a facility for local boats although visitor moorage is available if they have space; call ahead, 604-885-2100.

BOAT LAUNCH
Private, at marina.

Note: Fuel is not available, but the small marine workshop has a reputation for fixing just about anything!

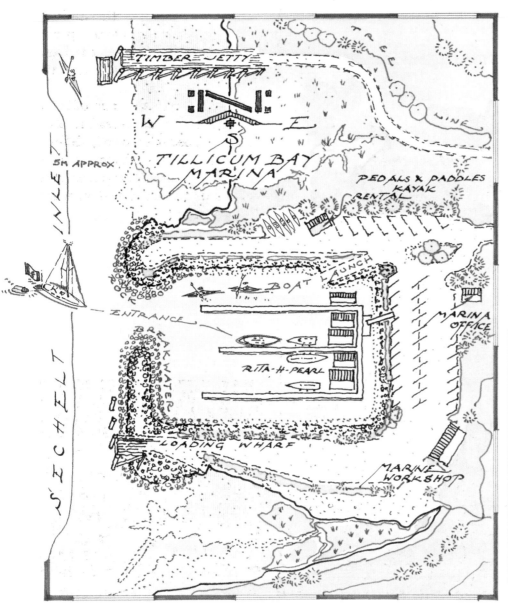

Not to scale. Not to be used for navigation.

This small low-key marina offers transient moorage when space is available. Visitors may be surprised to find *Rita-H-Pearl*, a beautifully maintained, half-size replica of the classic *Bluenose* built in Roberts Creek by the Pearl family. N of the marina is PEDALS & PADDLES, a well-run ocean kayak and canoe centre offering lessons, rentals and group programs. As Sechelt Inlet is a paddler's paradise, "jumping ship" for a day or two to explore the pocket marine parks and beaches by kayak is a fun alternative to anchoring. Call 1-866-885-6440.

The Rita-H-Pearl *moored in the marina.*

PORPOISE BAY PUBLIC WHARF AND MARINAS, SECHELT

CHARTS 3512. 3312, page 5

APPROACH
From the N. The red public wharf is the most conspicuous landmark.

ANCHOR
Anchorage is possible N of the public wharf in 12 m (39 ft). Bottom condition not recorded.

PUBLIC WHARF
The three-finger floats are mainly used by local or commercial boats. Raft-up if a spot is not available.

MARINA
ROYAL REACH MOTEL & MARINA; call 604-885-7844.
CHOQUER & SONS offers visitor moorage and haul-out facilities, 604-885-9244.
A LIGHTHOUSE PUB MARINA is under development, phone 604-885-9494 for current facilities.

FUEL
Gas only at the floatplane office.

BOAT LAUNCH
Public, adjacent to the public wharf.
Note: Porpoise Bay is an active float plane landing zone.

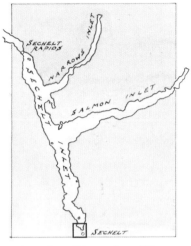

✵ 49°29.1'N 123°45.4'W

The well-worn public wharf is a convenient spot to tie up and take a stroll into Sechelt village (see 6.5, page 74). It is an easy 15-minute walk downtown

The LIGHTHOUSE PUB offers a waterfront patio, fresh seafood platters and a good selection of pub fare.

This is a busy floatplane area served by various companies that come and go. Check the yellow pages for current operators.

Porpoise Bay is busy with floatplane activity.

Not to scale. Not to be used for navigation.

HOTHAM SOUND, JERVIS AND PRINCESS LOUISA INLETS

Sailing up Jervis Inlet.

Chapter 11

HOTHAM SOUND, JERVIS AND PRINCESS LOUISA INLETS

Harmony Islands.

TIDES
Canadian Tide and Current Tables, Volume 5

Reference Port: Point Atkinson
Secondary Port: Saltery Bay

CURRENTS
The currents in Malibu Rapids run up to 9 knots on both the flood and ebb tides.
Reference Port: Point Atkinson
Secondary Port: Malibu Rapids

WEATHER
No specific reporting station covers these waters. In summer there are up-inlet breezes in Hotham Sound and Jervis Inlet that are accentuated by both moderate to strong NW and SE winds in Malaspina Strait. Overnight outflow winds are generally light in the summer but always listen for an outflow wind warning as the locally known Jervis Express can cook up on short notice — and a strong one can blow your socks off!

Hotham Sound branches off NE from the lower portion of Jervis Inlet (see Chapter 12) and extends for 10 km (6 miles) to the head of the sound with mountains rising steeply from its shoreline. There are few anchoring opportunities, the Harmony Islands being the best protected and most fun to visit. In this chapter we explore Harmony Islands Marine Park and the surrounding area, taking time to swim, snorkel and laze for a few days before embarking on a pilgrimage to Princess Louisa Inlet and the legendary Chatterbox Falls — a magical journey every boater should make at least once in a lifetime.

Imposing and steep-sided, magnificent Jervis Inlet penetrates a further 48 km (30 miles) north from Captain Islets and is divided into three long, sinuous reaches with few protected anchorages en route. Beyond Captain Island, the Prince of Wales Reach runs due north, then switches eastward to become the windy Princess Royal Reach. At Patrick Point the inlet turns northwest and becomes known as Queens Reach. By then most boaters have had enough breathtaking scenery and their fuel gauge is plummeting downwards, which makes the grand MALIBU LODGE at the entrance to Princess Louisa Inlet a surprising and welcome sight.

In settled weather it is possible to overnight in Dark Cove if you want to get an early start up Jervis Inlet. McMurray Bay makes a pleasant stop should you need to break your trip up Prince of Wales Reach. The nook behind Patrick Point in Queens Reach is a convenient holdover spot while waiting for the tidal gate at Malibu Rapids to open.

Lined with a magnificent backdrop of lush green forest and mini-waterfalls spouting out of its sheer granite cliffs, Princess Louisa Inlet is an idyllic and well-concealed stretch of water often described as the most beautiful fjord in the world. Stunning Chatterbox Falls at the head of the inlet is the "jewel in the crown" for visitors under Princess Louisa's spell.

Princess Louisa Marine Park would not be what it is today without the passion and determination of James F. "Mac" Macdonald. A longtime resident of the inlet, Macdonald fought his whole life to ensure that "this beautiful peaceful haven should never belong to one individual." In 1964 his treasured home was deemed a Class A marine park.

FEATURED DES-TINATIONS

Note: The anchorages around Junction and Sykes Islands in St. Vincent Bay have been inundated by aquaculture activity.

Not to scale. Not to be used for navigation.

11.1 HARMONY ISLANDS MARINE PARK, HOTHAM SOUND

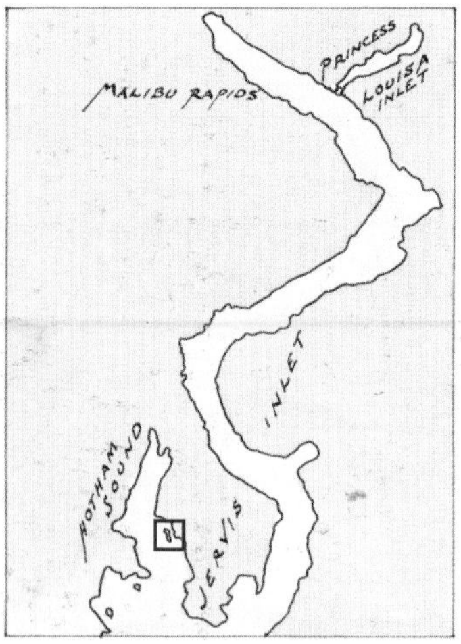

✲ 49°51.3'N 124°00.8'W

Kipling Cove has room for several boats, if everyone is considerate.

CHARTS 3514. 3312, page 3

APPROACH
From the SW. The islands are low-lying against a mountainous backdrop. The park's sign on the tip of the southernmost island is the most conspicuous landmark.

ANCHOR
Stern-to in the channel, swinging is also possible. Depths 5–15 m (16–50 ft), holding good in mud and shingle. (For "Kipling Cove" see 11.2, page 139)

Note: The channel acts as a wind tunnel. When anchoring stern-to, angle the bow as indicated in the shoreline plan to reduce windage.

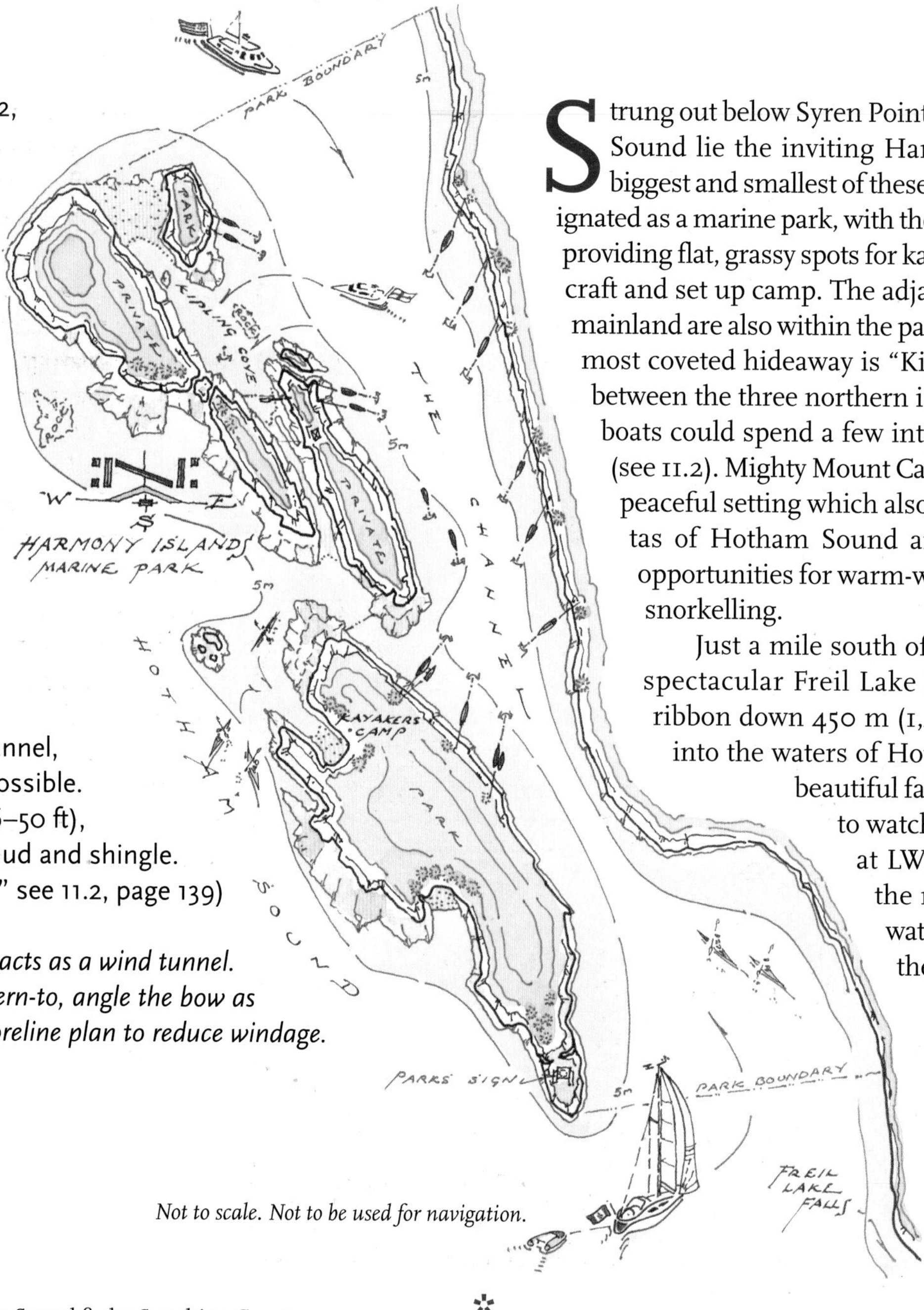

Strung out below Syren Point on the E of Hotham Sound lie the inviting Harmony Islands. The biggest and smallest of these four islands are designated as a marine park, with the southernmost park providing flat, grassy spots for kayakers to beach their craft and set up camp. The adjacent waters E to the mainland are also within the park's boundaries. The most coveted hideaway is "Kipling Cove," tucked between the three northern islands, where 5 or 6 boats could spend a few intimate days together (see 11.2). Mighty Mount Calder towers over this peaceful setting which also offers dramatic vistas of Hotham Sound and Jervis Inlet and opportunities for warm-water swimming and snorkelling.

Just a mile south of "The Harmonies," spectacular Freil Lake Falls cascades in a ribbon down 450 m (1,475 ft) of sheer cliff into the waters of Hotham Sound. These beautiful falls are mesmerizing to watch and fun to explore at LW. After heavy rains, the roar of the gushing water can be heard from the island anchorages.

See enlargement of "Kipling Cove" on facing page.

Not to scale. Not to be used for navigation.

APPROACH

With caution and best at low water. A rock just below chart datum lies in the cove's entrance.

ANCHOR

With a stern line ashore. The shoreline plan indicates the approximate number of boats that can anchor in the cove safely. Depths about 2.5 m (8 ft) around the rocky edge. Holding good in mud and shingle.

Note: In summer the cove is very popular. Stern lines should be tied below the HW mark as the island is private. Alternatively use a stern anchor. Up-inlet wind tends to whistle through "the Gap," but a taught stern line will help keep the boat's lateral movement in check.

A boarding party from Skookum.

Intimate "Kipling Cove" is a great place to get to know your neighbours while putting your finer seamanship skills to the test — these may include anchoring in a very restricted space, assisting with the next boat's stern line or coordinating a three-boat raft-up.

The islands backing the cove are private, please respect their boundaries. A trip to lovely Freil Lake Falls at LW will reveal two man-made pools, a deeper one for dunking under the falls and a smaller paddling pool a few rocks down.

The cove is great for swimming and snorkelling, as summer temperatures can reach 17 or 18°C (46°F). The "Dinghy Pass" between the private islands is fun to explore at HW with a shallow-bottomed boat, and provides a convenient route to the southern park.

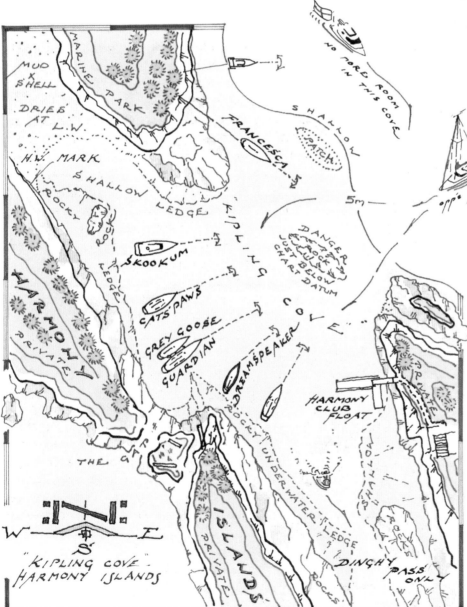

Not to scale. Not to be used for navigation.

11.3 DARK COVE, JERVIS INLET

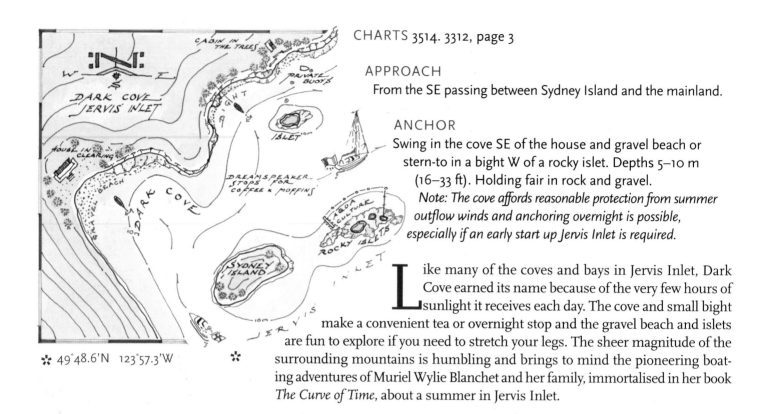

✤ 49°48.6'N 123°57.3'W   ✤

CHARTS 3514. 3312, page 3

APPROACH
From the SE passing between Sydney Island and the mainland.

ANCHOR
Swing in the cove SE of the house and gravel beach or stern-to in a bight W of a rocky islet. Depths 5–10 m (16–33 ft). Holding fair in rock and gravel.
Note: The cove affords reasonable protection from summer outflow winds and anchoring overnight is possible, especially if an early start up Jervis Inlet is required.

Like many of the coves and bays in Jervis Inlet, Dark Cove earned its name because of the very few hours of sunlight it receives each day. The cove and small bight make a convenient tea or overnight stop and the gravel beach and islets are fun to explore if you need to stretch your legs. The sheer magnitude of the surrounding mountains is humbling and brings to mind the pioneering boating adventures of Muriel Wylie Blanchet and her family, immortalised in her book *The Curve of Time*, about a summer in Jervis Inlet.

11.4 McMURRAY BAY, JERVIS INLET

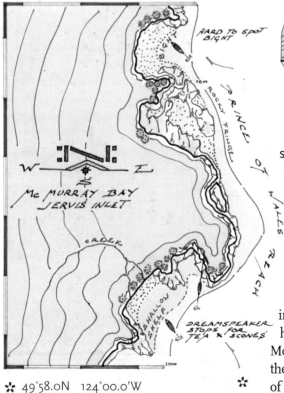

✤ 49°58.0N 124°00.0'W   ✤

CHARTS 3514. 3312, page 6

APPROACH
With caution. McMurray Bay lies on the western shoreline abeam of Moorsam Bluff in Prince of Wales Reach.

ANCHOR
Swing or stern-to off the shallow shelf if Jervis Inlet is silky smooth. If an up-inlet wind is blowing, "Hard to Spot Bight" about half a km N will afford more protection. Depths 5 m (16 ft) plus. The drop-off is dramatic. Holding fair in shingle.
Note: These anchorages are good picnic stops and can make a welcome break on the long trip north for sailboats and trawler yachts under diesel.

Anchoring off the delta in McMurray Bay makes for a pleasant stop in Prince of Wales Reach. Oysters can be found on the gravel and sand beach beneath the small creek and waterfall, and the sloping rocks on the point are mossy and soft. From here, with binoculars in hand, you can look across the inlet and take in the magnificence of Moorsam Bluff, with Soda Water Falls gushing out below. Be sure to avoid the first, rock-infested bight when looking for "Hard to Spot Bight" north of the delta.

MALIBU RAPIDS, PRINCESS LOUSIA INLET

CHARTS 3514. 3312, page 7

APPROACH

From the S. The gap in the wall of mountains indicates the entrance to the inlet from afar. As you get closer the light, islet and lodge become quite conspicuous.

MARINA

The lodge has a dock for short stays while visiting.

Note: The current runs up to 9 knots on the flood and ebb tide and entrance into Princess Louisa should be as close to slack water as possible — see Canadian Tide and Current Tables, Volume 5.

Reference Port: Point Atkinson
Secondary Port: Malibu Rapids
When entering on a strong flood tide, keep in mind that the current has a tendency to carry your boat towards the eastern shoreline.

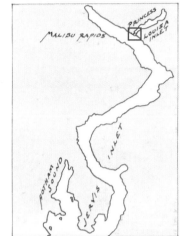

✳ 50°09.5'N 123°51.0'W

After travelling over 50 km (30 miles) up a stunning but near-deserted inlet, the boater is presented with an amazing sight at the entrance to Princess Louisa Inlet: grandiose MALIBU LODGE. Built as a luxury "rustic" resort for Hollywood stars during World War II, it fell into disuse until Young Life, a Christian group, turned it into a summer youth camp. The students give tours of the facilities. Monitor Channel 16 before transiting, as there is limited space in the narrowest part of the rapids.

Anne spies the entrance to the inlet.

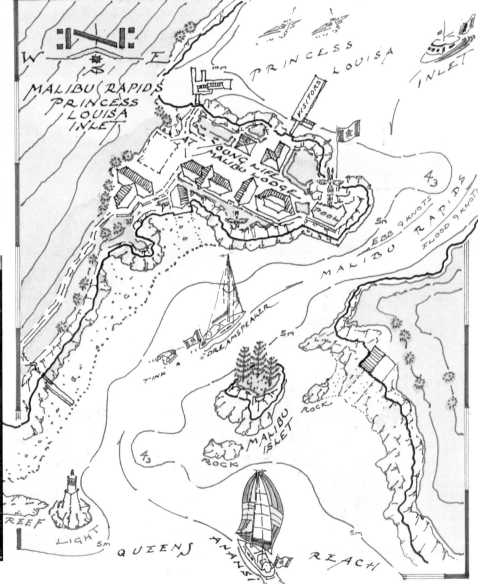

Not to scale. Not to be used for navigation.

11.6 PRINCESS LOUISA INLET

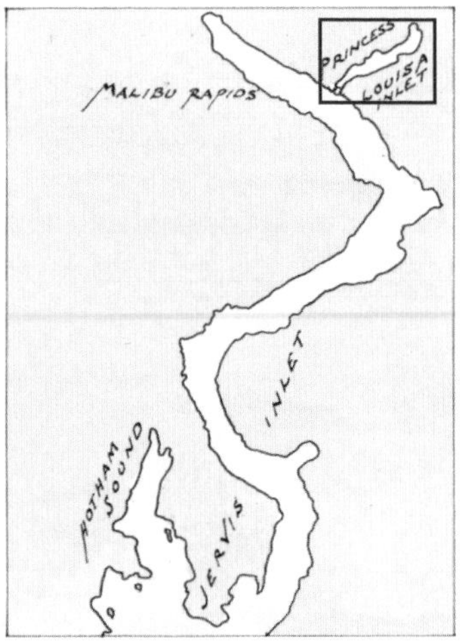

✲ 50°09.5'N 123°51.0'W

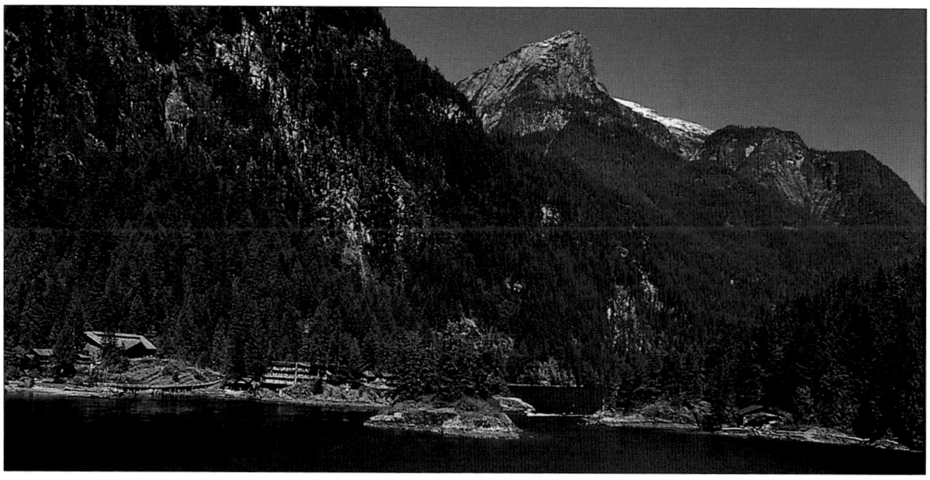

At the entrance to Princess Louisa Inlet lies the distinctive Malibu Lodge.

See enlargement of MacDonald Island on facing page.

CHARTS 3514. 3312, page 7

APPROACH
Once you are through the Malibu Rapids, the inlet is deep and without obstructions.

ANCHOR
The problem is finding suitable depths to anchor in. Fortunately there are parks buoys at Macdonald Island and a substantial parks float at the head of the inlet. For those with experience in deep-water stern-to anchoring (or in need of practice), there are plenty of trees and stern pins along the shoreline with opportunities to find your own special spot.

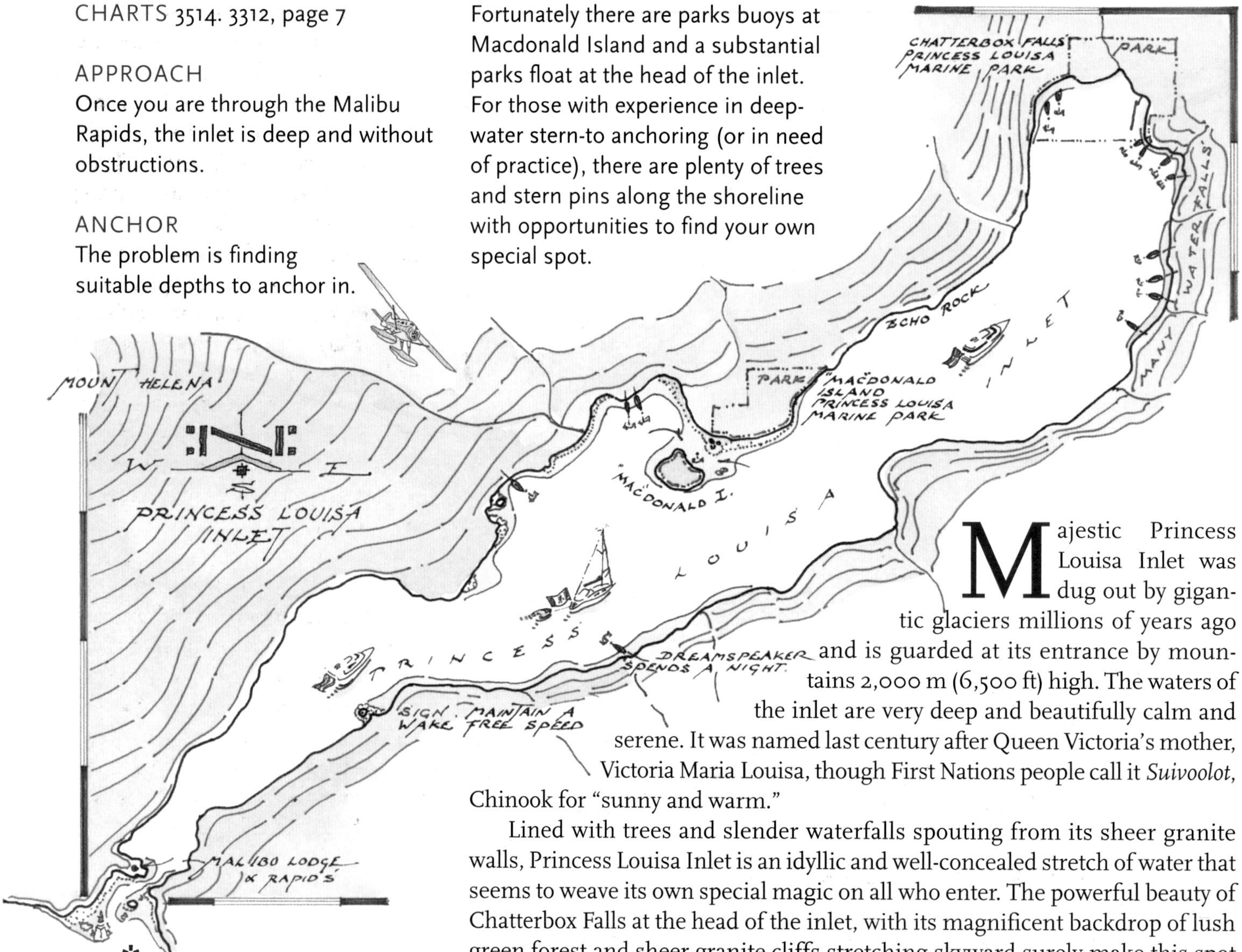

Not to scale. Not to be used for navigation.

Majestic Princess Louisa Inlet was dug out by gigantic glaciers millions of years ago and is guarded at its entrance by mountains 2,000 m (6,500 ft) high. The waters of the inlet are very deep and beautifully calm and serene. It was named last century after Queen Victoria's mother, Victoria Maria Louisa, though First Nations people call it *Suivoolot*, Chinook for "sunny and warm."

Lined with trees and slender waterfalls spouting from its sheer granite walls, Princess Louisa Inlet is an idyllic and well-concealed stretch of water that seems to weave its own special magic on all who enter. The powerful beauty of Chatterbox Falls at the head of the inlet, with its magnificent backdrop of lush green forest and sheer granite cliffs stretching skyward surely make this spot the eighth wonder of the world.

The glacier atop Mount Helena.

CHARTS 3514. 3312, page 7

APPROACH
The anchorage lies in the channel between Macdonald Island and the NW shore of the inlet.

ANCHOR
Pick up a park's buoy or anchor stern-to on the metal pins on the island's eastern shore.

Note: The rock that extends out from the island's eastern tip is barely covered at HW and difficult to see during a HW, low-light approach.

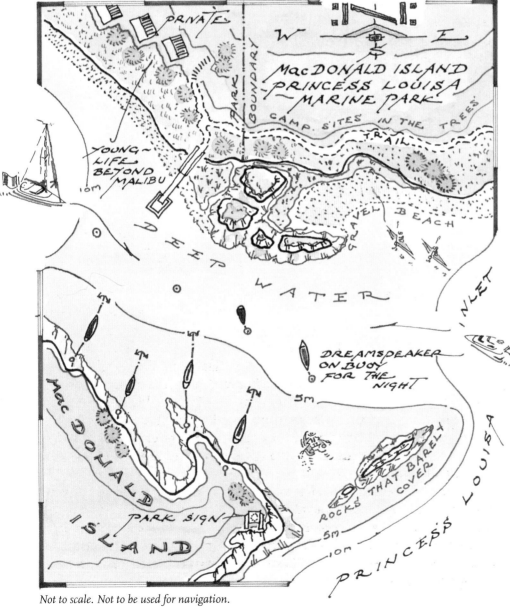

Not to scale. Not to be used for navigation.

Away from the hubbub of Chatterbox Falls, Macdonald Island and a section of the northern shoreline are part of the marine park. Convenient and peaceful overnight anchorage is available, especially if you have arrived late and plan to keep the thrill of Chatterbox Falls until the soft light of morning. "The rock that barely covers at HW" is fun to explore and makes a great photographic platform. Don't be alarmed if you are woken at an early hour by the "Young Life Beyond Malibu" camp preparing breakfast nearby. The sound of chainsaws, speedy runabouts and nervous teenage energy will either get you up or send you deeper under the duvet.

The park has a trail to rustic campsites in the trees and the gravel beach is perfect for kayakers to pull up their craft for the night and set up camp. The large and inviting grass-covered rocks slope gently into the water and are great to swim off or just laze, lizard-like, in the sun. Keep an eye out for black bears on the shores of Macdonald Island.

11.8 CHATTERBOX FALLS, PRINCESS LOUISA MARINE PARK

✾ 50°12.0'N 123°46.3'W

CHARTS 3514. 3312, page 7

APPROACH
Approach the head of the inlet very slowly and with minimal water disturbance.

ANCHOR
Stern pins are located atop rocks to the W of the falls and on the shore SE of the parks float.

MARINA
The parks float is substantial and is restricted to boats up to 18 m (55 ft) in length. Water is available.

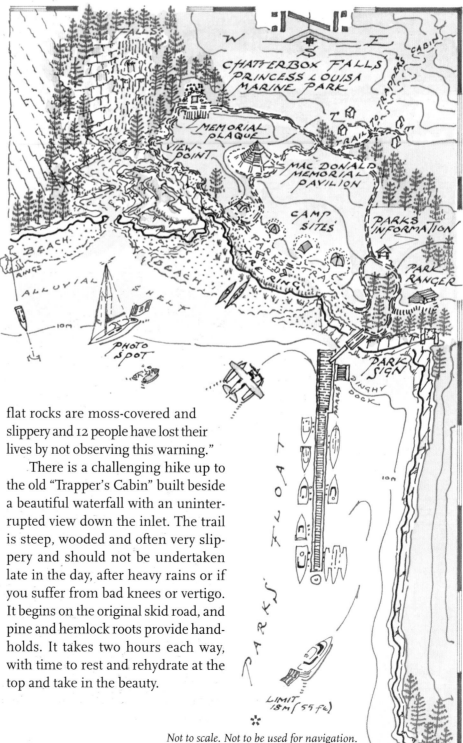

Chatterbox Falls tumbles and roars 500 m (1,600 ft) down over vast granite boulders, then bounces and rushes through a rock-jammed ledge before emptying into Princess Louisa Inlet, where a LW sandy beach has built up over the centuries.

The park's dock is a busy spot with boaters excitedly arriving or reluctantly preparing to leave. It's fun to spend a night or two here to visit the falls, explore the park and share anecdotes and a glass or two with the friendly dock crowd. Then it's off to find your very own nirvana and tuck into a little nook somewhere with the soul-soothing sounds of your personal waterfall slipping down through the trees.

From the dock, the first park trail leads to four waterfront campsites with picnic tables and a fire ring. This camping area allows kayakers or those without personal craft to visit the falls. Transportation by seaplane, water taxi or boat charter can be arranged; these services can be useful if family or crew need to leave paradise earlier than planned. From the park information booth, take the circular boardwalk trail to the Macdonald Memorial Pavilion and Chatterbox Falls viewpoint. A sign here reads "DANGER: Do not go near the top of the falls. The surrounding flat rocks are moss-covered and slippery and 12 people have lost their lives by not observing this warning."

There is a challenging hike up to the old "Trapper's Cabin" built beside a beautiful waterfall with an uninterrupted view down the inlet. The trail is steep, wooded and often very slippery and should not be undertaken late in the day, after heavy rains or if you suffer from bad knees or vertigo. It begins on the original skid road, and pine and hemlock roots provide handholds. It takes two hours each way, with time to rest and rehydrate at the top and take in the beauty.

Not to scale. Not to be used for navigation.

The plaque honouring "The Man From California."

Note: The Princess Louisa International Society actively supports Princess Louisa Marine Park with capital investments to provide additional and enhanced facilities. Membership and tax receipts for donations are available from the society at P.O. Box 17279, Seattle, WA USA 98107-0979, or P.O. Box 33918, Station D, Vancouver, B.C. Canada V6J 4L7. Visit their web page at www.princesslouisa.bc.ca.

W ithout the passion and determination of James F. "Mac" Macdonald, who took possession of the 115–hectare (292–acre) property at the head of Princess Louisa Inlet from the B.C. government in 1927, a very different sight might welcome visitors today. Macdonald turned down generous re-sale opportunities and offers from large hotel chains to purchase "The Princess." His only dream was to preserve her natural beauty for himself and future generations, as he believed that "this beautiful peaceful haven should never belong to one individual."

In 1964 his dream came true when his treasured home was deemed a Class A marine park. The non-profit Princess Louisa International Society passed the administration of the property to the Government of British Columbia and the property was named Princess Louisa Provincial Marine Park.

Those who have read and re-read the adventures of Muriel Wylie Blanchet and her five children in *The Curve of Time* will remember how the family also cherished Princess Louisa and their solitude while exploring the inlet. "The Man from California" (which he was not) changed all this and although the family resented his intrusion into their once deserted spot, Mac won them over with his generosity and friendship. Their one regret seemed to be the loss of privacy when indulging in their favourite pastime of rock sliding *au naturel* while their clothes dried.

Mac died in a Seattle rest home in 1978. His ashes are planted inside a boulder at the head of Princess Louisa, beneath an inscription that reads: "Laird of the inlet, Gentleman, friend to all who came here."

Ready to receive lines.

Chapter 12

NELSON AND HARDY ISLANDS AND LOWER JERVIS INLET

A Jervis jewel awaits discovery.

Harry Roberts' house on Nelson Island.

Chapter 12
NELSON AND HARDY ISLANDS AND LOWER JERVIS INLET

TIDES
Canadian Tide and Current Tables, Volume 5

Reference Port: Point Atkinson
Secondary Ports: Saltery Bay & Blind Bay

CURRENTS
Tidal rapids with very strong currents form at the entrances to both Cockburn Bay and Hidden Basin and we do not recommend them as destinations.

WEATHER
The nearest reporting station is Grief Point, approximately 15 nautical miles NW of Cape Cockburn. Similar conditions will prevail in Malaspina Strait.

O n the eastern seaboard of Malaspina Strait between Cape Cockburn and Scotch Fir Point lie the shorelines of Nelson and Hardy islands and lower Jervis Inlet, an area where the cruising boater will discover a selection of sheltered stop-off points en route to Desolation Sound and Princess Louisa Inlet. A mini-cruising ground in its own right, this section of coastline is blessed with hidden anchorages tucked into protected bays, cosy nooks and secluded one-boat havens. Panoramic vistas up Jervis Inlet and Hotham Sound and dramatic sunset views W to Texada Island are the reward for battling the frequently strong southeasterly or northwesterly winds in Malaspina Strait.

In calm seas or if a northwesterly is blowing, make a detour at Cape Cockburn and pop into welcoming "Sunray Bay" on Nelson Island. Peaceful "Harry Roberts Beach," backed by mounds of driftwood, is prime beachcombing land, and allows for a visit to Roberts' charming heritage home.

Popular Ballet Bay is often crowded in the summer as it provides a cosy, sheltered retreat, especially when a gale is forecast in Malaspina Strait. The neighbouring land and islets are private, but the shorelines, reefs and coves are a treat to explore by dinghy or kayak.

A favourite with boaters in search of hidden coves, Hardy Island offers excellent protection along the Blind Bay shoreline, although the anchorages in Jervis Inlet and Malaspina Strait are open to the northwest. On the island's SW corner, tiny Musket Island Marine Park is protected from NW winds and reputed for its peaceful stern-to anchorages and idyllic warm-water swimming. Secluded "Dogfish Nook" will enchant you with its spectacular sunsets, and the snug one-boat hideaway in "Pearl Islets" will lure the adventurous boater in and test his anchoring abilities.

Convenient and protected anchorage is also available in Thunder and Saltery bays. At the entrance to Jervis Inlet, Thunder Bay offers two anchorages, the most popular west of the T-shaped peninsula in a cove known locally as Maude Bay. The B.C. Ferry service from Earls Cove terminates at Saltery Bay, a pleasant rendezvous spot to pick up and drop off crew, or stock up on blackberries in season.

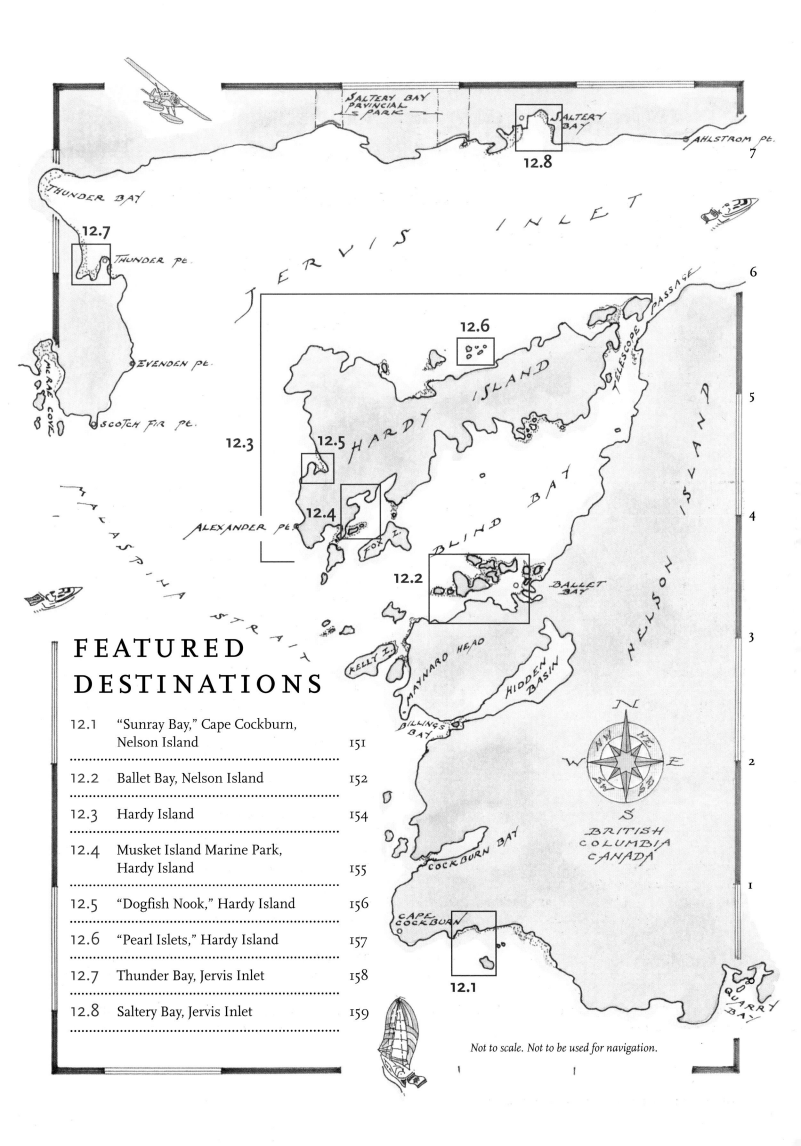

SALTERY BAY
PROVINCIAL
PARK

SALTERY
BAY

12.8

AHLSTROM PT.

7

J E R V I S   I N L E T

THUNDER BAY

12.7

THUNDER PT.

6

12.6

HARDY   ISLAND

TELESCOPE   PASSAGE

5

MC RAE COVE

EVENDEN PT.

12.3

12.5

BLIND   BAY

N E L S O N   I S L A N D

SCOTCH FIR PT.

12.4

ALEXANDER PT.

FOX I.

12.2

BALLET
BAY

4

M A L A S P I N A

KELLY I.

MAYNARD HEAD

3

S T R A I T

HIDDEN
BASIN

FEATURED
DESTINATIONS

BILLINGS
BAY

N
NW NE
W E
SW SE
S

2

BRITISH
COLUMBIA
CANADA

COCKBURN BAY

1

CAPE
COCKBURN

12.1

QUARRY
BAY

Not to scale. Not to be used for navigation.

PIONEER OF THE SUNSHINE COAST: HARRY ROBERTS, 1884–1979

Harry in his later years, at the typewriter.

We have to agree with Howard White, who in his insightful book *The Sunshine Coast* (Harbour Publishing) argues that "the candidate for Founding Spirit of the Sunshine Coast is indeed Harry Roberts, the patron saint of Roberts Creek. He didn't arrive until 1900 but was much more of the classic Sunshine Coast personality than George Gibson," the rather dour founder of Gibsons Landing. "Imaginative, visionary, non-conforming to a fault, he literally put the Sunshine Coast on the map. Roberts was the first Sunshine Coast pioneer to put into practice the idea that there are other things to do here just as important as cutting the trees, catching the fish and doing the developments."

Harry decided that the coast's many far-flung settlements and wonders should be packaged together under one evocative name. In typical style he then gave credit for the expression "Sunshine Coast" to his aged grandmother, Charlotte Roberts, who had retired to the coast north of Vancouver in 1890 (one of the pioneers of this flourishing tradition). Harry claimed that "Granny Roberts" liked to call the area around her home in Roberts Creek "the Sunshine Belt." He went a few steps further by painting the moniker in foot-high letters across the wall of the freight shed on the Roberts Creek steamer dock. After Roberts left the creek, White writes, "less imaginative promoters continued to exploit his brainwave, changing the acrid-sounding 'Belt' to the saltier 'Coast.'" Blackball Ferries then linked Pender Harbour to the Gibsons road to the Pacific Coast Highway, and "The Sunshine Coast" reached all the way from Port Mellon to Egmont.

After Harry left Roberts Creek, "he took to sea in his trusty yawl *Chack-Chack* where he could paint, write and philosophize full-time, eventually resettling on a paradisical south-facing beach at Cape Cockburn on Nelson Island. There he constructed his celebrated second home *Sunray* (the first being a castle, albeit a wooden one, in Roberts Creek), raised his three children and kept house with his second and third wives, give or take." Harry died at the age of 95.

Note: Harry Roberts wrote a book, The Trail of Chack-Chack, *hard to find these days.*

Sunray, Harry's cottage on Nelson Island, is still in remarkably good shape.

"SUNRAY BAY," CAPE COCKBURN, NELSON ISLAND

An expansive pebble and driftwood beach.

CHARTS 3152. 3311, Sheet 4. 3312, page 2

APPROACH
"Sunray Bay" lies midway between Cape Cockburn and the conspicuous gravel operation.

ANCHOR
Off "Harry Roberts Beach" in depths of 3–5 m (10–16 ft). Holding fair in shingle.

Note: The anchorage affords good protection from the NW but is open to all other quarters.

✿ 49°40.0'N 124°11.5'W

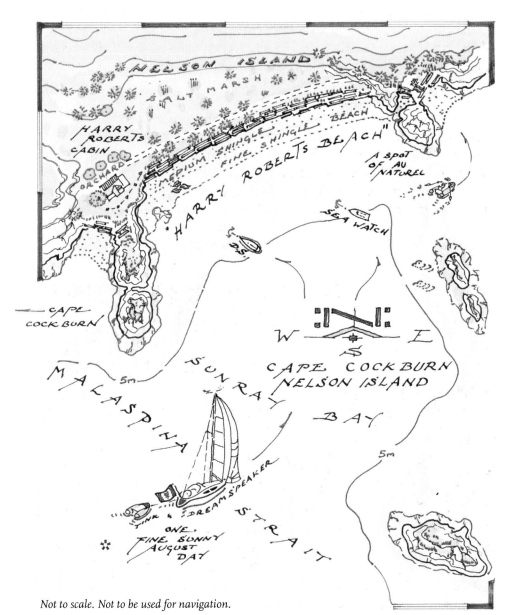

Not to scale. Not to be used for navigation.

Acquired by B.C. Hydro in the 1980s, Cape Cockburn now serves as the mainland terminus for the hydroelectric transmission line to Vancouver Island. Locals have resisted development, favouring the future establishment of a park that would safeguard the heritage home of Harry Roberts south of the cape and preserve the surrounding land.

On most trips north or south, *Dreamspeaker* has either been happily surfing beyond hull speed or battling against a strong southeasterly when passing Cape Cockburn. However, on a calm day or if a northwesterly impedes progress, take a quick detour, tuck into the calm of "Sunray Bay" and explore the delights of "Harry Roberts Beach." You will be rewarded with an expanse of smooth, rounded pebbles backed by mounds of driftwood, hidden picnic spots and a salt-water marsh frequented by a medley of wildlife. A stroll to the extraordinary log house "Sunray," the last home designed and built by Harry Roberts, is a must; please heed the sign installed by the caretakers of the house requesting visitors to "keep it clean and tidy, enjoy the apples and respect Harry's memory."

12.2 BALLET BAY, NELSON ISLAND

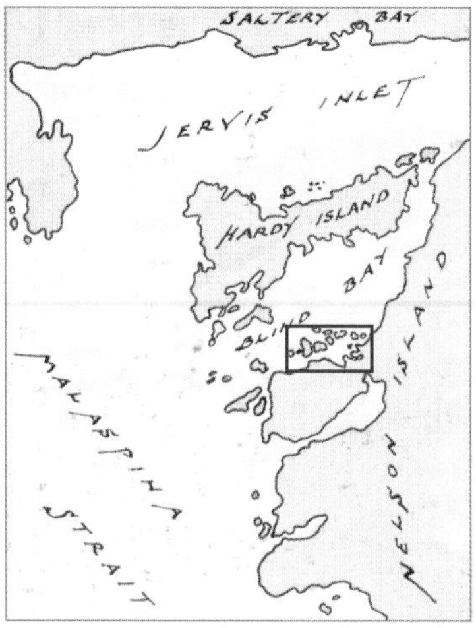

49°43.0'N 124°11.8'W

Approaching the entrance to Ballet Bay.

A large all-weather anchorage.

This is perhaps the only spot in these parts that did not take on the names of early naval explorers. Instead the bay was dedicated to the ballerina Audree Thomas, daughter of Harry and Midge Thomas, who owned property around the bay.

Tucked in behind the cluster of islets south of Blind Bay, this sheltered bay is often crowded in the summer, especially when a gale is howling out in Malaspina Strait. It has lovely vistas across to Hardy Island and up towards Telescope Passage and provides a cosy retreat to spend a few days reading, catching up on the cruising log or exploring the neighbouring shorelines, reefs and coves by dinghy or kayak. The small islet displaying the leading marks at the head of the bay is known locally as "Barbecue Island," being connected to Nelson Island by a constructed walkway. Note that the land surrounding the bay is private and should be respected as such. This includes the local trail to Hidden Basin, which is well used by the island community and visitors stretching their boat-weary legs.

Note: A small bronze plaque dedicated to Harry and Midge Thomas can be found in the SE nook of the bay.

CHARTS 3514. 3311, Sheet 4 (inset). 3312, page 2

APPROACH
From the W and best at LW. The safest entrance lies between Clio and Nelson islands. A cabin on Baker Point is quite conspicuous. The alternative northern entrance is rock-fringed and should only be approached at LW and at slow speed, keeping the local ranges (leading marks) on the small islet in line, as there is little room for error.

ANCHOR
Good all-weather anchoring may be found throughout Ballet Bay in depths of 2–10 m (6–16 ft). Holding good in mud and shell.
Note: "Sunset Cove" is open to the NW and has dinghy-only access to Ballet via "the Gap," as illustrated on the shoreline plan.

Checking out a Dreamspeaker *Guide.*

Not to scale. Not to be used for navigation.

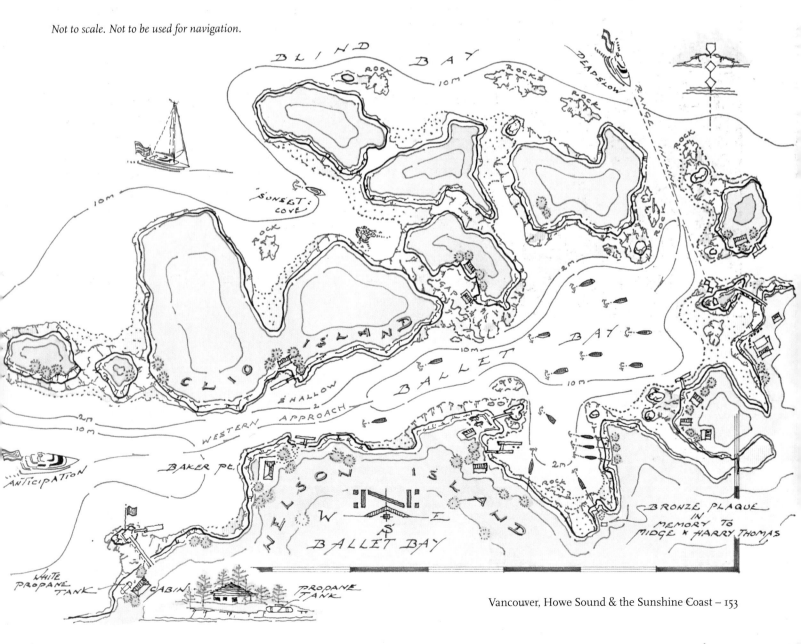

12.3 HARDY ISLAND

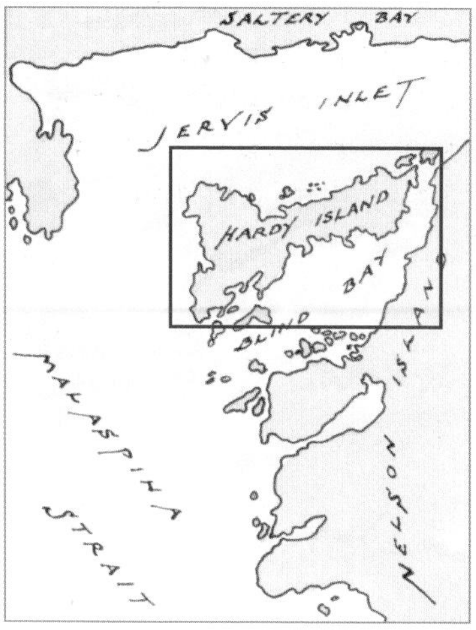

✣ 49°43.2'N 124°12.9'W

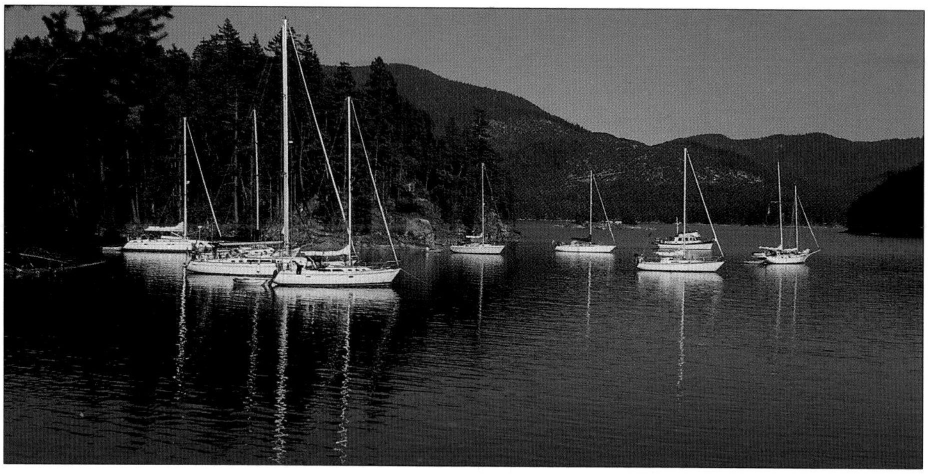

A favourite summer anchorage: Musket Island Marine Park on Hardy Island.

CHARTS 3514. 3311, Sheet 4 (inset). 3312, page 2

APPROACH

Hardy Island lies between Nelson Island and the mainland shore, and its numerous coves, bights and nooks provide many anchoring opportunities.

ANCHOR

The waypoint on the shoreline plan is for the approach to Musket Island Marine Park anchorage (see 12.4, page 155).

Note: It is best to explore the Hardy Island shoreline at LLW as there are a number of rocks and reefs that can catch you unawares.

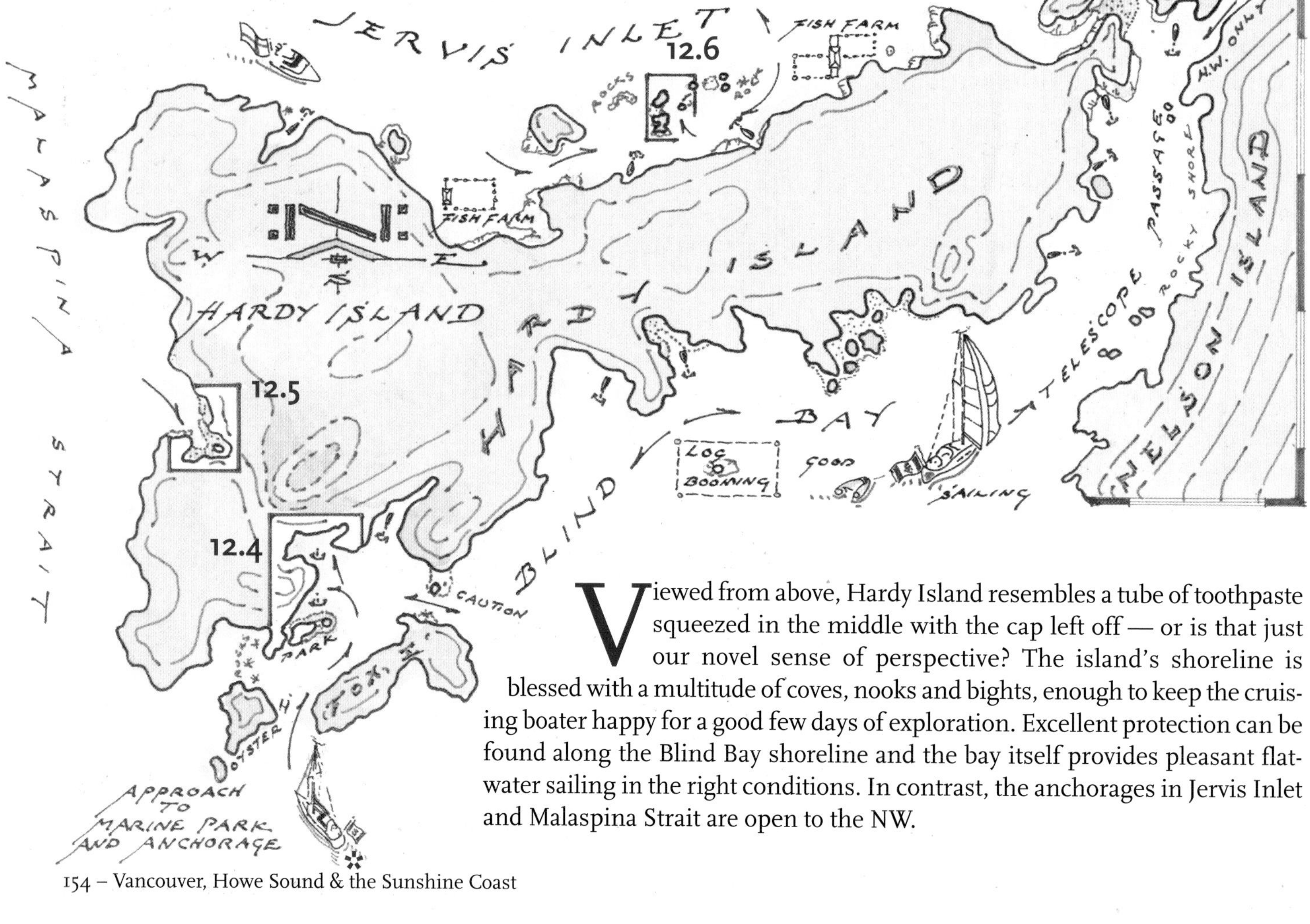

Viewed from above, Hardy Island resembles a tube of toothpaste squeezed in the middle with the cap left off — or is that just our novel sense of perspective? The island's shoreline is blessed with a multitude of coves, nooks and bights, enough to keep the cruising boater happy for a good few days of exploration. Excellent protection can be found along the Blind Bay shoreline and the bay itself provides pleasant flatwater sailing in the right conditions. In contrast, the anchorages in Jervis Inlet and Malaspina Strait are open to the NW.

MUSKET ISLAND MARINE PARK, HARDY ISLAND

Sailboats like Musket Cove.

APPROACH
From the S between Oyster and Fox islands. Musket Island is made conspicuous by the park sign.

ANCHOR
With a stern line ashore. This anchorage affords excellent protection from the NW but only fair protection from the SE. Anchor in depths of 2–4 m (6–13 ft). Holding good in mud and shell.

Note: Strong southeasterly winds penetrate the anchorage, followed by surface chop. The SW wall in "Musket Cove" offers the best protection.

Tiny Musket Island is connected to Hardy Island at LW and the shallows provide idyllic warm-water swimming on a rising tide. Musket Island Marine Park, once just Musket Island itself, was expanded in 2001 to include 16 hectares (40 acres) of land on Hardy Island's NW shore, giving boaters and their ever-eager pooches an alternative spot to stretch their legs. The surrounding real estate is private.

The park is a convenient hopping-off spot for boaters en route to Desolation Sound or Princess Louisa Inlet, making it very popular in summer. The SW shore in "Musket Cove" offers the best protection when a strong southeasterly wind prevails, although the stern-to anchorages off the rocky islets also afford some refuge. The shoreline plan gives a good indication of where to anchor in a northwesterly wind or settled weather.

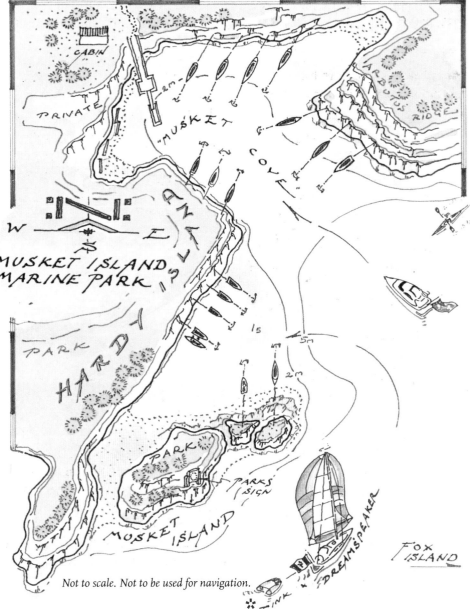

Not to scale. Not to be used for navigation.

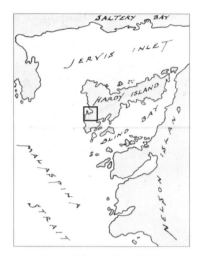

✳ 49°44.2'N 124°13.4'W

Sunset over Scotch Fir Point.

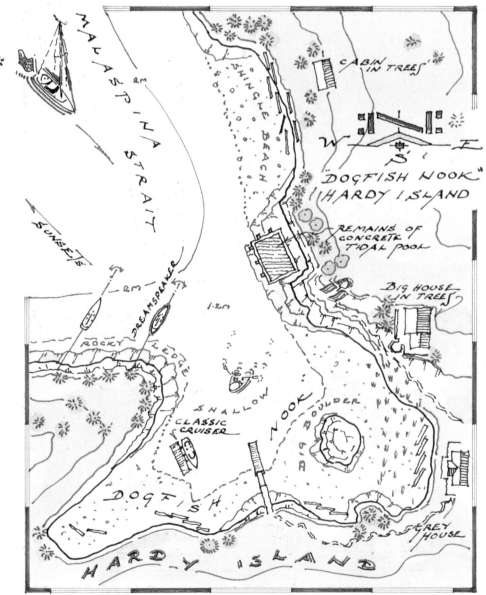

Not to scale. Not to be used for navigation.

CHARTS 3514. 3311, Sheet 4 (inset). 3312, page 2

APPROACH
From the NW. The nook opens up on Hardy Island's western shoreline and is best approached at LLW.

ANCHOR
With a stern line ashore as indicated on the shoreline plan. Good protection from the SE but open to the NW. Anchor in depths of 2–3 m (6–10 ft). Holding fair in mud and shingle.

Forever in search of dramatic sunset views, we were delighted to discover hidden "Dogfish Nook," as the evening's performance was truly spectacular.

Although private homes dot the shore, anchoring as indicated in the shoreline plan will ensure privacy and protection from southeasterly winds. The cosy nook and surrounding shallows are fun to explore at LW. At mid-tide, take a refreshing dip in the "pool." Before sundown, pack a picnic supper, set up camp on the rocky ledge beside the remains of the old tidal pool and experience a colourful West Coast treat while dining alfresco.

A gem, tickets not available.

CHARTS 3514. 3312, page 2

APPROACH
With caution at LLW as manoeuvrability between the rocks is limited.

ANCHOR
This anchorage is a "one-boat spot" not for the faint of heart. Use a taught stern line secured as indicated. Reasonable protection from both NW and SE winds. *Note: The "Alternative Spot" indicated on the shoreline plan also makes a good overnight anchorage.*

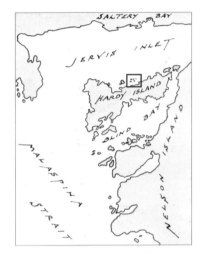

✿ 49°45.0'N 124°11.0'W

Low water exploration of Hardy Island's northern shoreline will reveal an interesting assortment of nooks and bights; however, the semicircle of islets, rocks and reefs clustered between the two fish farms challenged us to nose our way into the gap to investigate further. To our delight we discovered a tricky but cosy one-boat hideaway with great sunset prospects and lovely views up Jervis Inlet to Hotham Sound. We named this special spot "Pearl Islets" as that evening, while indulging in a platter of local oysters, the crew discovered a perfect teardrop-shaped pearl just before swallowing it. To date this little haven has not unveiled another gift from the sea, giving hope to other adventurous boaters who visit these charming islets.

Not to scale. Not to be used for navigation.

12.7 THUNDER BAY, JERVIS INLET

✳ 49°45.9'N 124°15.8W

CHARTS 3514. 3312, page 2

APPROACH
Thunder Bay lies north of Thunder Point on the mainland shore at the entrance to Jervis Inlet.

ANCHOR
The anchorage in Maude Bay (local name) lies to the W of the T-shaped peninsula. It offers good protection to all summer winds in depths of 5–10 m (16–33 ft). Holding fair in mud and shingle.

Note: Deep-water anchorage is possible at the head of Thunder Bay where the holding is good in sand, though the beach shallows rather quickly.

Convenient and protected anchorage is available in Thunder Bay for boaters cruising up Jervis Inlet or en route to Desolation Sound. The most popular spot is in a cove S of the bay, known locally as Maude Bay and home to an active summer community. Houses and cabins line the T-shaped peninsula and the southern shoreline, while the western shoreline is undeveloped thus far. On a rising tide it is possible to anchor close to the sandy foreshore, which is reasonably rock-free apart from an isolated boulder indicated on the shoreline plan.

Thunder Point: Maude Bay is just to port.

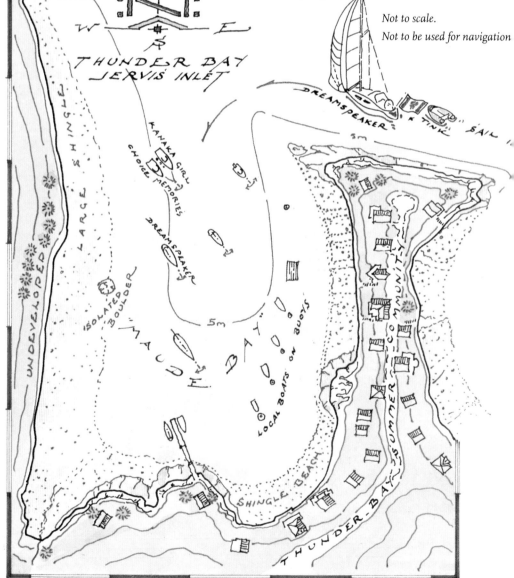

Not to scale.
Not to be used for navigation

CHARTS 3514. 3312, page 2

APPROACH
From the S. The B.C. Ferry terminal is highly conspicuous, especially if a ferry is in.

ANCHOR
Between the public wharf and the log float or stern-to on the SE shoreline, as illustrated in the shoreline plan. Holding and bottom condition unrecorded.

PUBLIC WHARF
Extensive deep-water moorage alongside two long fingers. The wharf is used by local runabouts heading to Hardy and Nelson islands.

BOAT LAUNCH
Public, on the NE shore. This is a gravel launch for small, light craft at HW. *Note: Be aware of the large arc required by the Queen of Tsawwassen for manoeuvring, and keep well clear. Float planes are also active in this area.*

✽ 49°46.7'N 124°10.4'W

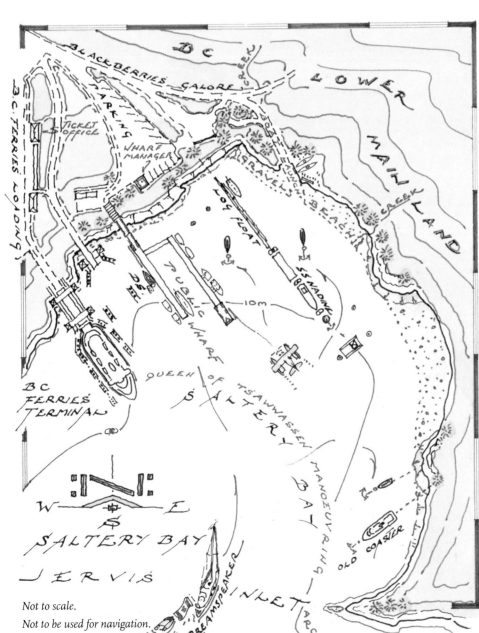

Not to scale.
Not to be used for navigation.

S altery Bay is the terminus of the B.C. Ferry service from Earls Cove and a convenient pickup and drop-off spot for family, friends and crew (see page 2 for travel information). It is a working harbour busy with boat, ferry and float plane activities but also provides protected overnight anchorage and moorage and is a pleasant stop to stretch your legs or pick blackberries in season.

Blackberry pie for dessert.

SOUTHERN TEXADA, LASQUETI AND JEDEDIAH ISLANDS

Dreamspeaker *and friends, Whiterock Bay, Jedediah Island.*

Chapter 13

SOUTHERN TEXADA, LASQUETI AND JEDEDIAH ISLANDS

TIDES
Canadian Tide and Current Tables, Volume 5

Reference Port: Point Atkinson
Secondary Port: False Bay

CURRENTS
Tidal streams may be encountered in Sabine Channel, but they seldom exceed 2 knots.

WEATHER
Strait of Georgia, North. The lighthouse at Sisters Islets is the nearest weather station covering this area.

Sunset Cove on Jedediah.

CAUTIONARY NOTES: *Winds tend to grow in strength through Sabine Channel. Exceedingly rough seas may be encountered when the wind opposes the current.*

The long, mountainous spine of Texada Island runs parallel to the Sunshine Coast with Mount Shepherd dominating the skyline. Tucked below the island's southern shores across Sabine Channel are a group of low-lying islands that form a varied and exciting cruising ground. This chapter begins with charming Anderson Bay on Texada, then covers the two largest playgrounds, Lasqueti and Jedediah islands. We also give you a glimpse of lovely "Otters Pool," a tranquil anchorage in the Finnerty Island group.

Before venturing into these islands, top up with fuel and food, as the only hope of replenishment is in the small village of False Bay on Lasqueti Island; in 2007, neither eastern Lasqueti, Jedediah nor southern Texada had even a basic local store. It is also wise to prepare the boat's bug screens because the Lasqueti Island mosquito has a fearsome, well-deserved reputation!

The Squitty Bay public wharf on Lasqueti Island is a popular, often crowded "storm hole" providing all-round protection once the tricky entrance has been negotiated. The expansive parkland is a fine place to stretch your legs and relax with nature. In contrast, Rouse Bay is a lovely spot to drop your anchor and observe the resident ospreys and kingfishers hunting.

Historic and well-preserved Jedediah Island was designated a Class A provincial marine park in 1995. It is a joy to explore, from the original homestead, orchard and meadows of Mary and Al Palmer, the former owners, to your first encounter with the flocks of woolly sheep and wild goats. There are numerous anchoring opportunities around the island with Deep Bay and Boho Bay (on nearby Lasqueti) providing the best protection.

Scottie Bay is a busy place when gale-force winds threaten the tranquility of Lasqueti Island. In settled weather "Maple Bay" is a perfect place to drop your hook and crab trap, laze on the white-shell spit and float in the warm water. Popular False Bay provides a convenient stop-off for boats heading N and has the added advantages of a hotel pub and restaurant and a small store.

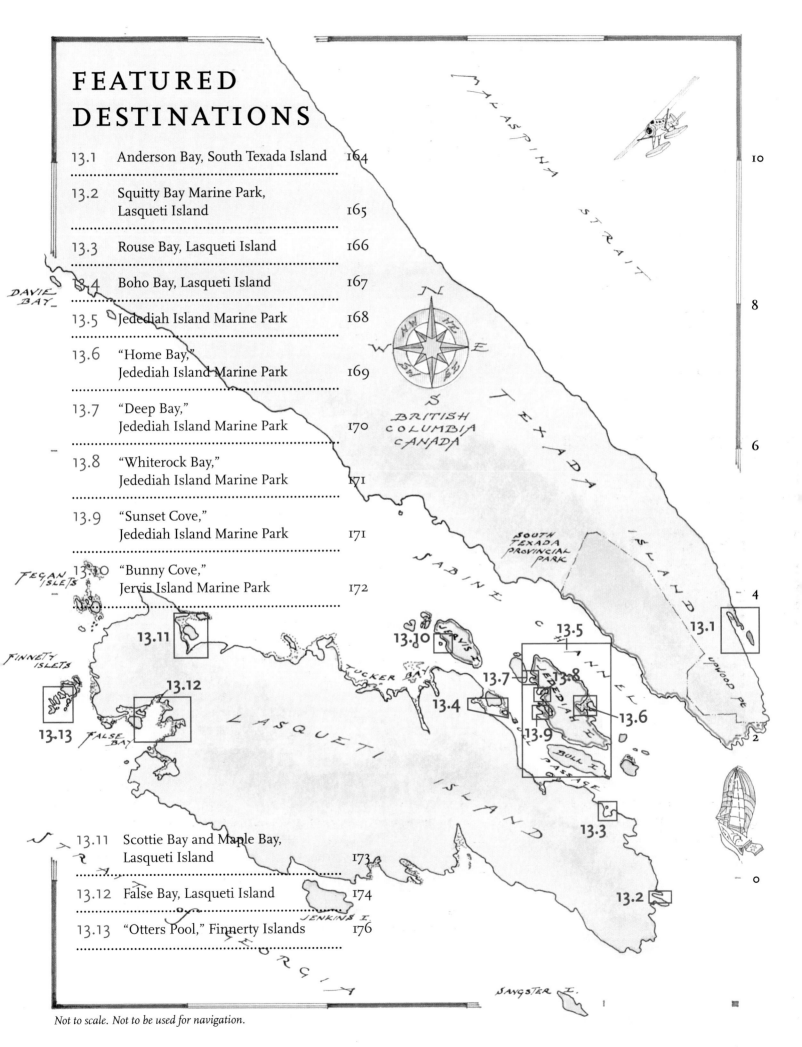

FEATURED DESTINATIONS

Not to scale. Not to be used for navigation.

13.1 ANDERSON BAY,
SOUTH TEXADA ISLAND

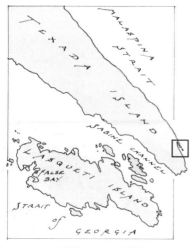

❀ 49°30.6'N 124°7.7'W

CHARTS 3512. 3312, page 1

APPROACH
From the SE or between "Stella's Island" and the peninsula, which is best negotiated at LW.

ANCHOR
At the head of the bay or stern-to the sheer granite wall. Good protection from the NW, but open to the SE. Depths 5–10 m (16–33 ft), holding fair in mud and rock.

Tink, *Anne and a watchful eagle.*

The new South Texada Provincial Park also includes "Stella's Island" (named by us) and the peninsula at Anderson Bay, on south Texada's eastern shoreline. The head of the bay offers protected anchorage in a peaceful setting in all winds except a southeasterly, and the gap between the park peninsula and "Stella's Island" is the perfect spot to drop your hook for a picnic lunch. Strewn with weathered driftwood and shaded by a cluster of arbutus trees, the island's small, crescent-shaped gravel beach is a lovely spot to relax and enjoy the variety of wildlife.

Not to scale. Not to be used for navigation.

Masts appear and the channel becomes clearer.

CHARTS 3512. 3312, page 1

APPROACH
From the W, favouring the southern shoreline to avoid the rocks that lie along the northern edge of the entrance.

ANCHOR
Not recommended, as cables that anchor the float criss-cross the bay.

PUBLIC WHARF
Used extensively by local boats — be prepared to raft up.

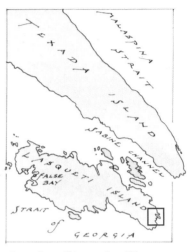

✿ 49°27.2'N   124°9.4W

P repare your mosquito screens well before docking at the public wharf in Squitty Bay: the *Dreamspeaker* crew nicknamed it "Mozzie Bay." Although the bay provides all-round protection and is a popular "storm hole," entering the rock-strewn entrance requires full concentration. Once inside there is little room to manoeuvre as the dock is usually crowded, with boats often rafted 2 to 3 deep. Squitty Bay is also closed to the discharge of sewage. Skittish feral sheep roam the natural parkland and a reserve has been established on the point to protect the grove of windswept juniper trees, reshaped over the years by the prevailing southeasterlies. Picnic tables and a brass cairn to commemorate "The Spanish discovery of Lasqueti Island in the year 1791" overlook the bay and some mossy rocks connected to the island by a driftwood isthmus.

Not to scale. Not to be used for navigation.

13.3 ROUSE BAY, LASQUETI ISLAND

✳ 49°28.6'N 124°11.1'W

CHARTS 3512. 3312, page 1

APPROACH

From the N, passing between the marked rock and "Telephone Islet" (day beacon absent in 2007). It is also possible to approach between the marked rock and the Lasqueti Island shore.

ANCHOR

Stern-to as indicated, or swing in the bay. Reasonable protection from light to moderate winds. Depths 2–4 m (6–13 ft). Holding fair in sand and weed.

Note: Strong SE winds create a surge in Bull Passage making Rouse Bay uncomfortable.

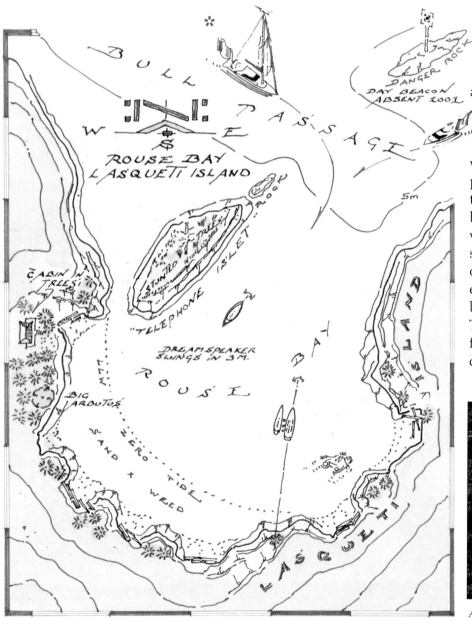

The quiet backwater of Rouse Bay is a lovely spot to drop your anchor, untie the dinghy and take a peaceful exploratory row. Private land grazed by laid-back local sheep surrounds the bay. Apparently the stunted tree on "Telephone Islet" was once fitted with an emergency telephone, a lifesaver for local craft and tugboats needing to communicate between islands or with the outside world. On our last visit the bay was silent and calm and we had the privilege of observing a pair of elegant ospreys engrossed in their vigilant "wash and brush-up" routine at the water's edge. They were followed by a trio of kingfishers performing magnificent diving displays to procure lunch.

A pair of ospreys patrol the bay.

Not to scale. Not to be used for navigation.

BOHO BAY, LASQUETI ISLAND

CHARTS 3512. 3312, page 1

APPROACH
From the E. The bay is clear of obstructions.

ANCHOR
As indicated in the shoreline plan. Although the bay is open to the SE it offers reasonable protection in light to moderate southeasterly winds. In strong northwesterly winds it is the preferred anchorage off Bull Passage, with plenty of room in deep water. Depths vary, holding good in mud.

Note: Skerry Bay has an active fish farming operation with associated commercial noise.

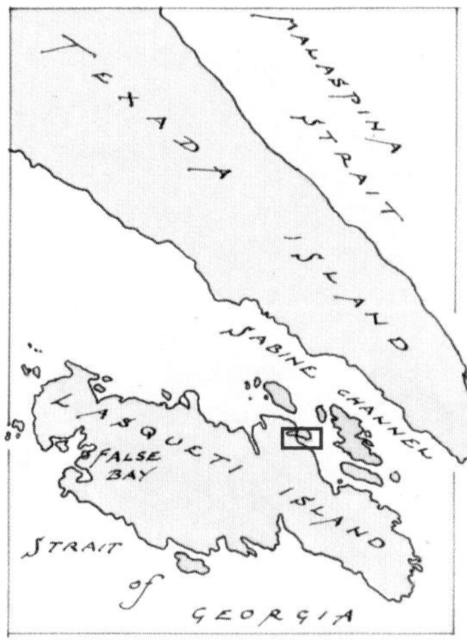

49°29.7'N 124°13.3'W

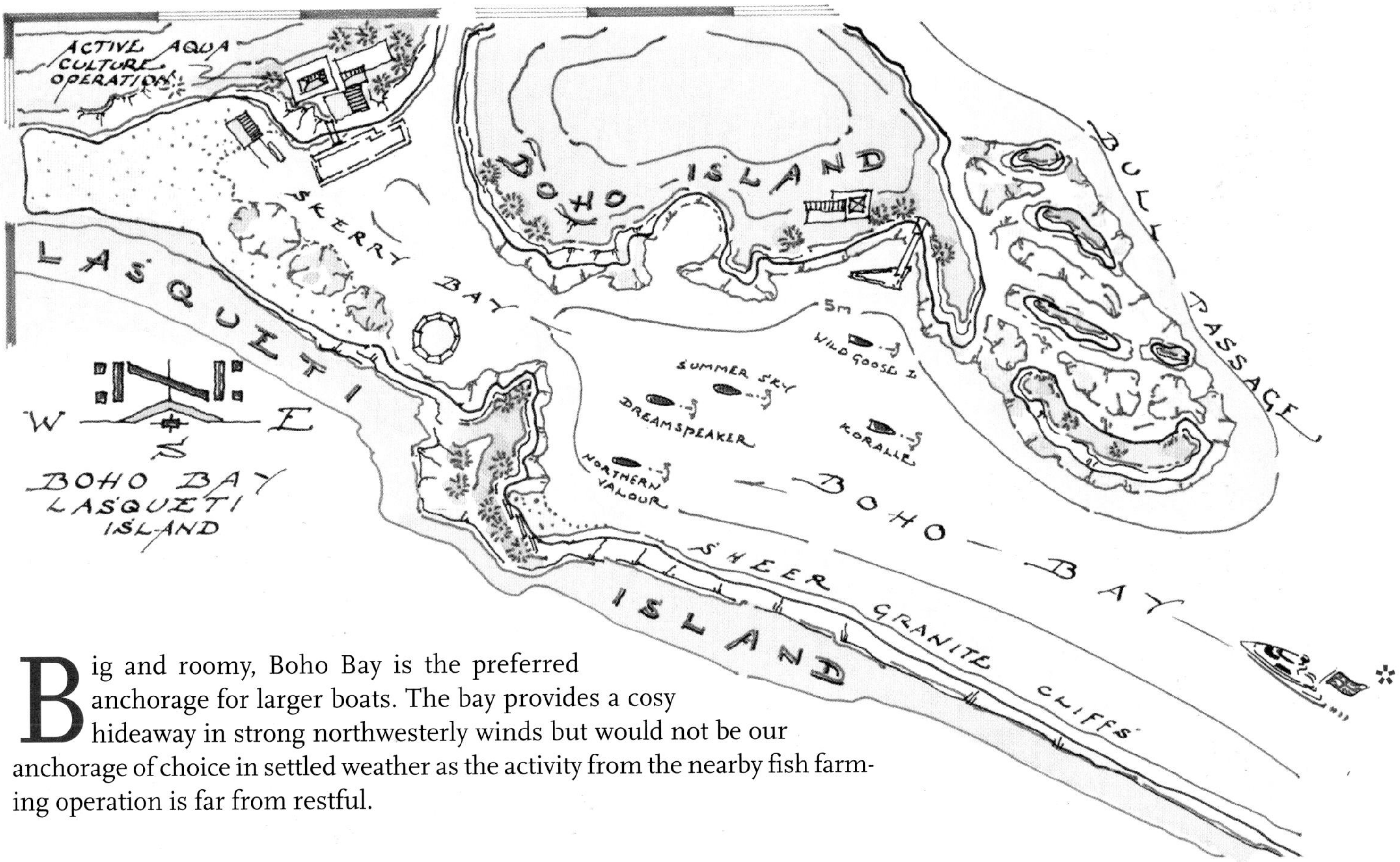

Big and roomy, Boho Bay is the preferred anchorage for larger boats. The bay provides a cosy hideaway in strong northwesterly winds but would not be our anchorage of choice in settled weather as the activity from the nearby fish farming operation is far from restful.

Not to scale. Not to be used for navigation.

13.5 JEDEDIAH ISLAND MARINE PARK

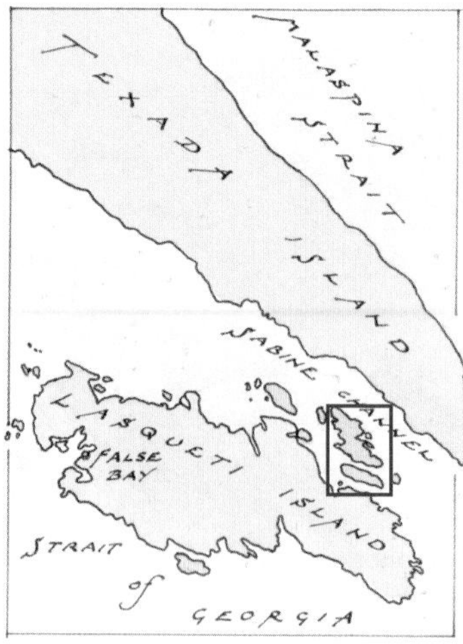

✲ 49°29.8'N 124°11.2'W

APPROACH
Jedediah Island may be approached from both Sabine Channel and Bull Passage. Little Bull Passage is also used by small recreational craft.

ANCHOR
Numerous anchoring opportunities around the island depending on wind strength and direction. The bays and coves all have local names:

"Deep Bay" — All-weather protection, 13.7, page 170
"Whiterock Bay" — Temporary anchorage open to NW winds, 13.8, page 171
"Boom Bay" — Dries at LW
"Long Bay" — Dries at LW
"Sunset Cove" — Temporary anchorage open to NW winds
"Codfish Bay" — Temporary anchorage, open to SE winds
"Home Bay" — Dries at LW, 13.6, page 169

Note: You will find good anchorage for larger boats long the southwestern edge of Jedediah Island towards the entrance to Little Bull Passage, with protection from both SE and NW winds.

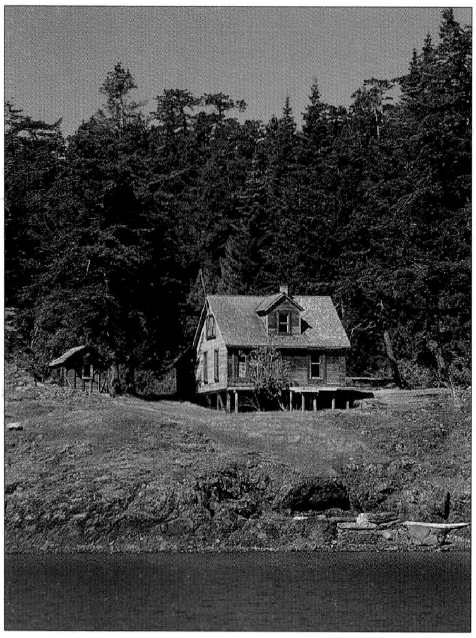

The Palmers' homestead.

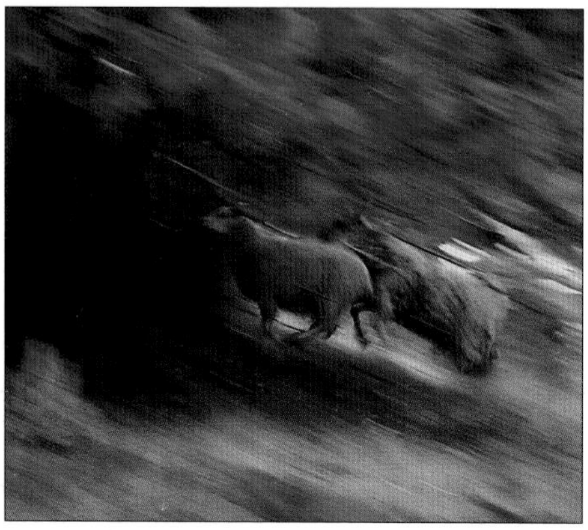

Wild goats in full flight.

Ruggedly beautiful and abundant with wildlife, Jedediah Island was officially designated a Class A provincial marine park in 1995, ensuring the preservation of its native plants, old-growth trees, beaches and countless unique features. This was made possible by the foresight of the island's former owners, Mary and Al Palmer, a generous gift from the Dan Culver estate, the fundraising efforts of the Friends of Jedediah and contributions from hundreds of individuals, groups and corporations.

The monument erected to the environmentalist Dan Culver above "Home Bay" features an inspiring quote from Goethe: "Whatever you can do or dream you can, begin it. Boldness has genius, power and magic in it. Begin it now!"

There is so much to discover and enjoy on Jedediah that we suggest an early start, good walking shoes, a swimsuit, binoculars and a packed lunch with a good supply of water (no water is available on the island). Dipping into Mary Palmer's very readable memoir *Jedediah Days: One Woman's Island Paradise* beforehand is an added bonus.

Some of Jedediah's highlights include: a ramble from "Sunset Bay" through open fields of ferns and wildflowers (in the summertime expect native foxgloves and camas, a blue hyacinth-like flower that was an important food source for First Nations people); your first thrilling encounter with herds of woolly sheep and the wild goats that historians believe were left behind by Spanish explorers in the eighteenth century; an energetic climb to the top of Mount Gibraltar, Jedediah's highest point, with stunning panoramic views; a hike to the Palmers' original homestead through beautiful meadows; lying in the shade of the Palmers' apple, pear and plum orchard; picking oysters or taking a turn on the swing rope on the lovely white sandy beach of "Home Bay"; and visiting "Driftwood Beach," created by years of winter storms. The island is also a kayaker's haven with a wide choice of cosy nooks and tenting sites to call home for a night or two.

"HOME BAY," JEDEDIAH ISLAND MARINE PARK

APPROACH
From Sabine Channel. The bay is shallow and dries at LW.

ANCHOR
In the lee of "Mother Goose Island," in calm weather or northwesterly winds.

Note: Beware of the rock that dries in the entrance to the bay. The anchorage is open to the wash from commercial vessels transiting Sabine Channel.

Not to scale. Not to be used for navigation.

"Home Bay" provides convenient access by dinghy or kayak to the Palmers' homestead, barn and orchards. Boaters can anchor in the lee of Mother Goose Island Bird Sanctuary and, by taking advantage of a rising tide, slip into the bay by tender and beach their craft below the main house or on the fine sandy beach south of the bay. At LW the bay provides plump oysters for the evening's chowder.

Not to scale. Not to be used for navigation.

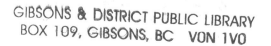

13.7 "DEEP BAY,"
JEDEDIAH ISLAND MARINE PARK

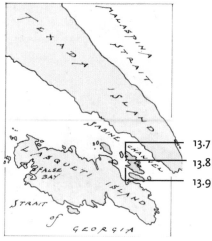

✳ 49°30.6'N 124°12.9'W

CHARTS 3512. 3312, page 1

APPROACH
"Deep Bay" lies in the passage between Paul and Jedediah islands. The approach from the N or S is quite straightforward.

ANCHOR
As indicated in the plan, taking a stern line to one of the lines provided by the park. Good protection from the SE, only moderate protection from strong NW winds. Depths 2–5 m (6–16 ft). Holding fair in soft mud.

Note: Plan shows ideal summer conditions in calm weather. Do not swing in the bay, as this will restrict anchoring for other vessels. Larger boats of 15 m (50 ft) and more may want to give this anchorage a miss. Alternative protected deep-water anchorage is available in nearby Boho Bay or "Whiterock Bay."

At anchor in Whiterock Bay.

It is deep and relatively small with iffy holding, but "Deep Bay" is the primary all-weather anchorage on Jedediah Island. The "full house" shown on the shoreline plan is quite common in the summer, but with a little forethought, considerate stern-to anchoring (rings with chains and rope are provided) and comradely co-operation, space is available for smaller boats to tuck deep into the bay. The water is clear and clean for swimming, the mossy cliffs are great for exploring and trails lead from the head of the bay through old-growth forest to the southern portion of the island.

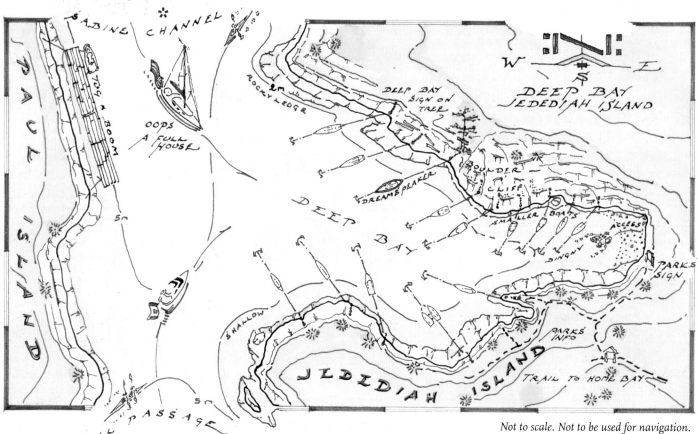

Not to scale. Not to be used for navigation.

"WHITEROCK BAY,"
JEDEDIAH ISLAND MARINE PARK

CHARTS 3512. 3312, page 1

APPROACH
From the SW, out of Bull Passage. The bay is deep and open to the W.

ANCHOR
With a stern line ashore. Well protected from the SE and comfortable in a light to moderate northwesterly wind. Depths 3–5 m (10–16 ft), holding good in mud.

T his large, deep-water bay has an open, friendly feeling and can accommodate numerous boats when anchored stern to the shoreline. Popular with yacht clubs and cruising flotillas as a rendezvous spot, Whiterock Bay has the added bonus of brilliant watercolour sunsets. The "one-boat cosy corner" in the NW nook has become a coveted spot for early arrivals. Good cellular reception is possible at "Reception Bluff" on the southern shore.

❊ 49°30.1'N 124°12.9'W

SUNSET COVE,
JEDEDIAH ISLAND MARINE PARK

CHARTS 3512. 3312, page 1

APPROACH
From the W out of Bull Passage. Leave the big rock in the entrance to the S.

ANCHOR
A one- or two-boat spot, open to the W and uncomfortable in a northwesterly. Depths 2–4 m (6–13 ft), holding poor in weed and sand. *Note: If a northwesterly springs up overnight, it can cause your anchor to drag in the weed and sand bottom.*

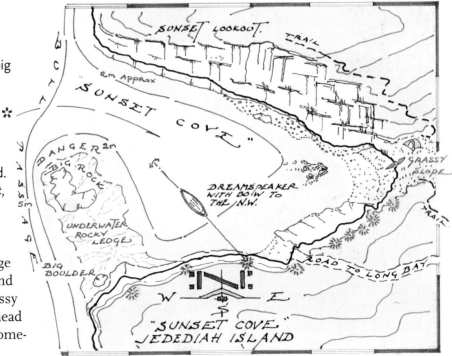

T his quiet little two-boat anchorage offers warm-water swimming and great sunset views from the mossy boulders above the cliff. A trail from the head of the cove leads to the Palmers' original homestead at "Home Bay."

Not to scale. Not to be used for navigation.   ❊ 49°29.8'N 124°13.0'W

13.10 "BUNNY COVE," JERVIS ISLAND MARINE PARK

✽ 49°30.8'N   124°15.1'W

CHARTS 3512. 3312, page 1

APPROACH
From the W. It is possible to enter the cove either N or S of Bunny Island.

ANCHOR
Bunny Island affords only moderate protection from the NW. Jervis Island screens the anchorage from SE seas, but the wind tends to wrap around from Bull Passage. Depths 3–5 m (10–16 ft), holding fair in gravel.

Note: The temporary anchorage indicated in the shoreline plan is in a natural wind-shadow when the wind is from the NW. Other stern-to combinations are also possible.

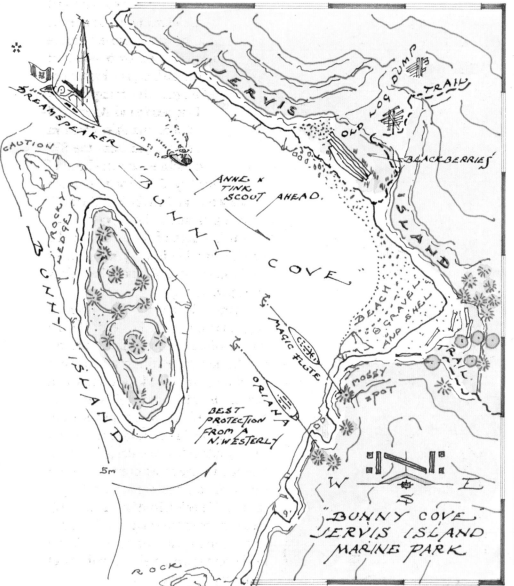

Jervis Island Marine Park is rather short on anchorages with "Bunny Cove," in the lee of Bunny Island, affording only moderate protection in northwesterly winds. In settled weather the cove makes a good hopping-off spot to visit the small beach and undeveloped marine park. The solitary blackberry bush just up from the beach produces plump, juicy fruit for breakfast treats well into late September; leaving a few for the next visiting boat would be a neighbourly gesture.

No sign of bunnies, but the blackberries were good.

SCOTTIE BAY AND MAPLE BAY, LASQUETI ISLAND

Magic Flute *joins the party in Maple Bay.*

CHARTS 3512. 3312, page 1. See inset 1B

APPROACH
Scottie Bay with caution as boulders extend S on a rocky ledge from Lindbergh Island. Stay close to the Lasqueti Island shore. Entering Maple Bay is straightforward.

ANCHOR
Scottie Bay affords excellent all-weather protection. Maple Bay is well protected from the NW but open to the SE. Depths 2–6 m (6–20 ft), holding only fair over a varied bottom.

✳ 49°31.0'N   124°20.2'W

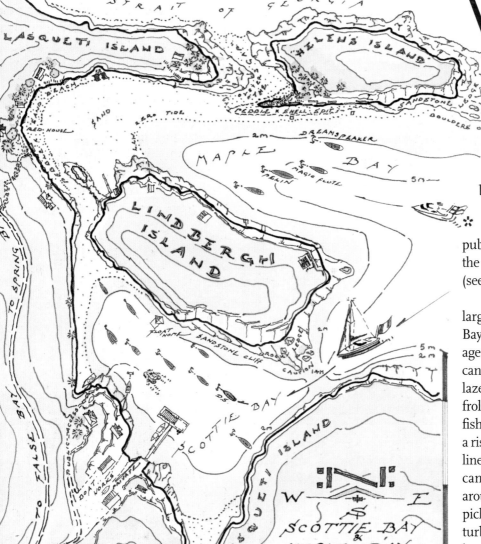

Not to scale. Not to be used for navigation.

Well known by commercial and recreational boaters as a "hurricane hole," Scottie Bay is filled with boats at anchor when gale-force winds threaten the tranquility of Lasqueti Island. A local trail to Mud and False bays can be accessed from the SW shoreline near the head of the bay. Once you're past the boatworks and on the island road, it is a pleasant 1.5-hour walk to the small village of False Bay and the public wharf in Mud Bay, terminus of the Lasqueti Island/French Creek ferry (see 13.12, pg 175).

Named locally for the cluster of large maple trees at its head, "Maple Bay" is a little-known but lovely anchorage. In the right weather conditions you can drop your hook close to shore and laze on the white-shell spit, watch the frolicking seals and dive-bombing kingfishers, bathe in the warm shallows on a rising tide or just row along the shoreline on a voyage of discovery. At LW you can walk on the sandstone ledges around "Helen's Island" (named by us), pick oysters in "the Gap" (without disturbing the oyster lease) or visit the lovely sand and pebble beach at the head of the bay.

13.12 FALSE BAY, LASQUETI ISLAND

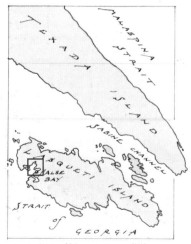

✴ 49°29.4'N 124°21.9'W

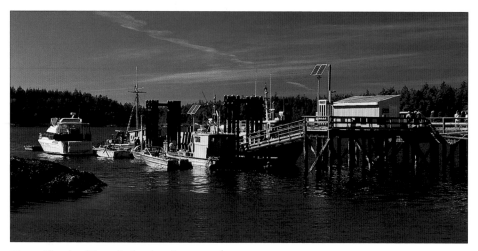

The public wharf from the hotel and resort.

Three-masted junk China Cloud.

False Bay is Lasqueti Island's most protected and popular anchorage in the busy summer months as it provides a convenient stop-off for boats heading north to Desolation Sound and a safe rendezvous spot for exploring the local area. Lasqueti is a protected and undeveloped island whose residents have chosen to leave it in its natural state. By choosing not to install electricity and to operate a foot passenger ferry service, they have managed to restrict development, minimize traffic disturbance and maintain the island's tranquility.

The small village of False Bay (situated in Mud Bay) has a mellow charm all its own, with the snug resort pub and sociable STORE and coffee shop providing a friendly gathering spot for locals and visitors. LASQUETI ISLAND HOTEL AND RESORT includes a restaurant. Their pub sells cold beer to go and the small store stocks some basics and ice. Lovely sunset views can be enjoyed from the patio (call 250-333-8503).

The quaint store and coffee shop by the sea also offers delicious, generous sandwiches and devilish baked goods. The store stocks all the necessary basics, local fruit and vegetables, grains, delicious peasant bread and free-range eggs. A short walk up the road will take you to the lovely OLD BAKERY BED AND BREAKFAST overlooking placid Mud Bay. This heritage cottage allows visitors to "step back in time and enjoy nature and island life at its finest" (call 250-333-8890 for a brochure or reservations). When we visited, the legendary *China Cloud*, an elegant, hand-built three-masted junk, was quietly resting in her mud berth at the head of the bay; to learn more about the boat and Alan and Sharie Farrell, the extraordinary couple who built and sailed her, read *Sailing Back in Time: A Nostalgic Voyage on Canada's West Coast* by Maria Coffey.

Continuing on your walk you will pass the post office (not open Tuesdays and Sundays), a fascinating gift shop, the FREE STORE and THE UPPER CRUST BAKERY (open Fridays only). It is a pleasant 1.5-hour walk to and from Scottie Bay (see 13.11, pg 173) with a few "honesty stands" along the way offering freshly picked chanterelle mushrooms and tasty homegrown fruit and vegetables.

CHARTS 3536. 3312, page 1.
See inset 1B

APPROACH
False Bay (proper) lies NE of Olsen Island and Heath Islet. The inner portion is entered S of Higgins Island.

ANCHOR
Close to shore in the northwestern anchorage of False Bay (Orchard Bay), which provides good holding and protection from both northwesterly and southeasterly winds. Listen out for Qualicum wind warnings on the weather channel as False Bay is open to these strong westerly winds, notorious for their swift and unexpected arrival. Depths 5–10 m (16–33 ft), holding good in mud.

PUBLIC WHARF
Situated in Mud Bay with little room for visiting craft. The wharf is also frequented by the Lasqueti Island/ French Creek passenger ferry service (in summer every day except Tuesdays). The old fuel float is now a designated dinghy dock.
Note: The fuel dock no longer dispenses fuel. It is possible to purchase emergency supplies at the LASQUETI ISLAND HOTEL AND RESORT *if you supply the jerry cans.*

A Lasqueti resident joins Anne outside the store.

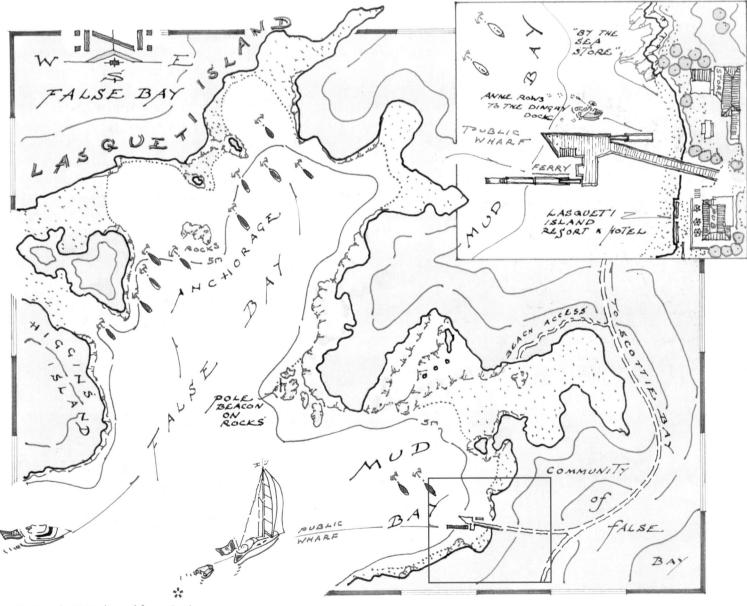

Not to scale. Not to be used for navigation.

13.13 "OTTERS POOL,"
FINNERTY ISLANDS

✳ 49°29.7'N 124°23.6'W

CHARTS 3512. 3312, page 1

APPROACH
From the S, between the isolated boulder and the cluster of islands to the E.

ANCHOR
Temporary anchorage for one or two boats in "Otters Pool." Depth 3 m (10 ft), holding fair over shingle and mud.

Note: Open to the S and to Qualicum Winds.

The temporary anchorage between the islands.

Not to scale. Not to be used for navigation.

A family of otters was gleefully at play when we slipped into the uninhabited Finnerty Islands and dropped our hook one sunny summer morning. The small temporary anchorage now named "Otters Pool" is a terrific day/picnic stop for the whole family, kids and dogs included. Hours can be spent playing Robinson Crusoe and exploring the lovely island group with its lagoons, tidal pools and rocky outcrops or identifying the abundant varieties of moss, grasses, flowers, and trees.

Chapter 14

VANCOUVER ISLAND: DEPARTURE BAY TO FRENCH CREEK

The Yeo Islands, a lunch stop in the middle of the strait.

Sunset over Northwest Bay.

Chapter 14
VANCOUVER ISLAND: DEPARTURE BAY TO FRENCH CREEK

TIDES
Canadian Tide and Current Tables, Volume 5

Reference Port: Point Atkinson
Secondary Ports: Nanoose Bay, Winchelsea Islands and Northwest Bay

CURRENTS
No reference or secondary stations cover this area.

WEATHER
Strait of Georgia, N of Nanaimo — weather reporting station "Ballenas Islands" will give a fair indication of conditions along this portion of the coast.

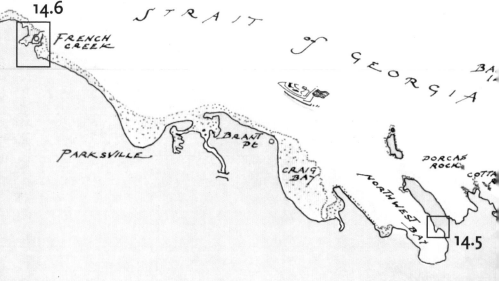

CAUTIONARY NOTES: *Boaters transiting this portion of the coastline need to be aware of the status of area "Whiskey Golf" (WG). When active, this is a testing area for underwater vehicles, including surface- and air-launched torpedoes that are extremely hazardous to all vessels. Range status is broadcast on the weather channel daily and the area is monitored vigilantly.*

FEATURED DESTINATIONS

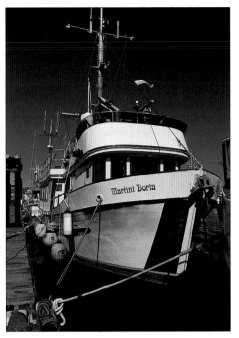

French Creek is still a predominantly working harbour with an active fishing fleet.

This chapter incorporates the "missing link" between "Volume 1, Chapter 14: Nanaimo" and "Volume 2, Chapter 3: Baynes Sound" on Vancouver Island's eastern shoreline. It includes six destinations north of Departure Bay, Nanaimo, as far as French Creek Harbour, just south of Deep Bay.

We begin the final chapter with peaceful Pipers Lagoon Park in Hammond Bay and a trip to the eccentric cluster of colourful shanties on "Shack Islands." With a sandy beach on the outside of the pebble spit and a protected warm-water lagoon for swimming on the inside, the park and its trails make for a fun day out.

Historic Nanoose Harbour has not been included because the harbour itself is a large expanse of open water far more suited to the naval ships that frequent its docks and buoys than to small recreational craft.

North of Nanoose Harbour lies the Winchelsea Islands, part of the Ballenas-Winchelsea Archipelago. South Winchelsea Island is protected by The Land Conservancy (TLC) as an ecological reserve because of its invaluable biodiversity. Visitors are welcome to explore certain sections of the island or rent the roomy three-bedroom cabin. North Winchelsea Island is a navy tracking station surrounded by hostile barbed wire that monitors area "Whiskey Golf."

Nearby SCHOONER COVE MARINA AND RESORT has all the facilities you will need to relax and pamper yourself for a day or two. Laze in the hot tub or heated pool, ride a bike along the numerous trails and meet the resident beaver family, play a game of golf or dine at the waterfront restaurant with superb views out to the Sunshine Coast. A kayaking trip to one of the lovely island hideaways for a sunset BBQ can be arranged and a boat picnic on the serene Yeo Islands offers absorbing LW exploration and a chance to swim with the otters.

The orderly and kid-friendly BEACHCOMBER MARINA provides a convenient stop on the seemingly endless Vancouver Island shoreline and has a grassy picnic point with lovely sunset views. In sharp contrast French Creek, home to the Lasqueti Island ferry terminus, is a bustling commercial harbour with a friendly but crowded public wharf. It's a great place to eat or buy fish and seafood straight off the work boats, stock up on provisions or enjoy a locally brewed beer at the pub while the laundry dries.

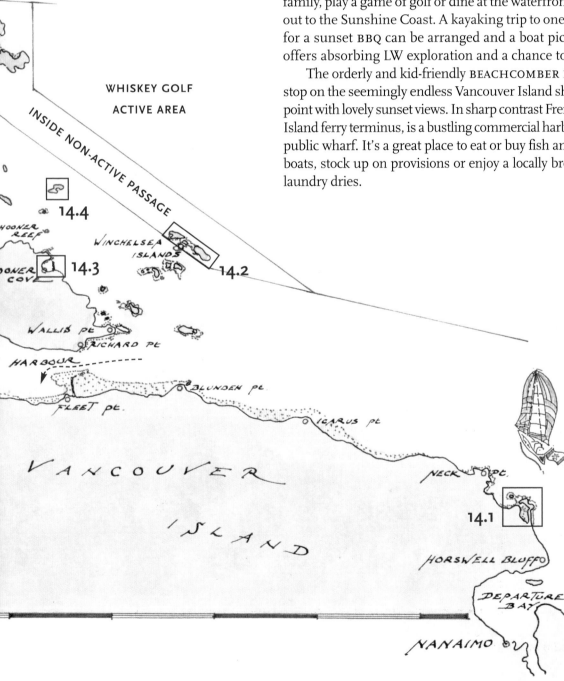

WHISKEY GOLF
ACTIVE AREA

INSIDE NON-ACTIVE PASSAGE

14.4

HOONER REEF

WINCHELSEA ISLANDS

14.3

OONER COVE

14.2

WALLIS PT

RICHARD PT

HARBOUR

BLUNDEN PT

FLEET PT.

ICARUS PT.

V A N C O U V E R

I S L A N D

NECK PT.

14.1

HORSWELL BLUFF

DEPARTURE BAY

Not to scale.
Not to be used for navigation.

NANAIMO

14.1 PIPERS LAGOON PARK, HAMMOND BAY

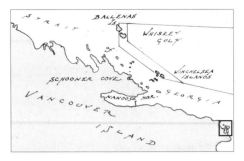

✽ 49°14.0'N   123°57.2'W

CHARTS 3458

APPROACH

By rounding Lagoon Head and the "Shack Islands" (local name), conspicuous by the clusters of colourful squatters' shacks hugging the shoreline.

ANCHOR

As indicated in the shoreline plan, W of the local mooring buoys. Good protection from the SE in depths of 5–10 m (16–33 ft). Holding fair in shingle.

BOAT LAUNCH

Public, with access from Hammond Bay Road.

Summer shacks add colour to Hammond Bay.

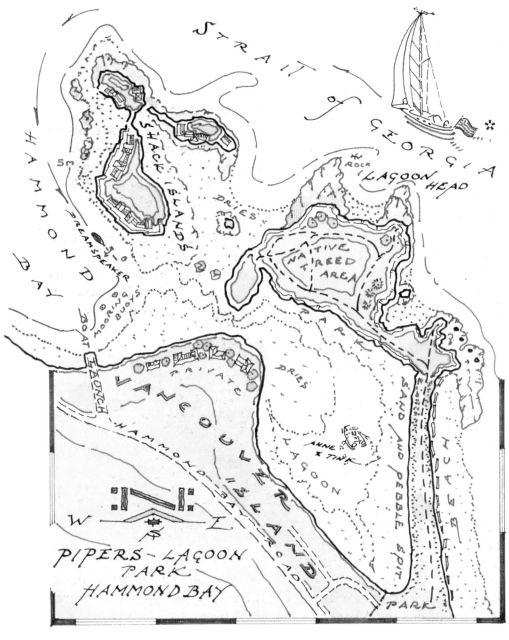

Once home to a gruesome whaling station, Pipers Lagoon is now part of a peaceful 8-hectare (20-acre) regional park that also encompasses Lagoon Head, a well-forested rocky islet joined to Vancouver Island by a sand and pebble spit. With a sandy beach on the outside and a protected lagoon providing warm-water swimming on the inside, Pipers Lagoon Park is wonderful to explore. Hammond Bay affords suitable overnight anchorage in southeasterly winds.

A full day could be spent puttering around this charming haven, beginning with the colourful and eclectic shanties dotted around "Shack Islands," originally constructed from found materials by squatters and fishermen. The lagoon is patronized by a variety of wildlife including common loons, lively black oystercatchers, bobbing surf scoters and fluffy-headed mergansers. Treat yourself to a quiet row at HW to observe the feeding rituals and energetic diving displays.

Not to scale. Not to be used for navigation.

WINCHELSEA ISLANDS

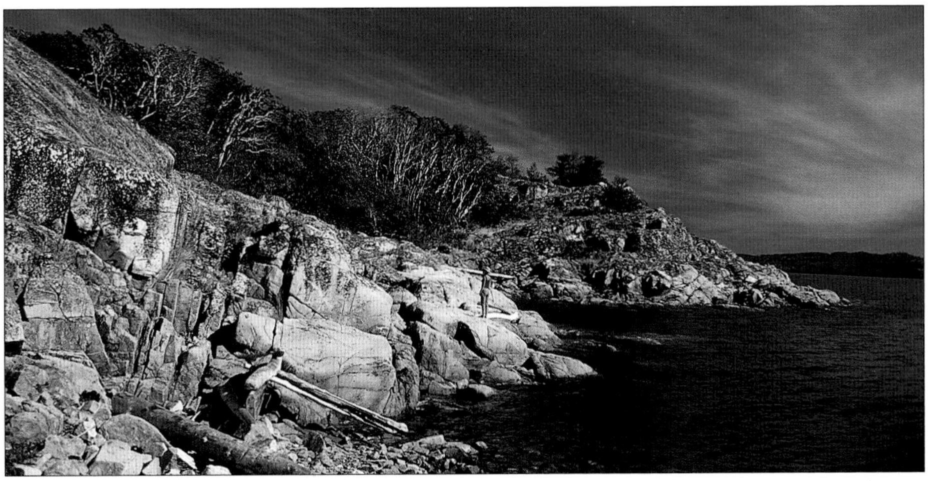

The diverse and remarkably intact ecosystem.

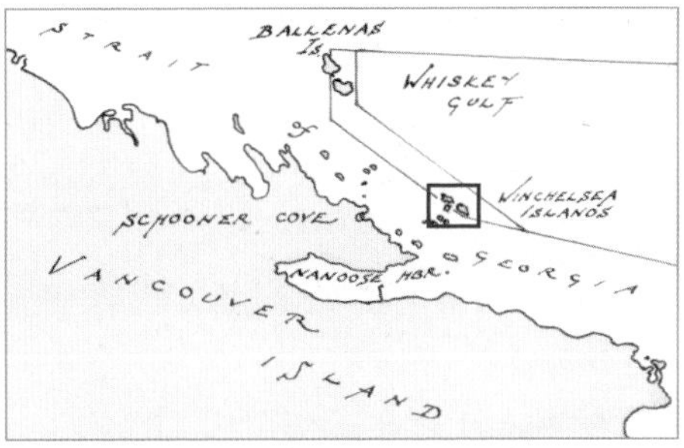

✲ 49°17.3'N 124°4.8'W

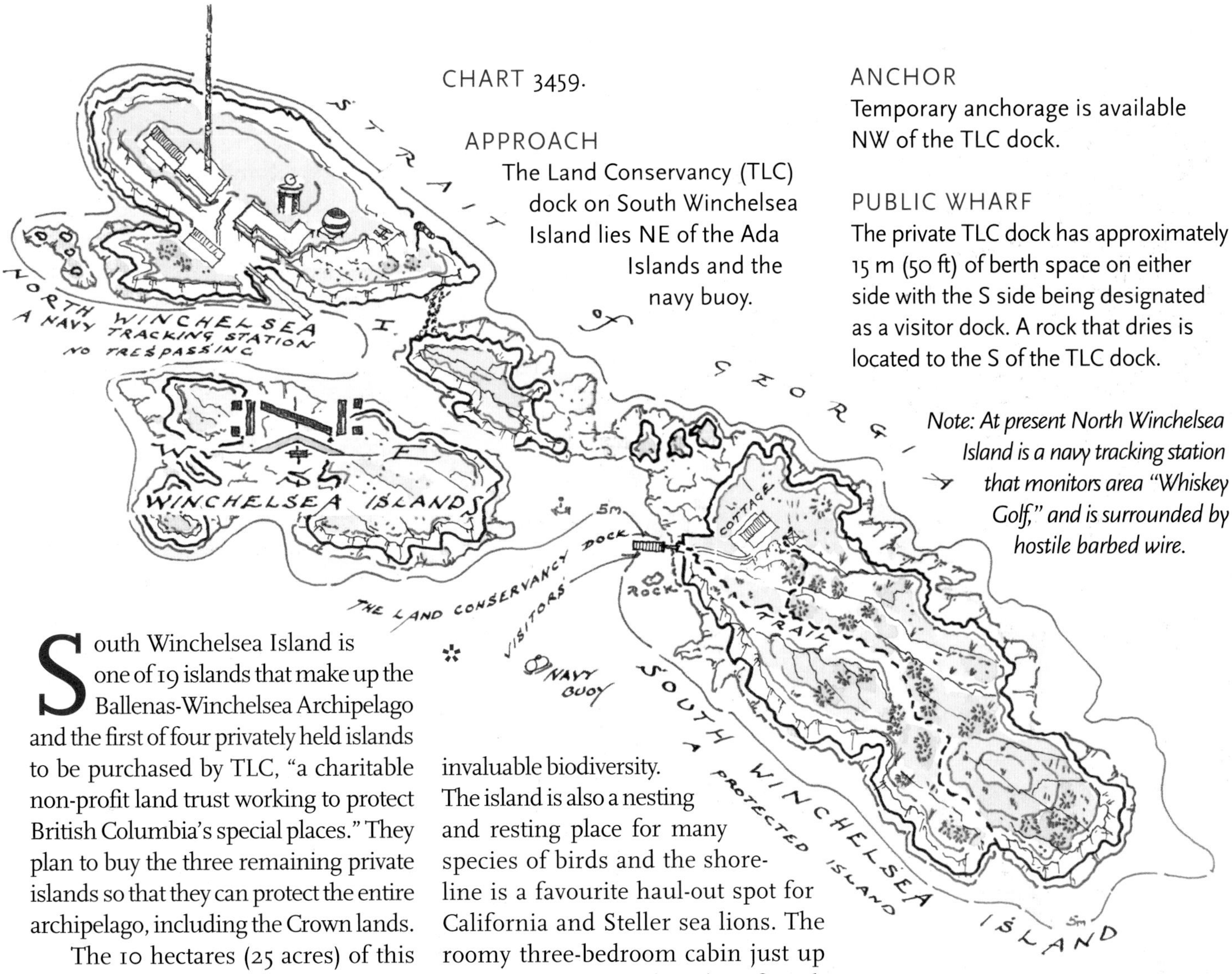

CHART 3459.

APPROACH

The Land Conservancy (TLC) dock on South Winchelsea Island lies NE of the Ada Islands and the navy buoy.

ANCHOR

Temporary anchorage is available NW of the TLC dock.

PUBLIC WHARF

The private TLC dock has approximately 15 m (50 ft) of berth space on either side with the S side being designated as a visitor dock. A rock that dries is located to the S of the TLC dock.

Note: At present North Winchelsea Island is a navy tracking station that monitors area "Whiskey Golf," and is surrounded by hostile barbed wire.

South Winchelsea Island is one of 19 islands that make up the Ballenas-Winchelsea Archipelago and the first of four privately held islands to be purchased by TLC, "a charitable non-profit land trust working to protect British Columbia's special places." They plan to buy the three remaining private islands so that they can protect the entire archipelago, including the Crown lands.

The 10 hectares (25 acres) of this fascinating island are heavily forested with a largely undisturbed Garry oak–arbutus ecosystem that is managed as an ecological reserve because of its invaluable biodiversity. The island is also a nesting and resting place for many species of birds and the shoreline is a favourite haul-out spot for California and Steller sea lions. The roomy three-bedroom cabin just up from the dock is used as a base for volunteer work parties and is also available for rent at very reasonable rates (the income is used to pay off the mortgage). For rental and tour information call TLC at 250-479-8053 or visit their web site at www.conservancy.bc.ca.

14.3 SCHOONER COVE MARINA AND RESORT

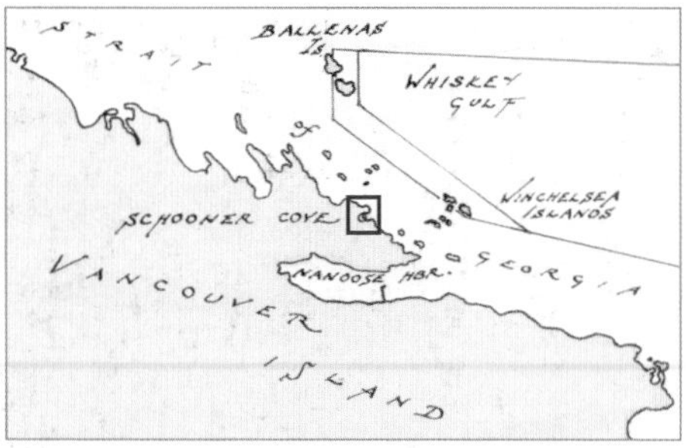

49°17.3'N 124°7.8'W

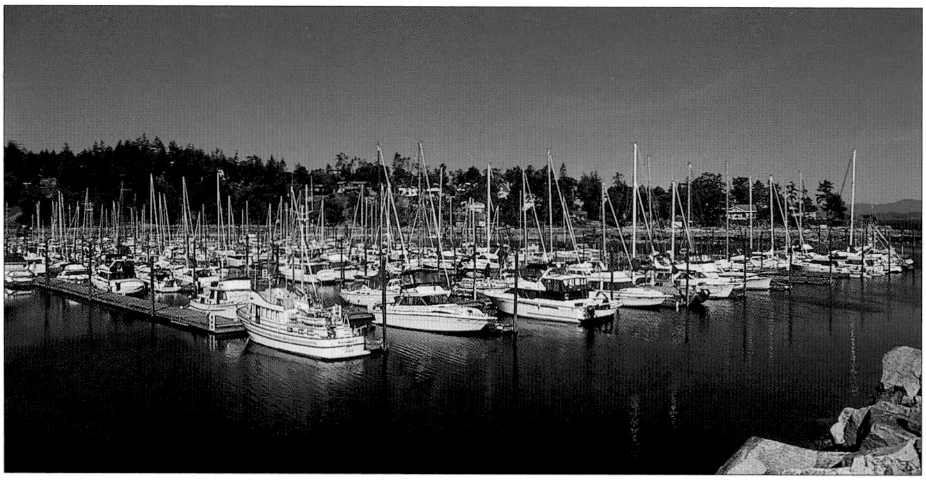

Schooner Cove, a four-star marina.

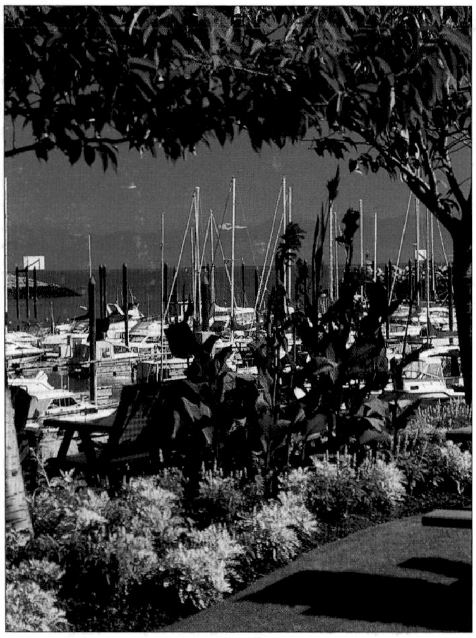

The marina garden offers great views out.

Well-maintained SCHOONER COVE MARINA with its friendly harbour staff and convenient Fairwinds Resort facilities is a fun spot to plug in, relax and pamper yourself for a day or two. Laze in the hot tub or heated pool, catch up on a little exercise in the fitness room, play a few rounds of golf or a game of tennis. Squeaky clean showers (no loonies needed) and laundry facilities are also available.

The resort and marina complex houses a cold beer and wine store and a coffee shop that serves breakfast and lunch. They also stock milk, juice and a few basics. If you fancy a break from the galley, the waterfront restaurant offers fine dining with views beyond the Ballenas Islands to the Sunshine Coast.

Transportation, transit timetables and the use of a rental car can be discussed with the efficient marina staff if you wish to venture beyond the resort complex. Local attractions include Qualicum and Englishman River falls, Horne Lake Caves and Parksville Beach. ARBUTUS MEADOWS specializes in scenic horseback rides through lovely forested trails, and the WILDLIFE RECOVERY CENTRE offers an educational walk-through display of West Coast animals and their habitat. Nanaimo's rejuvenated downtown and harbour-side boardwalk will provide a day of shopping, sightseeing and bistro-hopping.

Mountain bikes are for hire at the harbour office and an energetic uphill tour along scenic Dolphin Drive with its array of waterfront homes is well worth the venture. Hours can be spent exploring the many trails that loop around Dolphin and Enos lakes and the resort's golf course. Look out for the beaver colony.

A favourite with the locals, Brickyard Bay is a lovely 2-hectare (5-acre) waterfront park where brick remains from the original plant built in 1911 can still be seen on the beach and among the roots of maple and fir trees. Public beach access is also available south of the park. Sometimes you don't have to go far to find a special spot — a short walk past SCHOONER COVE RESORT will take you to a flat rocky point with magnificent views and solitude.

Kayaking trips to some of the loveliest island hideaways in Georgia Strait can also be arranged at the marina dock. Take a guided or overnight beach camp tour and enjoy the delights of Yeo, Amelia, Ada, Ruth and Maude islands, among the 19 islands of the Ballenas-Winchelsea Archipelago. For information and reservations call 1-866-468-5778.

CHART 3459

APPROACH
From the E, Schooner Cove is conspicuous by its long breakwater, with masts, condominiums and hotels breaking the skyline. Enter by rounding the end of the breakwater.

MARINA
SCHOONER COVE MARINA AND RESORT has extensive and secure visitor moorage; for reservations call 250-468-5364 or VHF Channel 66A.

FUEL
The marina has a fuel float.

BOAT LAUNCH
Private at the marina.

A good spot for kayaking lessons.

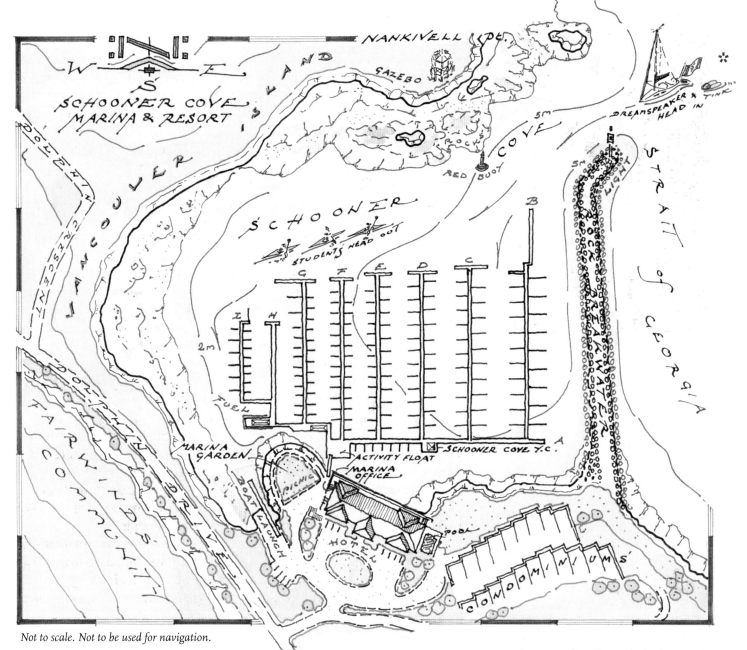

Not to scale. Not to be used for navigation.

14.4 YEO ISLANDS

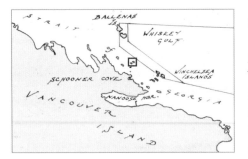

✻ 49°18.2'N   124°7.6'W

CHART 3459.

APPROACH
The approach waypoint on the shore-line plan indicates the entrance to the southern cove on Yeo Island, with shelter from NW winds. The northern cove is protected from SE winds.

ANCHOR
These are temporary anchorages only. Anchor in depths of 2.5 m (8 ft) with fair holding in shingle.

Note: Rocks extend E and W from the islands.

Yeo Island scenery.

Joined by a slim isthmus awash at HW, the serene low-lying Yeo Islands offer boaters a choice of two temporary picnic anchorages and fun LW exploration. A favourite with kayakers who can set up camp on the flat, grassy spots, this small haven is also home to a family of otters whose trails can be seen criss-crossing the islands. The crescent-shaped isthmus is a beachcombing delight piled high with enticing flotsam and jetsam, sun-bleached driftwood and smooth rounded pebbles deposited on the beach during ferocious northwesterly and southeasterly storms.

Not to scale. Not to be used for navigation.

BEACHCOMBER MARINA, NORTHWEST BAY

CHARTS 3459.

APPROACH
BEACHCOMBER MARINA lies on the eastern shoreline of Northwest Bay. Enter between the red and green channel buoys.

MARINA
Visitor moorage is available at the well-maintained BEACHCOMBER MARINA; call ahead for reservations at 250-468-7222.

BOAT LAUNCH
Private, at the marina.
Note: Good anchorage can be found at the head of the bay with protection from all quarters except the NW.

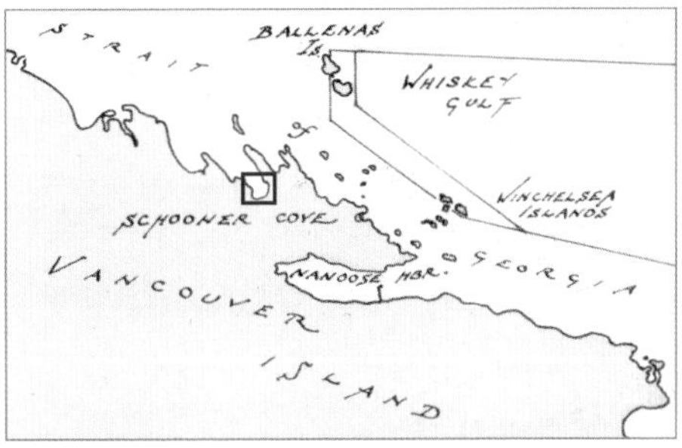

✲ 49°18.0'N 124°12.3'W

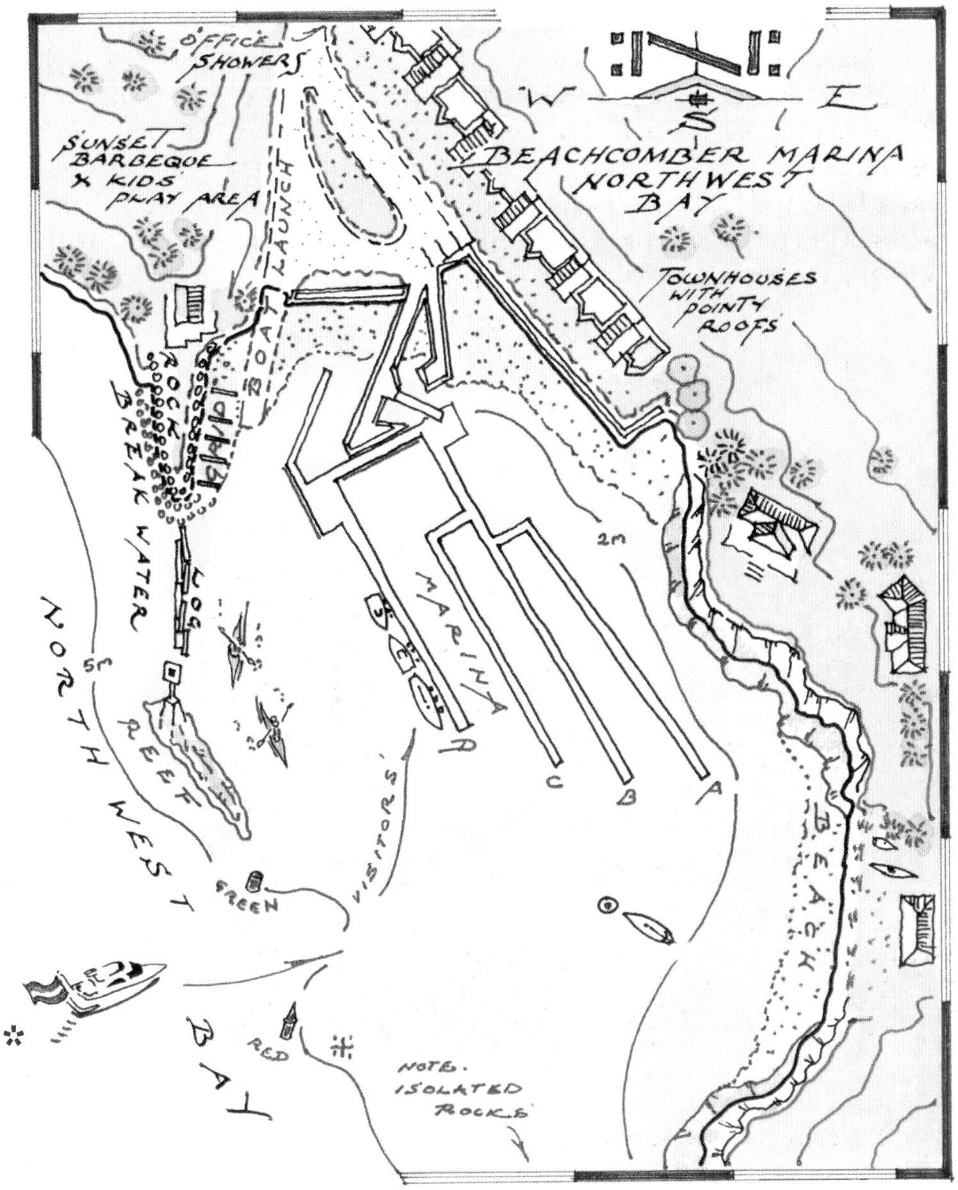

Not to scale. Not to be used for navigation.

Neat and well organized, the BEACHCOMBER MARINA has a number of well-maintained docks, and showers are available. A kids' play zone has been set up on the point behind the log and rock breakwater—as the marina enjoys lovely sunset views, take advantage of the grassy picnic area and experience a memorable sunset BBQ. Good anchorage in a southeasterly is possible at the head of Northwest Bay, to the east of the log-booming operations.

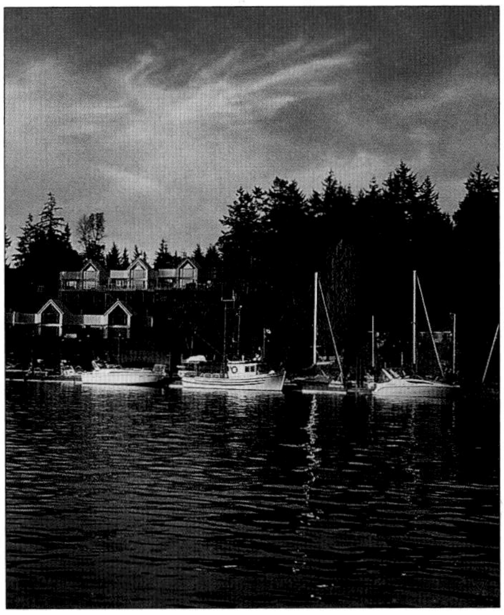

The approach channel to the marina.

14.6 FRENCH CREEK HARBOUR

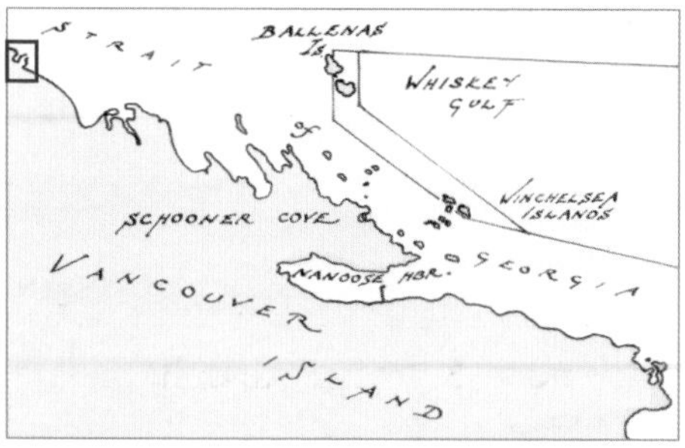

✲ 49°21.1'N 124°21.1'W

CHARTS 3512.

APPROACH
From the NE. The extensive breakwater and commercial activity makes the harbour conspicuous. Enter between the port and starboard beacons placed on top of pilings on either side of the breakwaters.

PUBLIC WHARF
An extensive public wharf lies behind the rock breakwater administered by the French Creek Harbour Authority; call 250-248-5051.

FUEL
Available on the French Creek Seafoods dock.

BOAT LAUNCH
Public, although a fee is charged for use of the launch.

Note: This is a very busy commercial harbour and the terminus for the ferry from Lasqueti Island to French Creek.

This is very much a working harbour and public wharf. It is also a great spot to tie up and throw in a load of laundry, stock up on provisions, sample fresh fish and chips at the WHEEL HOUSE CAFÉ or enjoy a locally brewed beer and at the BOAR'S HEAD PUB.

The FRENCH CREEK MARINA STORE stocks marine charts and supplies, tackle and bait, groceries and newspapers. The FRENCH CREEK MARKET carries fruit, vegetables and tasty sausages, and bread and pastries can be found at the FRENCH CREEK BAKERY AND CAFÉ at Breakwater Village. For the catch of the day, call on one of the fishing boats, visit FRENCH CREEK SEAFOODS behind the fuel dock or dine at the CREEK HOUSE RESTAURANT above the BOAR'S HEAD PUB.

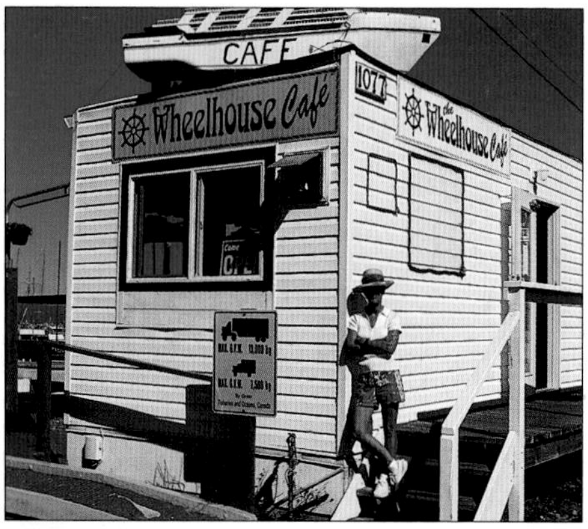

The Wheelhouse Café, serving good food on the wharf head.

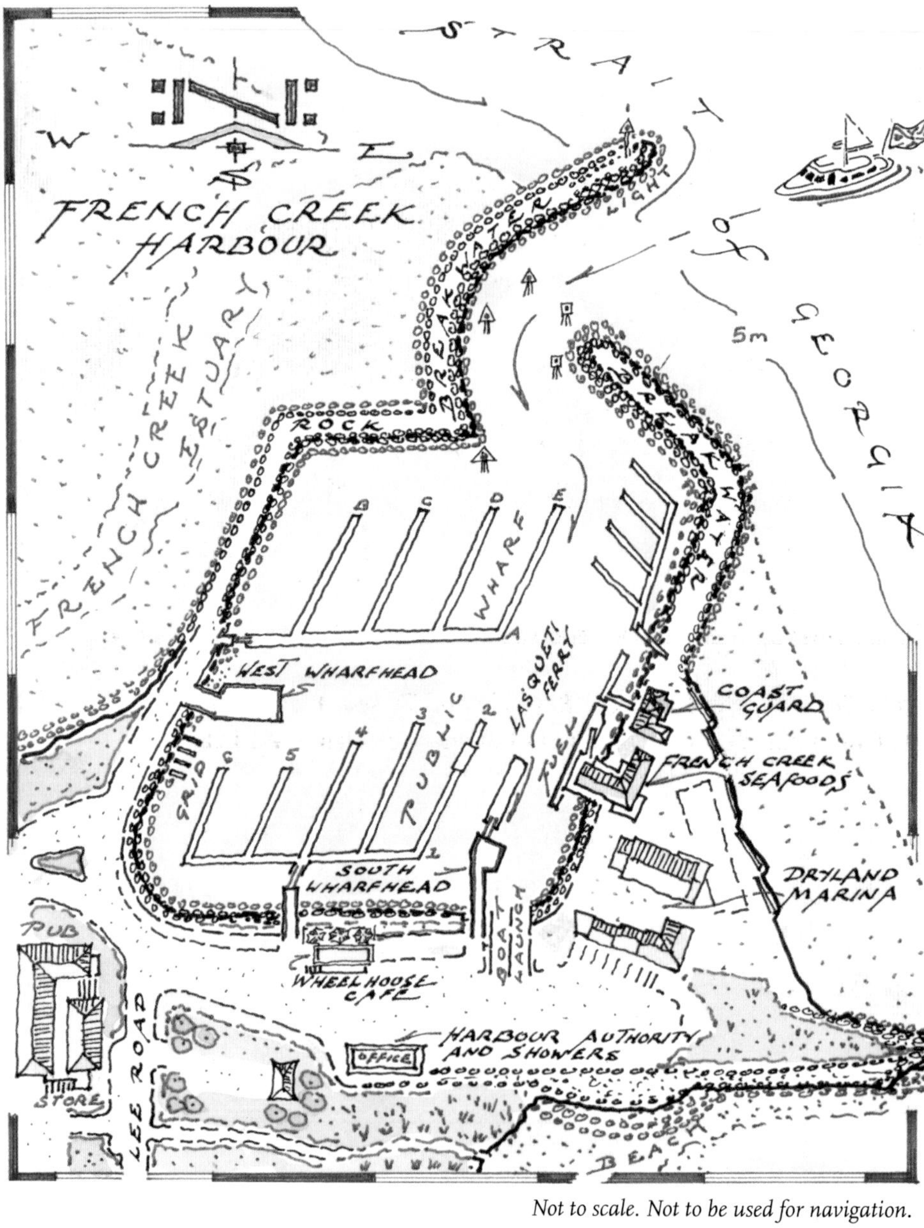

Not to scale. Not to be used for navigation.

FUEL FLOATS, VOLUME 3

The map below shows the main fuel floats for recreational boaters in the Vancouver, Howe Sound and the Sunshine Coast area. All are in Canada unless indicated otherwise.

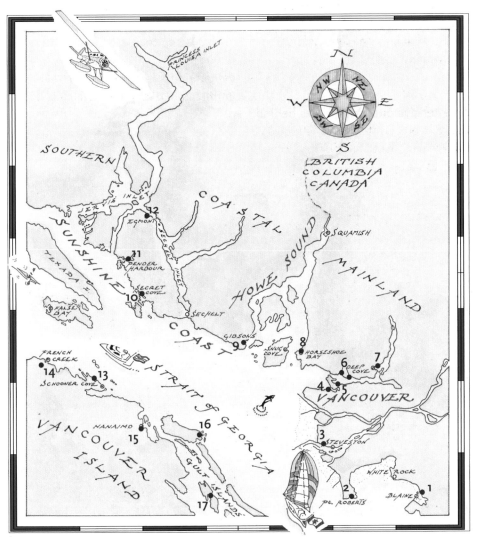

1. Blaine, U.S.A. (1.1., page 18)

2. Point Roberts, U.S.A. (1.3, page 19)

3. Steveston (1.4, page 19)

4. False Creek (2.3, page 29)

5. Coal Harbour (2.2, page 27)

6. Mosquito Creek (3.1, page 38)

7. Deep Cove, (3.5, page 43)

8. Horseshoe Bay (4.2, page 51)

9. Gibsons Landing (6.1, page 71)

10. Secret Cove (7.9, page 89)

11. Hospital Bay (8.6, page 101)

12. Egmont Marina and Village (9.4 & 9.5, pages 115 & 116)

13. Schooner Cove (14.3, page 183)

14. French Creek (14.6, page 186)

Note: For Nanaimo (15), Silva Bay (16) and Telegraph Harbour (17), see Dreamspeaker volume 1: Gulf Islands and Vancouver Island.

SELECTED READINGS

Armitage, Doreen. *Around the Sound: A History of Howe Sound — Whistler.* Madeira Park, BC: Harbour Publishing, 1997.

——. *Burrard Inlet: A History.* Madeira Park, BC: Harbour Publishing, 2001.

Barker, Terry. *Sunshine Sketches: An Artist's History of BC's Beautiful Sunshine Coast.* 2001

B.C. Marine Parks Guide. Vancouver: OP Publishing and *Pacific Yachting,* 1999.

Benson, Sara, and Chris Wyness. *Vancouver.* Melbourne: Lonely Planet Publications, 2002.

Blanchet, M. Wylie. *A Whale Named Henry.* Madeira Park, BC: Harbour Publishing, 1997.

Blanchet, M. Wylie. *The Curve of Time.* Sidney, BC: Gray's Publishing, 1968.

Clark, Lewis J. Wild Flowers of *British Columbia.* Madeira Park, BC: Harbour Publishing, 1998.

Cummings, Al, and Jo Bailey Cummings. *Gunkholing in Desolation Sound and Princess Louisa.* Edmonds, WA: Nor'westing, 1986.

Dawe, Helen. *Sechelt.* Madeira Park, BC: Harbour Publishing, 1990.

Douglass, Don, and Reanne Hemingway-Douglass. *Exploring the South Coast of British Columbia: Gulf Islands and Desolation Sound to Port Hardy and Blunden Harbour.* Bishop, CA: Fine Edge Productions, 1996.

Hale, Robert, ed. *Waggoner Cruising Guide.* Bellevue, WA: Weatherly Press, 1994 to present. Updated and published annually.

Hammond, Dick. *A Touch of Strange: Amazing Tales of the Coast.* Madeira Park, BC: Harbour Publishing, 2002.

——. *Haunted Waters: Tales of the Old Coast.* Madeira Park, BC: Harbour Publishing, 1999.

——. *Tales from Hidden Basin.* Madeira Park, BC: Harbour Publishing, 1996.

Hill, Beth. *Guide to Indian Rock Carvings of the Pacific Northwest Coast.* Surrey, BC: Hancock House, 1984.

——. *Seven-Knot Summers.* Toronto: Fitzhenry and Whiteside, 2002.

——. *Upcoast Summers.* Ganges, BC: Horsdal and Schubart, 1985.

Iglauer, Edith. *Fishing with John.* Madeira Park, BC: Harbour Publishing, 1988.

Living Oceans Society. *Fish for Thought.* Vancouver: Arsenal Pulp Press, 2000.

Pacific Yachting's Marina Guide and Boater's Blue Pages: The Complete Guide to B.C. Marinas and Marine Services. Magazine supplement (January issue), updated and published annually by *Pacific Yachting* magazine.

Peterson, Lester R. *The Story of the Sechelt Nation.* Madeira Park, BC: Harbour Publishing, 1990.

Pinkerton, Kathrene. *Three's A Crew.* Ganges, BC: Horsdal and Schubart, 1940.

Palmer, Mary. *Jedediah Days: One Woman's Island Paradise.* Madeira Park, BC: Harbour Publishing, 1998.

Sept, J. Duane. *The Beachcomber's Guide to Seashore Life in the Pacific Northwest.* Madeira Park, BC: Harbour Publishing, 1999.

Southern, Karen. *Sunshine and Salt Air: The Sunshine Coast Recreation and Visitors Guide.* Madeira Park, BC: Harbour Publishing, 1997.

Stewart, Hilary. *Looking at Indian Art of the Northwest Coast.* Vancouver: Douglas & McIntyre, 1979.

Turner, Nancy J. *Food Plants of Coastal First Peoples.* Vancouver: UBC Press, 1995.

Varner, Collin. *Raincoast Pocket Guides: Plants of Vancouver and the Lower Mainland.* Vancouver: Raincoast, 2002.

Vassilopoulos, Peter. *Anchorages and Marine Parks.* Vancouver: Seagraphic Publications, 1998.

——. *Docks and Destinations: Coastal Marinas and Moorage.* West Coast Cruising Dock-to-Dock Destination Guides. Vancouver: Seagraphic Publications, 1996.

Walbran, John T. *British Columbia Coast Names, 1592 to 1902.* Vancouver: Douglas & McIntyre, 1971.

White, Howard. *Raincoast Chronicles First Five: Stories and History of the BC Coast.* Madeira Park, BC: Harbour Publishing, 1995.

——. *Raincoast Chronicles Six/Ten: Stories and History of the BC Coast.* Madeira Park, BC: Harbour Publishing, 1983.

——. *Raincoast Chronicles Eleven Up: Stories and History of the BC Coast.* Madeira Park, BC: Harbour Publishing, 1994.

——. *The Sunshine Coast: From Gibsons to Powell River.* Madeira Park, BC: Harbour Publishing, 1997.

Wolferstan, Bill. *Sunshine Coast.* Vancouver: Whitecap, 1982.

CHS CHART DEALERS

The following are Canadian Hydrographic Service (CHS) authorized chart dealers in the Vancouver, Howe Sound and the Sunshine Coast area:

LOCATION:	NAME & ADDRESS:	TELEPHONE:
Bowen Island	Union Steamship Co., 1 Government Rd, P.O. Box 250, V0N 1G0	604-947-0707
Delta	Massey's Marine Supply, 4907 Chisholm St, Ladner, V4K 2V2	604-946-4488
French Creek	French Creek Marina Store, #5 – 1025 Lee Rd, V9K 2E1	604-883-2222
Garden Bay	Fisherman's Resort & Marina, P.O. Box 68, V0N 1S0	604-883-2336
	John Henry's Marina, 4907 Pool Lane, P.O. Box 40, V0N 1S0	604-883-2147
Gibsons	Gibsons Marina Hotel, 675 Prowse Rd, P.O. Box 1520, V0N 1V0	604-8868686
Nanoose Bay	Beachcomber Marina, #7 – 1600 Brynmarl Rd, V9P 9E1	250-468-7222
	Fairwinds Schooner Cove Resort, 3521 Dolphin Dr, V9P 9J7	250-468-7691 or 1-800-663-7060
Richmond	Nikka Industries, 3551 Moncton St, V7E 3A3	604-271-6332
	Pacific Net & Twine, 3731 Moncton St, V7E 3A5	604-274-7238
	Pacific Trollers Association, suite 625, 5960 No. 6 Rd, V6V 1Z1	604-273-4213
	Shelter Island Marina, 115 – 6911 Graybar Rd, V6W 1H3 604-270-6272	
	Steveston Marine & Hardware, 3560 Moncton St, V7E 3A2	604-277-7031
	Vancouver Marina (1971), 8331 River Rd, V6X 1Y1	604-278-9787
	Wolff Marine Supply, unit 130, 6751 Graybar Rd, V6W 1H3	604-270-7770
Sechelt	Sechelt Books & Stuff, 5755 Cowrie St, Trail Bay Mall, P.O. Box 1250, V0N 3A0	604-885-2625
	Trail Bay Sports, 5504 Trail Ave, P.O. Box 678, V0N 3A0	604-885-2512
Secret Cove	Buccaneer Marina & Resort, Sans Souci Rd, Box 2, Buccaneer Site, RR#2, V0N 1Y0	604-885-7888
	Secret Cove Marina, 5411 Secret Cove Rd / West Arm of Secret Cove, P.O. Box 1118, Sechelt, V0N 3A0	604-885-9368
Vancouver	Canadian Fishing Co, North Foot of Gore Ave, V6A 2Y7	604-681-0211
	Ecomarine Ocean Kayak Centre, 1668 Duranleau St, V6H 3S4	604-689-7575
	Kocher's Diving Locker, 2745 W. 4th Ave, V6K 1P9	604-736-2681
	Marine Training & Consulting, 2423 Burrard St, V6J 3J3	604-299-4626
	Maritime Services, 3440 Bridgeway St, V5K 1B6	604-294-4444
	Natural Resources Canada, Geological Survey of Canada, Sales Office, suite 101 – 605 Robson St, V6B 5J3	604-666-0529
	Redden Net, 1638 W, 3rd Ave, V6J 1K2	604-736-5636
	Steveston Marine & Hardware, 1603 W. 3rd Ave, V6J 1K1	604-733-7031
	The Quarterdeck, 1660 Duranleau St, V6H 3S4	604-683-8232
	Vick Enterprises, 1790 Powell St, V5L 1H7	604-254-7111
	Western Marine, 1494 Powell St, V5L 5B5	604-253-7721
	Wright Mariner Supply, 485 Broughton St, V6G 3E8	604-682-3788
West Vancouver	The Wet Shop, 6615 Royal Ave, V7W 2S2	604-921-6371
	Thunderbird Marine Supplies, 5776 Marine Dr, V7W 2S2	604-921-9011
White Rock	Boundary Bay Water Sports, unit #1, 15531 – 24th Ave, V4A 2J4	604-541-9191

INDEX TO CHARTS AS REFERENCED IN VOL III

NUMBER	TITLE	SCALE
3311	Sunshine Coast, Vancouver Harbour to Desolation Sound (Strip Charts)	40 000
3312	Jervis Inlet and Desolation Sound (Chart Atlas), the best coverage of Lasqueti Island	Various
3458	Approaches to Nanaimo Harbour	20 000
3459	Approaches to Nanoose Harbour	15 000
3493	Vancouver Harbour	10 000
3495	Vancouver Harbour, Eastern Portion	10 000
	Indian Arm	30 000
3512	Strait of Georgia, Central Portion	80 000
3514	Jervis Inlet	50 000
3514	Jervis Inlet, Malibu Rapids	12 000
3514	Jervis Inlet, Sechelt Rapids	20 000
3526	Howe Sound	40 000
3534	Plans – Howe Sound	
	Mannion Bay and Snug Cove	8 000
	Fishermans Cove	3 000
	Horseshoe Bay	8 000
	Shoal Channel	12 000
	Squamish Harbour	10 000
3535	Plans – Malaspina Strait	
	Pender Harbour	12 000
	Secret Cove and Smuggler Cove	10 000
	Welcome Passage	25 000
3536	Plans – Strait of Georgia	
	False Bay	12 000

To obtain a list of local chart dealers or to order navigational charts and publications directly from the Canadian Hydrographic Service, contact:

Sales and Distribution Office
Canadian Hydrographic Service
Department of Fisheries and Oceans
Institute of Ocean Sciences, Patricia Bay
P.O. Box 6000, 9860 West Saanich Rd.
Sidney, B.C., V8L 4B2
tel: (250) 363-6358 fax: (250) 363-6841
E-mail: chartsales@pac.dfo-mpo.gc.ca
Web site: http://www.ios.bc.ca/ios/chs

For dealers outside of the area covered by this cruising guide, refer to the Catalogue of Nautical Charts and Related Publications: Pacific Coast 2 (published by CHS) or contact the CHS Chart Sales and Distribution Office directly (contact information above).

INDEX

THE DREAMSPEAKER SERIES

BY ANNE & LAURENCE YEADON-JONES

A COMPREHENSIVE SET OF CRUISING GUIDES TO THE COASTAL WATERS OF THE PACIFIC NORTHWEST

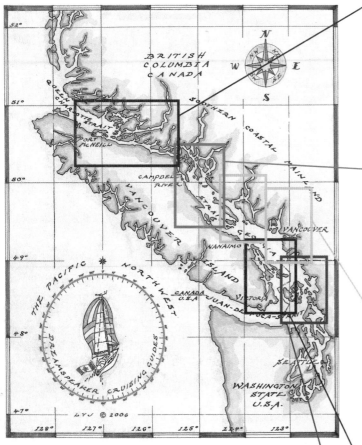

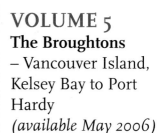

VOLUME 5
The Broughtons
– Vancouver Island,
Kelsey Bay to Port
Hardy
(available May 2006)

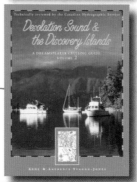

VOLUME 2
**Desolation Sound &
the Discovery Islands**

VOLUME 3
**Vancouver, Howe
Sound & the Sunshine
Coast**
– Princess Louisa Inlet
and Jedediah Island

Each volume is a colourful, illustrated cruising companion full of charts, data, tips and visitor information, and features more than 100 beautifully hand-drawn maps of public wharfs, marinas and small boat anchorages, including both popular and little-known highlights. You'll find everything from safe all-weather havens to secluded picnic spots and marine parks.

VOLUME 1
**Gulf Islands &
Vancouver Island**
– Victoria & Sooke
to Nanaimo

VOLUME 4
The San Juan Islands